lifemaps

a step-by-step method for
simplifying 101 of
life's most overwhelming
projects

Michael Antoniak

**Edited by Stephen M. Pollan
and Mark Levine**

A Fireside Book
Published by Simon & Schuster

New York London Toronto Sydney Singapore

This book is designed to provide readers with a general overview of consumer, business, career, and personal-finance strategies and tactics. It is not designed to be a definitive guide or to take the place of advice from a qualified financial planner, attorney, accountant, or other professional. If the reader requires expert assistance, a competent professional should be consulted. As each situation is unique, there is no guarantee that the methods suggested in this book will always be applicable. Thus, neither the publisher nor the author assume liability of any kind for any losses that may be sustained as a result of applying the methods suggested in this book, and any such liability is hereby expressly disclaimed.

FIRESIDE
Rockefeller Center
1230 Avenue of the Americas
New York, NY 10020

FIRESIDE and colophon are registered trademarks of Simon & Schuster, Inc.

For information regarding special discounts for bulk purchases,
please contact Simon & Schuster Special Sales:
1-800-456-6798 or business@simonandschuster.com

Designed by Ruth Lee

Manufactured in the United States of America

10 9 8 7 6 5 4 3 2 1

Library of Congress Cataloging-in-Publication Data
Antoniak, Michael.
    Lifemaps : a step-by-step method for simplifying 101 of life's most overwhelming projects /
Michael Antoniak; edited by Stephen M. Pollan and Mark Levine.
        p. cm.
    1. Life skills—Handbooks, manuals, etc.   2. Problem solving—Handbooks, manuals, etc.
I. Title: Step-by-step method for simplifying 101 of life's most overwhelming projects.
II. Pollan, Stephen M.   III. Levine, Mark, 1958–   IV. Title.
HQ2037 .A56 2002
646.7—dc21   2002021679
ISBN 0-7434-0061-5

For Liz

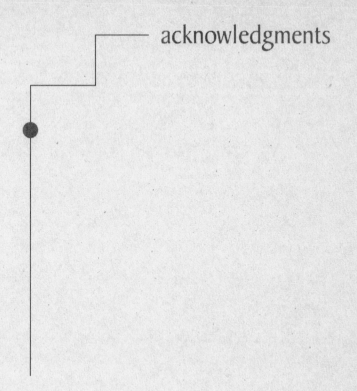

acknowledgments

Thanks to Stephen Pollan, Mark Levine, and Stuart Krichevsky for entrusting me with the Lifemaps concept.

contents

part two. lifemaps for career and business

part three. lifemaps for personal finance

part four. lifemaps for consumers

introduction

There aren't enough hours in a day.

Technology hasn't made our lives simpler. Actually, it has made them more complex. Having a cell phone means you'll never miss a call from an important customer and never be out of touch with your family. But it also means you'll never escape the office and will have a constant list of daily chores to be done.

After flirting with frugality and tightwad lifestyles, most Americans now realize that the real key to improving the quality of our lives is saving time. Having more time gives us not only the chance to make more money but the opportunity to get closer to our families and friends and to devote more attention to our hobbies and pastimes.

That's what *Lifemaps* is all about. By taking 101 of life's most problematic projects and offering quick and easily understood and followed solutions in a graphic format, *Lifemaps* gives us all the gift of more time. Mike Antoniak has searched out the best wisdom and advice on all these projects, digested the material, and reduced it to its essential elements for quick and easy consumption. No longer will you need to read myriad books on, for example, home buying, take notes, and come up with your own checklist. *Lifemaps* has done it all for you.

Not only that, but *Lifemaps* is a crash course in the school of hard knocks, a replacement for the wisdom of experience. Having explored problems and solutions thoroughly from beginning to end, Antoniak is able to warn you of potential problems and prepare you for possible potholes in your road to success.

Lifemaps is the ultimate how-to book, not just because it tells you how to address life's projects but because, behind the maps, lies a wonderful philosophy: you can handle all your problems, no matter how complex they seem or difficult they might appear. All that's required is for you to take a deep breath and then tackle them rationally.

Start by figuring out the basics, determining your goals and objectives, and learning the lay of the land.

Seek out inside information, such as the needs of the other side in a transaction, the established rules of a business or process, or the current trends in the field in question.

Learn the jargon, the special terms and language unique to the problem, so you'll both feel and be perceived as being on top of the situation.

Gather any supplemental information that could expand your knowledge.

Watch out for any warnings or alerts that explain potential obstacles to achieving your goals.

And finally, be open enough to consult any additional resources that might be available to add to your expertise.

It's a remarkably simple formula, but one that promises today's most sought after reward: more time.

Stephen M. Pollan

lifemaps: the basics

part one

how to use lifemaps

1

the basics

Each Lifemap begins with a section that briefly describes the premise of the map. When you're trying to get from one point to another, a map is a real convenience. It's the best resource for determining how to reach your destination, what landmarks you should look for, what turns to take. A map describes a path but not your journey. Although a road may not change, it's different for every traveler. Each Lifemap in this book is based on this same premise. In the pages that follow, you'll find information to help you deal with many issues you're likely to face in your personal or professional life. Today, with the demands of family and career pulling in several directions at once, it's often difficult to focus your energy where needed. Lifemaps can help prepare you for specific life challenges. Like any map, though, they only describe the landscape through which you must travel. Their value rests with how well you use and adapt the insights they offer for reaching personal goals.

inside information

The second section of each map provides more detail as it discusses the underlying strategy of the Lifemap. There's always something more you need to know in order to accomplish your goal. We come at many of life's challenges as outsiders; here you'll find a quick synopsis or refresher course that can help you implement the strategy described in the Lifemap. Sometimes that means knowing what forces are at work and the challenges each imposes. In other situations, the focus is on established policies and procedures. Occasionally the section presents a discussion of prevailing trends shaping the topic. The intent in each is to help you develop the understanding and insight necessary to effectively adapt the Lifemap to your life.

jargon

Here you'll find definitions of some key terms you're likely to encounter as you use the Lifemap. Every business and specialty has its own terms and terminology. Some are uncommon meanings of common words. Or there may be a word you're unlikely to see anywhere else. In a few situations, a definition may describe a document or process specific to the subject of the Lifemap.

fyi

The purpose here is to provide some supplemental information to enhance your understanding of the topic. The value of the Lifemaps depends much on what you bring or add to each. You can get a quick grasp of a topic and solution from these pages, but it may take additional research and work on your part to effectively adapt and implement each strategy.

warning

This section alerts you to common dangers, pitfalls, and false assumptions that can impede your progress. Every situation, every individual is different. Each Lifemap presents a plan as a linear progression of logical steps. Some you'll fly through; others pose obstacles to further progress; some may even present you with entirely new challenges. Lifemaps are not solutions but recommended strategies you can adapt to your situation.

Here you'll find sources of additional information to help you master each topic and realize your goals. You should be able to draw enough from these pages to tackle many problems. Sometimes, though, you'll need to supplement your understanding or turn to an expert for additional help. Depending on the topic, recommended resources may include books and publications; Web sites of companies or agencies; organizations; or any combination of these.

Note: The Internet URLs were correct at the time this book went to press; however, all URLs are subject to change.

As illustrated here, each Lifemap is a "map" of landmarks you will pass on your way to a specific goal. Each provides a basic strategy you can refer to and adapt to your life and challenges.

1. Read Part I to understand the underlying strategies used throughout the rest of the book.

2. Define your challenge or goal.

3. Find the Lifemap most closely related to this topic; if none is included, use the information from Part I to develop your own Lifemap.

6. Which landmarks are easily achieved?

5. Review the Lifemap with regard to your personal situation.

4. Read the entire relevant Lifemap entry.

7. Which present unique challenges?

8. Do you have the required expertise? If not, consult other Lifemaps.

9. Use the Resource list to enhance your understanding as necessary.

12. Refer to the Lifemap as a gauge of your progress until your goal is achieved.

11. Use this as a guide to assist you in planning and implementing an appropriate course of action.

10. Personalize the Lifemap to your situation as needed.

how to approach any problem

2

the basics

Problems—"challenges" might be a more appropriate term—present themselves at every turn, in every day of our lives. They can be as simple as finding directions to an uptown location; as straightforward as figuring out how to frame in a new window; or as complex as bringing warring parties in the office to the table to resolve their differences. In these and countless other situations, we need to draw on our knowledge and experience to achieve a goal or to recognize our limitations and identify the expertise that will allow us to do so. In school, we were presented problems in math and science to develop our thinking. The same skills and intuition that got you through geometry or physics, together with your own intuition, will equip you for solving the many problems and challenges of life.

inside information

The toughest and most important part of solving any problem is identifying your goal: what you need to know or what you must accomplish. Once you've identified that, it's simply a matter of determining what's required to reach that goal. Consider each step in that process as an individual goal, and break each down into manageable tasks. The more complicated the goal or the less prepared you are to reach it, the more steps are involved. A written plan can help focus your energy and resources. For some people, it's enough to describe the problem and desired outcome. Others prefer a detailed plan: a checklist of things you must do as you progress or a diagram outlining all steps. Each Lifemap in this book describes a plan that can be applied to common problems and challenges. A written plan offers several advantages: it organizes your thoughts and actions; serves as a measure of your progress; and reinforces your accomplishments, making it easier to stay focused. When striving for any goal, always be prepared for the unexpected. There will be unforeseen obstacles. Flexibility and the ability and willingness to adapt will be critical to your ultimate success. Many problems you face will involve personal relationships. A formal training course may meet some of these challenges, but your own sensitivity, intuition, and ability to hear what people are really saying can prove crucial to success. The golden rule always applies: Treat others as you want to be treated, respect the basic equality of all, and personal problems will present you with opportunities for growth.

jargon

Intuition: Instinctive knowledge of or insight into a situation without conscious reasoning. A conviction more felt than known, which proves true.

Manageable tasks: Small steps or modest goals, easily achieved, which ultimately contribute to the progress toward reaching a goal or solving a problem.

fyi

There are some problems, some personal challenges, for which there are no easy answers, no practical solutions. In such cases it's better to walk away and remove yourself from the situation rather than waste energy pursuing elusive answers. You may find that stepping outside the problem lends you the new perspective you need to solve it. It's easier to summon up the energy to meet a challenge when you consider it an opportunity rather than an obstacle. Many of life's challenges, by forcing us to reconsider our path, awaken us to possibilities otherwise missed.

Solving a problem requires completing manageable tasks at a sustainable pace. Try to accomplish too much at once, and your problems will overwhelm you. Blaming others for your problems only distracts you from what you need to do. Regardless of how you got into a situation, only actions you initiate can remove you from it. You'll be able to meet many minor challenges on your own. Recognize, too, that some challenges are more than you can handle alone. Never let pride get in the way and prevent you from turning to others for the skills, experience, or emotional support you need.

resources

When Families Feud: Understanding and Resolving Family Conflicts by Ira Heilveil (Berkeley, 1998): A psychologist's observations on the roots of family problems, with specific advice on how to restore harmony.

Turning No into Yes: Six Steps to Solving Your Financial Problems (So You Can Stop Worrying) by Stephen M. Pollan and Mark Levine (HarperBusiness, 2000): Using examples from real life, the authors present an easily adapted six-step plan for resolving even the most vexing financial problems.

1. Define your problem in writing.

2. Define any other factors that are contributing to the problem.

3. Identify and isolate the core issue, the root of the problem.

12. Periodically refer to your plan to measure your progress.

11. Proceed, based on your plan, one goal at a time to solve the problem.

10. Educate yourself or turn to others for help.

13. With personal problems: if you have an adversary who is the primary cause of the problem, identify his or her motivations.

14. Try to understand the cause of this problem from his or her perspective.

15. Why has this problem occurred?

22. If you realistically foresee the problems escalating, move on.

4. What major goal must you achieve in order to overcome this challenge?

5. What minor goals must you achieve in order to reach this goal?

6. Identify the obstacles that must be addressed in order to achieve each goal.

9. Decide if you must develop these yourself or can turn to someone else for help.

8. Identify any skills, knowledge, or experience you currently lack that prevents you from completing each task.

7. Develop a plan: define your strategy for solving the problem as a series of manageable tasks.

16. Approach the other person and explain how this problem is impacting you.

17. Listen to what the other person says, and be sensitive to feelings he or she may not express.

18. If you are wrong or a misunderstanding has occurred, admit your mistake and apologize.

21. Weigh the merits of either proceeding further or simply removing yourself from the situation.

20. If the other person refuses or is unwilling to work with you, reconsider the premise of the relationship.

19. Work together to resolve any differences and create a strategy for dealing with them in the future.

how to research anything

3

You already have the skills to discover the answers to almost all your questions. All that's involved is the patience to plan your research and the tenaciousness to follow it through. One of the tricks in doing research is knowing what you are looking for. The more specific you can be in identifying what that is, the quicker you'll find the answer. Think of all research as trying to answer a question: the who, what, when, where, how, or why of what you need to know. Often, how to define that question is obvious. Sometimes it's not. Everything else about the process depends on how well you've posed the question. The second key to effective research is to use multiple sources for your information. No matter what the research topic, you'll rarely find a single source that has all the information. Use as many sources as it takes to develop a breadth of understanding about the subject you are investigating. Depending on the type of information you are after, research can get extremely tedious. There are people who do research for a living, and you can hire their services. But you'll still need to define the information you seek before they can help you.

The Internet has made researching any topic much simpler. In fact, it's such a valuable source of all types of information that Lifemap 4 is devoted to helping you learn how to conduct research online. That said, local public and college libraries, as well as area bookstores, are your best alternative sources for research information. They usually have an abundance of reference materials on hand as well as access to magazines, journals, and newspapers with the latest information. Experts on the subject you are researching are also good sources. Most don't have the time to spend answering a confused telephone call. But they may enthusiastically offer answers and suggestions to a person who sends them an organized, concise letter requesting specific information. It never hurts to ask. College professors and graduate students can be good sources, as their knowledge is highly specialized and focused on your research topic. If other sources fail, try calling the local college or university.

Abstract: A concise summary of the information contained in an article. Commonly used in medical and academic journals, it briefly introduces the reader to the key points of the research explained in the article.

Archive: A repository of information of general or specific interest.

Bibliography: The list of references used to produce a book or research article. The bibliography of any written document can help identify sources for additional information.

Reader's Guide: Shorthand for Reader's Guide to Periodical Literature, a reference book that provides an index to all articles on all subjects covered in major periodicals. Available in most public and school libraries.

Your research is only as good as your sources—and your notes. Get into the habit of keeping notes on the information you uncover as the work proceeds. Also, keep records of the sources you use. Thorough research can be a time-consuming process. You must be willing to devote whatever time it takes to answer your question fully. It can't be rushed.

The New York Public Library Book of How and Where to Look It Up, edited by Sherwood Harris (Macmillan, 1994): A solid introduction to research procedures with advice and sources for locating information on a range of subjects.

Online: **Amazon.com** (www.amazon.com) and **Barnesandnoble.com** (www.bn.com) are two major online booksellers that feature search engines that can help you quickly identify the books, both in print and out of print, available on any topic.

Almanacs, dictionaries, encyclopedias: Basic reference guides for refining your research subject and gathering preliminary information and identifying sources.

Your local library's reference room and reference librarian: A logical start for any research project. The librarian can be especially helpful in identifying resources you may not be familiar with.

1. Describe what you want to know—in writing.

2. Refine the topic to a few words or concepts.

3. Based on our description, what are the questions you need to answer? Write them down.

5. If you know and have access to an expert, contact that person and ask for help with your specific questions.

4. Start by looking up your topic(s) in a standard reference book such as a dictionary, encyclopedia, or other standard reference. Take notes and, if necessary, further refine the description of what you need to know.

6. Visit a library and/or bookstore. Borrow or purchase pertinent books, using their index, table of contents, and any available reviews as a guide; consult the *Reader's Guide* and other reference works for up-to-the-minute information.

7. Conduct an online search, based on keywords (see Lifemap 4); visit sites and save or print helpful information.

10. If the information seems too specialized or personal for you to find or the search becomes too time-consuming, consider hiring the services of a professional researcher.

9. Periodically review what you have learned to see if you have adequately answered your question. If not, continue your research.

8. Compile your information; read and absorb it. Use multiple sources; no single reference can tell you everything.

11. Look in the yellow pages under researchers or research services, or conduct an online search, based on the topic.

12. Contact an area college or university to see if there's anyone there who could help you.

how to do research on the Internet

4

the basics ●

Today, any research project should begin on the Internet. Even if you plan to do most of your research in books and publications, an Internet search can save you hours in trying to identify the best sources of that information. The information you seek is out there somewhere in cyberspace. To find it you have three basic tools: Web directories; search engines; and Usenet groups, also called newsgroups or forums. A directory, as the term implies, organizes Web information by category. A search engine allows you to search for relevant Web sites, based on keywords. Newsgroups are open forums where people the world over can share ideas and opinions about common interests by posting and responding to messages left by other members.

inside information ●

It takes time to master the nuances of different directories and search engines, since they determine and categorize Web content using different criteria. That's why it's important to use more than one search engine or directory in your search. Choosing the right "key-words" will be critical to your success. Defining a very broad topic in one or two words is an art. Newsgroups can prove especially valuable when you are trying to use research to develop a new skill or investigating a topic about which people are passionate. These are great places to find "experts" who will take the time to step you through whatever you are trying to accomplish.

jargon

Domain name: The name of a particular location on the Internet. The domain name identi-fies the Web site and is used in its Web address, or URL.

Hyperlinks: Sometime referred to as hot links, these are links from one Web site to another. When appearing as text, hyperlinks are underlined or in a color different from the rest of the text. If photos, hyperlinks usually have a box around them.

Uniform Resource Locator (URL): The address of a Web domain or page on the Internet, for example, www.something.com.

warning

You have to be careful to validate the research you do on the Internet. Many Web sites and personal home pages present opinion masquerading as information. Before you fill out any form online, check into the Web site's privacy and security policies. Everything you do online is tracked, and some Web sites compile and sell or exchange information about those who visit and what information they seek.

fyi

Conducting an online search will become even easier as more information resources are put online. Several companies are already experimenting with search engines that allow you to ask questions in simple English, rather than use keywords, when looking up infor-mation.

Find It Online: The Complete Guide to Online Research by Alan M. Schlein (Facts on Demand Press, 2000): A complete guide to identifying sources of and finding information online.

Online: Directories and search engines, including **Yahoo** (www.yahoo.com), **Excite** (www.excite.com), **AltaVista** (www.altavista.com), and **WebCrawler** (www.webcrawler. com). Each includes a detailed directory of Web sites that have listed themselves with the site, as well as a search engine that uses keywords to search the content of these sites.

Ask.com (www.ask.com): Lets you pose questions in plain English. The information brought back includes information from Web sites as well as messages posted in user groups.

I. Define the topic.

2. Break its definition down into one or two keywords that describe the essence of the information you seek.

3. Log on to the Internet.

4. Visit one of the major Internet directory sites, and follow the category and subcategory listings until you reach likely sources of the information you seek.

5. In the search box of the search engine site, enter your keywords and hit "Return."

6. Review the list of Web sites on your screen. If practical, set the page to show summaries of the sites.

7. Click on links to the sites that have most in common with your query.

8. Visit these sites, and if possible conduct a search of the site using your keywords.

9. Print out or save to disk any pertinent information.

10. Check the "related links" or "other links" listing on any site of interest.

11. Visit those that seem most appropriate.

12. Print or save relevant information.

13. If your first query yields disappointing results, try broadening your search using different keywords.

14. Repeat this entire process using at least two other search engines.

15. Review all the information you've gathered.

16. Determine if your research has provided adequate information.

17. If the information is not sufficient, identify likely sources of information or experts from your research.

18. Revisit these sites and try to e-mail these sources with a concise query, describing the information you seek.

19. In the "newsgroups" section of your Web browser or e-mail program, use keyword searches to try to identify user groups where the information you seek may be available.

20. Try combining your keywords with the word "newsgroup" in the search bar of the search engines visited earlier.

21. Review the postings in these groups to see if the messages relate to your topic.

23. Visit the relevant newsgroups on a regular basis to increase your knowledge of the topic.

22. If so, post a message containing your query and check back later for responses.

how to tap into online resources

5

the basics

What would you like to do? Whatever your response, it's likely that the Internet, and its global reach, has made it somehow easier to accomplish. You can uses the resources of the Internet to find your next job, book a summer vacation on the other side of the world, complete your education, enhance your knowledge of any subject, or meet people who share your passions, whatever they may be. Sitting before your computer screen, you can read the world's great books; tour the galleries of museums you will never visit; or listen to play-by-play action of your favorite team from the hometown you left behind. The possibilities are literally endless. The Internet is everything and anything you want it to be. Explore and use its World Wide Web of interconnectivity ("the Web"), and the world will become a much smaller, yet richer place.

As with any tool, there are no real secrets of mastering the Internet. The more you use it, the more proficient you'll become at discovering ways in which it can serve you. The basic skill required is being able to conduct research online (see Lifemap 4). Once you understand that, the doors of information will open for you in every direction. Then you can begin to tap into the many resources that can enhance your life. The information available online can make you a smarter consumer, a more informed citizen, a better cook. All sorts of information awaits your discovery anytime, at your convenience. Whatever your interest, there's someone, somewhere else in the world, who shares it. The Internet provides a forum where like-minded people can connect and share their passions. It's truly an intellectual community where race, color, creed, and religious persuasion are inconsequential considerations. Without the Internet, you might never have access to much of this content. Archives of ancient maps, photographs, diaries, recordings—any vehicle of human communication—are now available online. If you have a problem or are facing some challenge, search the Internet for a recognized expert or someone who has already been through a comparable situation. Whatever you want from life, whatever you're trying to accomplish, the resources now available to you on the Internet can make it easier to reach your goals.

Browser: The software interface that enables you to move around the Internet, and access Web pages and content; the most popular are Netscape Navigator and Internet Explorer.

Cookies: Bits of data that Web sites upload to your hard drive for future reference. Cookies can help personalize the content of the sites you visit and ads you see; they can also be used to track where you go and what you do online.

Online community: A Web location where people with similar backgrounds or interests can meet and share that interest. The typical community provides members with relevant content, an electronic newsletter tracking pertinent news developments, and a forum where members can meet and exchange ideas and comments.

Web site: A repository of information and graphics published on the Internet by an individual or company, identified and reachable via its own Web address.

The trend among businesses is to use their Web sites as the primary channels for distributing information. In fact, you may find it easier to get a response from a company's customer service department by e-mail than by telephone. You can make your Internet service pay for itself by taking advantage of special offers, discounts, and coupons available only online. In fact, it's even possible to make some long distance calls for free using your Web browser and Internet account. Many newspapers, magazines, and even local TV and radio stations now publish much or all of their content on the Internet, where you can review it at your convenience, free of charge.

fyi

warning

Too much of anything isn't good for you, including the Internet. It can be quite addictive, at least initially. Don't let this tool overwhelm you. Get up and walk away from the screen every one in a while. Be aware that every move you make online can be tracked. To protect your privacy, learn about cookies: what they are, how they work, and what you can do to disable or delete them. Cyberstalking is becoming an increasingly common form of harassment online. As a general rule, don't reveal personal information to strangers you meet in cyberspace, and if you suspect that someone is tracking you, consider changing your ISP and user name.

resources

The Internet for Dummies by John R. Levine, Margaret Levine Young, and Carol Baroudi (Hungry Minds, 2000): A guide to all aspects of the Internet, with tips on how you can get the most from your online experience.

Harley Hahn's Internet Yellow Pages, 2002 Edition by Harley Hahn (McGraw-Hill Professional, 2001): A directory of Internet resources, with Web addresses arranged by topic, such as finance, sports, travel, music, computers, and more.

Online: Web directories and search engines are the gateways to the resources of the Internet. Some of the most popular are **Netscape** (www.netscape.com), **MSN** (www.msn.com), **Yahoo!** (www.yahoo.com), and **Excite** (www.excite.com). Each offers a great starting point for discovering all the Internet has to offer.

1. Sign up with an Internet service provider.

2. Familiarize yourself with the features and functions of your Web browser.

3. Learn how to disable or delete cookies.

12. Always check a site's privacy policy before completing any electronic form to make sure your name and information will not be redistributed.

11. Visit these sites and sample their content before enrolling.

10. Identify online communities devoted to some Internet or life experience you have.

13. Monitor the activity and messages in chat rooms and newsgroups before deciding to participate.

14. If possible, join using a name that doesn't reveal your true identity.

15. Periodically revisit sites of interest for updates on content.

4. Learn how to use the "bookmark" feature.

5. Learn how to conduct re-search online (see Lifemap 4).

6. Whatever you are trying to accomplish, use the Internet as an information resource.

9. Bookmark relevant content.

8. Explore all the resources you have uncovered.

7. Conduct an online search.

16. Periodically review and purge your cookie file.

17. When buying any goods online, check the site's security guarantees before entering your credit card number.

18. Also review the company's shipment and return policies.

19. As you develop new information needs, continue to explore the resources available on the Internet.

should you do it yourself or hire a professional?

6

the basics

There's little you cannot do—as long as you believe in yourself and possess the time, resources, and initiative to get the job done. That said, there are times when it simply makes more sense to turn the job over to someone else—who has the expertise and experience you lack. Sometimes the decision to do so comes easily. At other times, it may be tempered by the cost of hiring a pro or by your desire to develop certain skills or gain a unique experience. Doing it yourself—whatever it may be—does breed a rewarding sense of accomplishment. But it can also overwhelm you with frustration. The difference comes down to knowing what you're getting into at the outset, and being realistic about whether your interests are better served by doing it yourself, or letting someone skilled and experienced handle the job.

Whatever the project, you're sure to find an abundance of "how-to" information to guide you through the process. You can also draw inspiration and guidance from others who have successfully done it themselves. On the other hand, don't expect fan mail from professionals who make their living doing what you're trying to do. They know more than you can expect to learn—unless you're embarking on a new career course—and usually can't spend a lot of time trying to help a novice through the process. Some may offer friendly advice, but if you want a lot of their time, let them handle the job.

jargon

Budget: The cost of the project. Do-it-yourselfers often overlook the cost of tools involved in a project when figuring the cost. In reality, the tools may be more expensive than the materials or other resources required for completion.

Time: Here, time means the total amount of time it will take to develop the skills required for the project, as well as its actual completion. Whatever you are doing, always allow more time than you think you'll need.

Tools: Everything that's required to complete the project. This means actual tools as well as the skills required to use them.

warning

Most do-it-yourself projects fail because the doer didn't allow her- or himself enough time, tried to rush things along, and dug a deeper hole with each advance. The seeds of that failure generally arise in the planning stage. Be realistic when you outline the project. Break it up into many small steps that logically should allow you to achieve specific goals. Create a detailed plan for what's involved and what you need to do to complete each step. Only with a realistic assessment of all a project requires can you evaluate your options.

fyi

Once you decide on a do-it-yourself project, the Internet can be one of your best resources for learning how to do it. There you'll find an abundance of information on every topic and people who are actually willing to share their knowledge with strangers (see Lifemap 7).

The Big Book of Small Household Repairs by Charles Wing (Rodale Press, 1999): Save money with this step-by-step guide to fixing more than two hundred things that break or wear out in the typical household. Easy-to-follow instructions.

Better Homes and Gardens New Complete Guide to Home Repair and Improvement, edited by Benjamin W. Allen (Better Homes and Gardens Books, 1997): Get ideas and solve problems with this guide for the do-it-yourselfer.

Homestore.com (www.remodel.com): A great Web site for do-it-yourself projects or finding someone to do the job for you. Good information on all sorts of tools and how to use them properly; help planning a project.

1. Describe your project.

2. Determine what's involved. Break the project down into steps that will lead to its completion.

3. Break each step down further into a list of things you must do to complete each step.

6. Do you have them?

5. Identify any special skills required to complete the project.

4. Determine your budget. Figure out how much you can afford to spend for the project.

7. List all tools required.

8. Do you own them?

9. If not, can you rent them?

12. Set a goal for when you want the project completed. How much time does that give you?

11. How long will it take to master them?

10. What will they cost to rent?

13. Do you have the time to devote to it?

14. If not, consider hiring a professional (see Lifemap 7).

15. If professional bids aren't within your budget, reconsider doing it yourself.

16. Can you break the project into smaller projects or goals you can accomplish by yourself, over a longer period?

17. Can you structure the project so you have more time to invest in learning to use the tools?

18. If you can, do it yourself.

19. If you can't, increase your budget and hire a professional.

how to evaluate a professional

7

the basics

No matter who you are or what your skills, there comes a time when you must rely on someone else's expertise to solve a problem or complete a task. Whatever you need done, there's some expert who has made a career of it. How do you know who's the right person for the job? Area of specialization is usually your first indicator: you would not hire a mechanic to represent you in court any more than you'd want an attorney fixing your car. Both professionals might carry credentials and licensing that let you know they meet certain minimum standards. Beyond that, though, much of the evaluation process is based on what you are able to learn about a professional from others, and whether his or her own demeanor and experience warrant your trust.

inside information

Word of mouth should be your first, and will possibly be your best, source for finding the right professional for any job. First ask for recommendations from friends and family. If they can't help, contact trade organizations, licensing boards, or vendors to the type of specialist you seek. As a last resort, try telephone directories. There are several ways to size up candidates. When you've narrowed your selection down, interview each one before you sign on for their services. See what kinds of licenses and accreditation they carry. Ask if they continue to take training courses to keep abreast of changes in their specialty. Make sure they have experience relevant to the specific work you want to hire them for, and ask for at least three references. Explain your needs and ask for suggestions. Pay attention to how well they listen to you, how well attuned they are to your particular needs, and what kind of advice they are able to offer initially. Always check the references and ask about the quality of the work or service; actual versus estimated costs; ability to stay on schedule and meet deadlines; and responsiveness to the questions or concerns of these former customers.

jargon

Accredited: A person who is accredited has met certain minimum standards as established by a professional organization, board, or educational institution. Depending on the organization, it may mean he or she has completed a course, passed a test, or met certain minimum standards for experience and skills.

Licensed: A professional who meets the minimum legal standards to perform a particular job or task is licensed in that profession. Licensing requirements can vary by state or municipality, so it's important to make sure a person is licensed to perform the job where the work will be done.

warning

A high price is no more an indicator of the quality of service than a low price is of your best buy. When evaluating any professional, your analysis must be based on much more than cost. Whatever the job you need done, the person needs to demonstrate the combination of skills, experience, and attentiveness to the needs of the client or customer to warrant your trust. Today, the trend is more and more toward specialization. One contractor might specialize in decks, another in kitchen renovation. An attorney may specialize in disability claims or job discrimination. Ultimately you'll save time and money by working with the specialists whose background and experience most precisely match your present need.

Before hiring anyone, you should always check with your local chapter of the Better Business Bureau to make sure there have not been a significant number of complaints against them. Then make sure the candidate carries any and all current licenses or certifications required by local or state government to perform this service. If applicable, also inquire if he or she is insured and bonded so that you do not assume any unnecessary risk by hiring them. Make sure you understand how the work is to be done, the estimated completion date, who will be performing the work, and the schedule of payment before signing any contract. It's okay to work out a partial payment schedule as work progresses, but you should never pay in full for any service until you are completely satisfied with the quality of the work.

Personal references: Always start your search by asking friends and family for recommendations. Their past experience should help you decide who you want to hire.

Professional organizations: Membership in a professional or trade organization demonstrates a professional commitment. These organizations are good resources for finding candidates and learning what you should expect.

Licensing/certification board: If a professional doesn't show proof that he or she is licensed, check the local government agency regulating that profession. It can also advise you on what various license or certification levels qualify a given individual to do.

1. Determine the type of professional whose services you require. Be as specific as possible in defining that need.

2. Ask family, friends, and neighbors for recommendations.

3. If they can't supply you with a list of candidates, contact trade and business associations for a list of professionals in your area.

12. Request a detailed written bid or estimate.

11. Inquire about fees, and what they are based on.

10. Explain any concerns you have about how or when the project should be completed.

13. Request at least three customer references.

14. Contact these references and ask about their experiences working with these professionals.

15. If necessary, visit and examine the quality of work done for these past customers.

4. Check with the Better Business Bureau and drop any candidates with a significant number of complaints against them.

5. Contact at least two candidates and explain the type of work you need done.

6. Ask how much experience they have with this specific type of project.

9. Explain what you need done and listen to the candidates' suggestions.

8. Arrange a meeting with the best candidates, on site if this involves building, renovations, etc.

7. Inquire, as needed, if they have the appropriate licenses, certification, insurance, etc., as required locally.

16. If a candidate refuses to put anything into writing, drop him or her from consideration.

17. Make sure the bid or estimate details how the work will be done, by whom, estimated date of completion, payment schedule, and who is responsible for paying for materials and any subcontractors, if applicable.

18. The agreement should also outline procedures for terminating the contract.

20. Raise any concerns or voice complaints immediately.

19. Continually monitor the quality of the work or service throughout the project period.

how to protect your interests in a contract

8

the basics

You've probably been a party to more contracts than you realize. Whenever you agree to pay for a service, sign up for a credit card offer, or agree to let your doctor file insurance claims on your behalf, you've entered into a contractual agreement. A contract need not be in writing in order to be an enforceable, legally binding agreement. And you don't need to have an attorney draw up every legal document. It is often in your best interest, though, to involve your attorney in contract preparation and negotiations, particularly when a large amount of money is involved or your agreement is especially complex. To protect your interests, always read every legal document before signing. Make sure you understand all clauses and their implications for you. If there's no document, make sure both you and the other party agree on all terms of your agreement. Once you close the deal, by handshake or signature, it's too late to make changes.

Putting something into writing, defining the terms of your agreement, is the best protection for both parties. With a written contract, everyone understands the terms of the agreement and mutual obligations and responsibilities. If either party fails to live up to those responsibilities, a signed document defining the agreement is your best proof if you end up in court for breach of contract. Since the legal implications of the language used in a contract escape most consumers, it's advisable to have your attorney at least review any complicated contract and advise you on its contents. Signing a contract or accepting an offer is the final step in a process that usually begins with informal discussions. Consider the purchase of a house as an example. Initially you talk with the real estate agent about the home, its features, and its price. Once you express an interest, you enter into preliminary negotiations. You make an offer, and if the home owner accepts you have got a deal. Usually, though, the seller comes back with a counteroffer. The process goes back and forth until you arrive at a mutually acceptable price. At that point, the seller removes the house from the market so your attorney can negotiate the sales contract. It will define the details of the sale: what you get for what you've agreed to pay. Any contract you negotiate will follow a similar pattern: discussions, negotiations, offers, and counteroffers, until an agreement is reached, with or without a written agreement. Once an offer is accepted by the other party, you have a contract. The person making the offer can pull it at any time prior to its acceptance by the other party. It's in both parties' interest to define how long an offer will stand. No matter what verbal agreement the parties think they have, it's the written document they sign that becomes the enforceable contract. What's written there ultimately defines the agreement and the obligations of all parties. Only a thorough review of this document by you and your attorney can guarantee that it's the agreement you want and can accept.

jargon

Addendum: An addition to a preexisting contract. Often an addendum is a revision of the original document or an change that imposes new or additional conditions on the terms of the original contract.

Boilerplate: A "generic" fill-in-the-blank contract, available for purchase, often used for rental, lease, or sales agreements.

Consideration: Something of value that is promised to be delivered or received as a condition of a contract. It can mean a seller's product or service, as well as the amount to be paid by the buyer.

Electronic signature: The electronic equivalent of a signature on the Internet. Recent federal legislation has given electronic signatures the same legal status as regular signatures, making it possible to sign and transmit contracts and other legal documents on the Internet and by e-mail.

fyi •

Often you are presented with a contract without having any opportunity to negotiate its terms. For example, a service provider may present you with a contract to sign before work begins, or you may be required to sign a contract agreement in order to receive a new credit card. Review these with the same scrutiny as any other contract you negotiate. Hidden in the details may be terms unacceptable to you. Certain federal and state laws may give you the option of reconsidering, even canceling, a contract within a limited time after signing. For instance, you have three days to cancel a contract for products costing more than $25 bought from a door-to-door salesman. You have the same amount of time to cancel contracts for loans in which you pledge your home as security. To learn what other rights you may have, check with your state's Department of Consumer Affairs.

warning •

Any contract, any legal document you endorse with your signature, is an agreement enforceable by law. If you fail to uphold your responsibilities, your case may be turned over to a collection agency or you may be summoned into court, where fines and court costs might be judged against you. Certain transactions require a written contract. These include transactions involving the sale of real estate; the leasing of real estate for a year or more; any promise made to pay off someone else's debts; service agreements that will take more than one year to complete; and the sale of goods worth more than $500.

resources •

101 Law Forms for Personal Use, 2nd edition, by Robin Leonard and Ralph Warner (Nolo.com, 2001): Book and companion CD-ROM containing 101 legal forms and contracts ready to use in many common day-to-day transactions and situations.

Business Contracts Kit for Dummies by Richard D. Harroch (Hungry Minds, 2000): A basic yet thorough guide to business contracts, with dozens of sample contracts on the enclosed CD-ROM.

1. Recognize that a contract is any legally binding, enforceable agreement.

2. Realize that a verbal agreement is an acceptable form of contract.

3. Understand that as soon as you sign a legal document or accept an offer involving the exchange of money, goods, or services, you have a contract agreement.

6. Although a contract does not need to be in writing, in order to protect your interests, it is advisable to have a written contract, signed and dated by both parties.

5. Make, reject, or revise offers and counteroffers until you arrive at a mutually acceptable agreement.

4. When entering into an agreement with another party, develop a contract agreement through the process of negotiation.

7. Although an attorney's help is not required when negotiating a contract, it's advisable to rely on your attorney's advice when negotiating and drafting a contract for any agreement that involves significant amounts of money or complex issues.

8. You have the right to reject any terms and continue negotiations until you sign a contract.

9. Always read any contract or legal document before you sign it.

12. Make sure a contract includes a description of who the signatories are.

11. Make sure a contract includes the accurate names and addresses of any individuals and/or representatives of businesses who will be signing it.

10. If you don't understand any aspect of the agreement, have the other party and/or your attorney explain it to you.

13. Make sure a contract includes a detailed description of what each party promises to do and is obligated to do.

14. Make sure a contract includes an accurate description of any goods to be exchanged, including their condition.

15. Make sure a contract specifies any warranties or guarantees the agreement carries.

18. Make sure a contract specifies the conditions under which either party can terminate it.

17. Make sure a contract specifies when these fees are due and how they are to be paid.

16. Make sure a contract specifies any fees, how they will be determined, and how they will be applied.

19. Make sure a contract specifies whether or not the terms of the contract can be transferred or assigned to any other party, and under what circumstances.

20. Make sure a contract specifies who will be liable for any damages resulting from the agreement, if applicable.

21. Make sure a contract specifies the procedures that will be followed to determine if there has been a breach of contract, such as arbitration or a court hearing.

24. Keep an original and a copy of the contract for future reference.

23. Make sure a contract specifies the length of time the contract will remain in effect and includes the signatures of all parties, with the date.

22. Make sure a contract specifies who will be responsible for paying the legal fees if breach of contract is proven.

how to resolve disputes

9

Disputes are an inescapable component of human interaction. Usually we agree to disagree, but there are times when minor differences have the potential to become major distractions, disrupting home or business life. The best strategy: settle disputes early so the situation never progress so far that anyone's ego is pummeled or anyone's wallet emptied. Both at home and at work, escalating arguments easily spill over into the other sphere, making life, in general, pretty miserable. Disputes in the workplace can also extract a financial toll in lost productivity and missed earnings opportunities. For a business owner, an unsettled dispute can prove especially damaging if it results in a lawsuit by some irate or dissatisfied customer and others learn of it. In almost every difference of opinion, there is an early opportunity to reach a mutually acceptable resolution. It's always the best strategy: the longer a dispute is allowed to fester, the more damaging its impact.

inside information

Every dispute is rooted in some difference of perception. A wife may become angry because she expected her husband to pick her up at five, while he thought he had until after the ball game. A customer demands that a contractor clean up, because he never read the contract stating that it is his own responsibility. In a personal dispute, it's best to reach some compromise before an argument turns into resentment, then something more. In a business setting, being able to establish the facts is crucial to early, quick compromise and resolution. Each side in any dispute expects something from the other. Before you can resolve any difference, you must know what the other party wants. If that's more than you're willing to give, work together toward a compromise. It's always best to try and resolve any business dispute before turning to the legal system. And there are other options short of a lawsuit: you might work through a mediator or agree to abide by a decision reached through arbitration. If you do resort to the courts, it will drain your time and energy, even if you prevail. Whenever a simple dispute arises, do all you can to prevent it from becoming anything more than that.

jargon

Arbitration: A legally binding process in which both sides in a dispute agree to sit down and work with an arbitrator or arbitration panel and abide by the resulting decision. This is usually less costly than taking a case to court and results in a quicker resolution of the dispute.

Mediation: Resolving a dispute through a mutually accepted mediator who acts as a go-between for both sides, trying to negotiate an acceptable settlement. The mediator may be anyone the parties choose, but usually it's someone with some expertise related to the cause of the dispute.

fyi

No one wants to lose face in a dispute, even if he realizes he is wrong. Always try to resolve a dispute in such a way that both of you can walk away feeling you've won something. There are instances when it simply isn't worth your resources or emotion to continue fighting. If the costs outweigh all you could ever hope to gain by continuing, consider looking for the easiest way out. Sometimes you will be better served by giving the other party what he or she wants, so you can get rid of him or her and move on.

Your best protection against disputes in any business setting is always a written contract. If you're a business owner, make sure your interests are adequately protected in all contracts, service agreements, and policy statements. If you're a consumer, make sure anything you sign spells out what you will get for your money, all warranties, terms of payment, and any additional requirements in your interest. Disputes can be promptly resolved when a contract defines exactly how disagreements can be settled. Many business contracts today include a clause stipulating that the parties go to arbitration in the event of breach of contract. The contract should also spell out who should be responsible for any fees when a judgment is made. Anger is your worst enemy in any dispute. Before you respond, give yourself the opportunity to calm down so you can think and react rationally.

Resolving Conflicts at Work: A Complete Guide for Everyone on the Job by Kenneth Cloke and Joan Goldsmith (Jossey-Bass, 2001): Using examples, the authors discuss the roots of conflicts in the workplace, then offer advice and guidelines on how to resolve those that do arise.

From Conflict to Cooperation: How to Mediate a Dispute by Beverly A. Potter and Phil Frank (Ronin Publishing, 1996): A handbook of effective and proven techniques for resolving disputes in any situation.

American Arbitration Association: This national organization with branch offices in major cities can provide additional information explaining the arbitration process, and where to find an arbitrator in your area. Call (212) 484-4000.

1. Minimize the potential impact of business disputes: write any necessary protection or warranties you require into any contract you negotiate.

2. Always read a contract or any legally binding document before signing.

3. When a dispute arises, listen to what the other party has to say.

12. Make what you consider to be a fair offer to the other party.

11. If the dispute arose out of a verbal agreement, explain your understanding of the terms of the agreement.

10. See if the contract states how disputes are to be resolved.

13. If he or she doesn't accept it, ask if he or she is willing to try to work the problem out.

14. If so, try to work out a mutually acceptable compromise, allowing both an opportunity to save face.

15. If compromise can't be reached, decide if it's worth your time and money to pursue the matter further.

24. Present your case to an arbitrator or panel.

23. Consult your local court clerk for arbitration guidelines and referrals to arbitrators.

22. If mediation is unacceptable, propose arbitration.

25. Abide by the decision.

26. If the contract does not stipulate arbitration for resolving disputes, consider filing a suit against the other party in court.

27. Weigh all potential costs of the action before filing suit: legal and court fees; lack of guarantee that the court will rule in your favor; publicity; loss of work time for court preparation and appearances.

4. Restrain from a knee-jerk reaction due to anger.

5. If necessary, give yourself an opportunity to calm down before you respond.

6. Determine exactly what the other side wants.

9. Consult written contracts or legal documents.

8. If the request is unreasonable, determine your obligations.

7. If it's a reasonable request, grant it.

16. If not, give the other person what he or she wants and be rid of that person.

17. Get a signed release stating that the dispute has been resolved and how.

18. If it is worth trying to resolve the problem further, propose that you try to mediate your differences.

21. Work with the mediator to negotiate a settlement of the dispute.

20. If the other party agrees, work together to identify an acceptable, appropriate mediator.

19. Make sure the other party agrees to abide by the mediator's decision.

28. If you decide to proceed, work with an attorney to prepare your case.

29. If the final resolution is unfavorable consider the merits, costs, and value of an appeal.

lifemaps for career and business

part two

how to conduct a job search

10

the basics

There are no absolute rules when it comes to finding a job. While your ultimate goal is to secure employment, the goal of the search is to get you an interview. At that point the search assumes a new dynamic (covered in Lifemaps 12 and 13). Unless the employer has approached you, a job search is an experience few enjoy but all must endure. This is truly one of those situations where you must pull out all the stops and try everything you can. Of course, before you can effectively search, you need to know what you are looking for. What do you want from your next employer? Where do you want to be? What matters most in employment? Are you looking for a job or a career? What can you offer? Only when you have the answers to questions such as these can you begin casting your net effectively.

Ask other people how they got their positions, and you'll likely receive responses reflecting the full menu of search tools in today's market: found it through a classified ad, employment agency, friend, or family; started as a temp; went to a headhunter; or just plain lucked out. Use every available resource to create opportunities. Hit the pavement, send out letters, answer ads, browse the online job postings, knock on doors, tell friends and peers that you're in the market. Use every opportunity to network. Be relentless in your pursuit, know your worth, and don't settle for less. The secret of finding a job is creative determination: you have to exhaust every resource.

Career counselor: A professional consultant who specializes in helping people redirect their careers or embark on new careers based on their skills and experience. If you're experiencing frustration in your employment search, it may be worth your while to have a career counselor provide an objective assessment of your career goals and how you are going about the search.

Résumé on file: A phrase often used when a company informs you that you didn't get the position or it has no openings: "But we'll keep your résumé on file." Don't believe it. If you really want a job with a particular organization, keep hammering and track its listings. Don't assume it reviews résumés on file to see whose skills match current openings. In fact, don't assume the "file" is anything other than a garbage can.

Temp: A temporary or contract worker. "Temping" is an excellent way to get your foot in the door, hone your skills and experience, and field-test a job and/or company.

Tenacity is essential to a successful job search. Never give up until you find the job you want. And don't wait around for employers to come to you. Call when you don't hear from someone who promised to get back to you. It is better to have your doubts removed and be able to resume your search than wait around only to be disappointed. Resist paying anyone who asks for a fee for finding you employment, and certainly never pay up front on the mere promise of a job.

Seriously consider any offer of temporary or contract employment. Often companies use this as a way of screening potential employees. They can assess skills and see how well a person fits in with the organization while being under no real obligation. If things work out, they may offer a position. In fact, you may want to register with a temp agency if you're intent on entering a particular field and want to keep your skills current.

resources •

The Complete Job-Search Handbook: Everything You Need to Know to Get the Job You Really Want by Howard Figler (Henry Holt, 1999): A complete guide to the job hunt, from matching a career to your skills and interests to locating that best match.

Jumpstart Your Online Job Search in a Weekend by Pat Kendall (Prima Publishing, 1999): Timely advice on how to use the job search resources available online to find your next job and advance your career. Includes CD-ROM.

Job-Search-Engine.com (www.jobsearchengine.com): A good place to start with an on-line employment search since it searches postings on all the major job sites, based on key-words, location, etc.

1. Prepare your résumé (see Lifemap 11).

2. If relevant, assess your present employment situation.

3. Decide what features, responsibilities, opportunities, and perks you must have in your next position.

12. Register with employment agencies handling positions in your field and requiring your experience.

11. Register with online employment sites. Search them daily.

10. Network: let your peers and contacts—anyone who may be able to help you—know you are seeking new employment.

13. Contact career counselors or consultants and determine if their services can aid your search. If so, arrange an appointment.

14. Peruse the classified ads on a daily basis. Respond as needed.

15. Conduct a cold-call campaign. Visit companies and fill out applications.

4. Define what you want in your position. Include salary and benefits, responsibilities, opportunities for advancement, perks.

5. Are you willing or planning to relocate?

6. Compile a list of types of jobs that require your skills and experience.

9. Draft a cover letter and send out your résumé.

8. Get the names of contacts at those companies in personnel or human resources or the department you wish to work in.

7. Work up a list of companies you'd like to work for.

16. Check with local temp agencies to see if they have any need for a person with your skills and/or if they provide employees to any of your target companies. If so, register with them.

17. If targeting a large corporation or organization, review their job postings at least weekly.

18. If you have had an interview and the employer does not contact you by a stated date, call and inquire if it has made a decision.

19. Continue all these efforts until your search results in employment.

how to prepare a résumé

11

the basics

Your résumé is your most important personal marketing tool in the preliminary stages of your job search. A résumé tells your story: who you are, your education, work experience, achievements, special skills or qualifications, and anything else of interest to a prospective employer. You may think that this information could fill a book, but your interests will be better served by a concise résumé that conveys all you have to offer a prospective employer. It should include personal contact information; work experience, with dates; a description of your achievements, duties, and responsibilities; relevant professional awards and special training; and educational degrees.

inside information

Your résumé may have only a few seconds to do its work. The fact is, employers may be overwhelmed with résumés, especially in the days after a Sunday newspaper listing of a job. In these quick reviews, the information in the top half of the résumé often determines if your application gets a second look. Most employers use résumés as negative screening devices. They're looking for a reason to discard your résumé, not keep it. The key is for the information at the top of the résumé to match whatever the ad specifically says the employer is looking for. Use bold type and a clean layout to make sure this information pops off the page, even at a quick glance. Obviously that means that whenever you apply to a specific company for a specific job you must adapt your résumé to the job or company, restating and rearranging the material based on the job description or the company's business.

jargon

Achievements: Specific accomplishments, preferably stated in some kind of numeric fashion. Examples are: "Cut department costs by 10 percent" or "Trimmed two days off production cycle."

Cover letter: A letter that accompanies your résumé when you respond to a job listing or offer. It should introduce you, state why you are interested in working for the company, and briefly summarize your best points, noting that they are "fully explained in the attached résumé."

References: People who know and can vouch for you, personally and professionally. Professional references carry more weight. Past employers make ideal references. Always check with a reference before you submit his or her name.

warning

Your résumé can do as much to hurt as help your job search. It must be neat, well organized, easily read and understood, and clearly printed on quality paper. Avoid garish colors or a rambling document. Also, unless you work as a consultant or in an industry where job-hopping is commonplace, having worked at many jobs over a short period of time raises a red flag to an employer.

fyi

You should strive to fit your résumé onto a single page. A longer résumé does not necessarily attract additional attention. If you need additional pages, make sure your first page highlights whatever it is that indicates you're a perfect candidate for the job in question, whether it's your achievements, your experience, or relevant training.

101 Best Resumes by Jay A. Block and Michael Betrus (McGraw-Hill, 1997): Learn from examples in this guide, which uses sample résumés to help you develop and produce the document that will speak best for you.

The Complete Idiot's Guide to the Perfect Resume by Susan Ireland (Macmillan, 2000): Don't let the title fool you; whatever your professional level, you'll find something here to help you build a better résumé.

1st Resume Store (www.freeresumetips.com): A Web site offering an abundance of inside information on how to prepare a résumé and cater it to a specific career or position, as well as professional résumé preparation services.

1. Compile a list of information you want to include on your résumé, including personal information, past employers and dates, achievements, skills, educational experience, and any awards or honors.

2. For each job, create a detailed list of your achievements and responsibilities. Describe your duties, the number and types of workers you supervised, the equipment you operated, the computer systems and software you used. Write down your reason for leaving.

5. Combine your relevant experience and skills with your long-term aspirations into a single paragraph that summarizes your employment skills and achievements.

4. Review all this information and make any necessary additions.

3. Make a list of what you enjoyed about each of these jobs and what you didn't like.

6. Create a chronological outline of your employment history.

7. If you need to conserve space, edit this list, concentrating on employment over the earliest five years of your career. Eliminate any jobs you held for a short period that aren't relevant to your career or from which you were fired. If these leave gaps in your employment history, be prepared to explain them.

9. Decide if you want to prepare the résumé yourself or take it to a professional. If taking it to a professional, take this information with you and explain your job goals and what achievements, skills, and experience you want to emphasize and why. If doing it yourself, investigate what resources are available to help you format the résumé.

8. Organize your information.

10. Review other résumés or templates available in books and word processing applications.

11. Choose a format, font, and font size that work well together for a résumé that's attractive, professional-looking, and easy to read. Put your information into the selected format.

12. Consider using boldface and italics to highlight important information.

15. Print and edit again.

14. If that is not possible, concentrate on telling your whole story on the first page, backing it up with details on the subsequent pages.

13. Print and edit the résumé. Ideally, you want a one-page document that will catch an employer's attention.

16. Make sure the dates of employment convey a consistent job history.

17. Have at least two other people read the résumé.

18. Make final edits and changes.

21. You don't need to include contact information for references, but at the bottom of the résumé you should mention that personal and professional references are available upon request.

20. Get their permission.

19. Choose your reference candidates.

22. Select a quality bond paper for the résumé.

23. Print several general copies and store them in a folder.

24. Review your résumé before responding to any position and revise it as needed for that job or employer.

how to prepare for an interview

12

the basics

Until you sit down with a prospective employer, you are your résumé. It was obviously impressive enough to open the door, but the interview is when you'll actually land the job or blow your chances. It's the half hour to an hour in which an employer passes judgment on you as a person and a professional. This is always a subjective decision, and the outcome depends on how well you connect with the interviewer and impress him or her with your knowledge, experience, and ambition. Remember the saying that the first impression is a lasting one? The interview is your one chance to make that impression and convince a potential employer that you belong on its team. With your future riding on the decision, it only makes sense to do all you can to prepare for this test.

inside information

By the time you arrive, the interviewer already knows something about you from the details provided in your résumé and cover letter. You should already know something about the company, its business, and its market as well. Knowledge is bound to impress—or at least demonstrate your enthusiasm—and will certainly help you through the interview process. Most interviews are in two parts: first the employer questions you about your work history, abilities, and goals; then there's a discussion about the company and its business. When the focus is on you, you're best served by honesty on all matters, emphasizing your personal responsibility and ability to articulate your strengths and ambitions. When you can pose pointed questions about the company and its market, it demonstrates the interest, knowledge, and enthusiasm employers value.

jargon

Career goals: In your interview, the employer will want to learn if your goals coincide with those of the company. When explaining them, mention the skills you want to improve, the contributions you want to make as an employee, and your ultimate professional ambitions.

Qualifications: In a job interview, the employer wants to know everything about you that qualifies you for the job. This can include actual work experience as well as pursuits outside work and your demonstrated abilities and ambition.

warning

There are so many ways to blow an interview that they can be easily forgotten. Some basic rules: dress neatly and appropriately; arrive on time for the interview or call if you are going to be late; don't put down your present employer; if you've made a mistake, accept the responsibility; answer questions thoroughly; look the interviewer in the eye.

fyi

Employment interviews, by their nature, are tense situations for both the interviewer and the job applicant. One of the keys to a successful interview is finding some way to break that tension and establish a rapport with the employer. Thank him or her for the opportunity for the interview; admire the office or view; mention the beautiful weather. Smile. Do what you can to clear the tension, and the interview will be over before you realize it.

101 Dynamite Answers to Interview Questions: Sell Your Strength! by Caryl Rae Krannich and Ronald L. Krannich (Impact Publications, 1999): Examples of how to answer even the toughest questions posed during a job interview to make the kind of impression that will help land the job.

The Complete Idiot's Guide to the Perfect Interview by Marc Dorio (Macmillan, 2000): A complete guide to all types of job interviews and how to use the interview process to your advantage.

1. Revise your résumé to match the job description closely.

2. Draft a cover letter noting how your experience and interests match the job description.

3. When contacted for an interview, write down the directions to the location, the appointment time, and the contact's telephone number.

12. Why would you like to work for this company?

11. Prepare and rehearse for the interview, developing answers to likely questions.

10. If possible, speak with present and former employees about working at this company.

13. What do you have to offer in terms of experience?

14. What skills do you have to offer?

15. What kind of opportunities are you looking for?

24. Where do this department and position fit into the overall company structure?

23. What does the job entail?

22. What are the job's responsibilities?

25. What are the company's policies and procedures?

26. Whom would you answer to?

27. Who will your coworkers or staff be?

36. Allow yourself sufficient travel time to arrive early for your appointment.

35. Dress professionally and conservatively for the interview.

34. Gather your support materials for the interview, including copies of your résumé, reference information, and work samples.

4. Educate yourself about the company.

5. If time allows, request a copy of the company's annual report from the public relations or investor relations department. Ask for any other available brochures on the company.

6. Visit the company's Web site and read up on the company's history, operations, markets, and products.

9. If time permits, visit your local library and check through business reference materials for additional information on the company, its operations, and recent news events.

8. Conduct an online search of news articles about the company.

7. Review online press releases for news of the company, such as its business strategy and new initiatives.

16. Where do you expect to be in your career five years from now, and how do you plan to get there?

17. Why are you leaving your present job?

18. What have you learned from your past experiences?

21. Compile and rehearse questions you would like to pose to the interviewer about the job opening.

20. What are your salary requirements?

19. How will hiring you benefit this organization?

28. Is any special equipment used?

29. What is the department's budget?

30. What are the business hours?

33. Are there any travel requirements?

32. Are there opportunities for advancement within the company?

31. What is the salary range for the position?

how to evaluate a company and a job offer

13

the basics

Your résumé landed you an interview, which you aced. Now the prospective employer is calling to let you know the job is yours. Think before you commit yourself. It's time for the final and perhaps most important phase of the successful job search: evaluating the offer. Whether you've actively pursued a new position or the company came after you, it's imperative that you weigh the offer and all it entails to make sure you're making a smart career move.

inside information

We usually think of a job offer in terms of position and salary, and often that's enough to elicit a yes or no from job candidates. Base your decision on these factors alone, however, and you could sell yourself short and actually end up worse off than you are in your current position. Before you even start looking for another job, make a thorough assessment of everything your present employer provides: wages as well as benefits, insurance, holidays and vacation, profit sharing, pension, and a working environment conducive to your talents and interests. What's your reason for seeking another position? You'd better define that well so you can make sure the next job measures up. On-the-job training, tuition reimbursement, and company-paid training all contribute to the worth of a position.

jargon •

Benefits package: This commonly used term can mean entirely different things from company to company. It could mean just health insurance, or it might mean a whole menu of programs and benefits that add to the value of the job. Ask the employer to define it for you in detail.

Contract employee: When you are offered a position as a contract or temporary employee, the job is yours for a limited period of time. This type of position can have other implications as well, including increasing your tax liability and denying you benefits available to regular employees.

Probationary period: Often, when new employees are hired, the position is not officially theirs until a probationary period has passed. If this applies to the position you are considering, have the employer explain the length of probation and the review process before you begin working there.

warning •

Don't assume anything about a job offer or accept a promise to iron out details after you're on staff. Know what you need up front, and don't settle for less. Take time to learn a little about the company and its business before signing on. What you learn about the company will allow you to make a more insightful evaluation of the job offer. You want to hitch your career to a rising star.

fyi •

If you want a job but are looking for a better offer, there's nothing wrong with sitting down to negotiate salary and benefits. You want this move to be a step up your career ladder. When an employer extends a job offer, it is essentially saying that you are its man or woman. You're the one with the leverage now. The deal you hammer out will go a long way toward determining what you're able to command the next time you switch employers. It's advisable to have any promises formalized in an employment contract.

resources

Get a Job in 30 Days or Less: A Realistic Action Plan for Finding the Right Job Fast by Matthew J. DeLuca and Nanette F. DeLuca (McGraw-Hill Professional, 1999): Written for career-minded professionals who want to find employment that matches their skills, interests, and ambitions.

National Compensation Survey: Statistics on prevailing salaries for most professionals, updated periodically. A useful reference for determining if a job offer is reasonable for those in a given profession. Available online at www.bls.gov/ncs/ or through the Bureau of Labor Statistics Office of Compensation and Working Conditions at (202) 606-6199.

1. Determine the salary range you are seeking and an absolute minimum requirement.

2. Compile a list of the health-related benefits and life insurance you are entitled to with your present employer. Note any costs to you.

3. Compile a list of vacation days, personal days, sick days, comp time, etc.

6. Is the salary within range for your profession and in your area? If yes, continue.

5. When a prospective employer calls with an offer, learn what the salary, job title, and responsibilities are.

4. Compile a list of your present employer's pension, profit sharing, stock plans, and benefits.

7. Express your interest, but arrange for a meeting as soon as possible to meet coworkers and superiors if you haven't already done so; review and discuss the benefits package and personnel policies; and negotiate an acceptable package, if needed.

8. Before the meeting, review what you learned in preparing for the interview.

11. What are the opportunities for advancement?

10. What is the salary period?

9. At this meeting discuss position, salary, and responsibilities.

12. What is the salary review policy?

13. Ask the employer or human resources manager to explain the benefits package.

14. Health insurance considerations: type of coverage, carrier, deductible, copayment, monthly cost to you, coverage of preexisting conditions, etc.

17. What are the policies on vacation and personal days and eligibility for them?

16. Is there a stock or profit-sharing plan?

15. Pension considerations: type of plan, who contributes, whether the company matches contributions, etc.

18. What training and educational support programs are available to employees?

19. What are the company's dress requirements?

20. Is business travel required? How will you be compensated for your time and expenses?

23. Is telecommuting or work-at-home days permissible?

22. Will the company reimburse you for the use of your own vehicle or equipment?

21. Will you be required to spend extended periods at trade shows or business gatherings?

24. After considering all of the above, would accepting this position mark a step up the career ladder?

25. Is this the type of organization you want to work for?

26. If you accept an offer, make sure any special conditions promised are detailed in an employment contract or agreement.

28. If you feel you've been misled on any point, try to resolve it immediately with the person who hired you.

27. Continue to evaluate this position and employer for at least the first month.

how to get a raise or promotion

14

In an ideal working world you'd never need to ask for a raise or promotion; your employer would value and appreciate your contribution so much that he'd make sure to let you know how deeply that appreciation was felt. In the real world, you need to make your own case. Unless your employer is reminded of all you are doing and shown proof, he or she may assume you're satisfied with the status quo. Whether you are seeking a raise or a promotion, you have to do the real work before you ever approach your superior or apply for that move up. Day to day, on the job, is where you build the case that's going to merit a serious reevaluation of your worth or establish the trust that merits additional responsibility.

inside information

Simply doing your job well will rarely warrant anything more than an annual cost-of-living increase. Your employer hired you to do a good job; it's the least that is expected of you. It's the things you do above and beyond your job description that do the most to make your case for a raise or promotion. Surpass the expectations inherent in your job, and you're building your case for a raise or promotion. Begin right away: when you accept a job or promotion, make sure you thoroughly understand the responsibilities it entails. Fulfill those responsibilities. At the same time, don't hesitate to assume additional responsibilities, help your boss do his or her job better, or help your department operate more efficiently. Document all you do so you can demonstrate to your superior just how much you are contributing. You can strengthen your petition for a raise by knowing what peers in comparable positions are being paid. When courting a promotion, be prepared to explain how you can better serve the company in a new position, as well as how your present responsibilities can be shifted without detracting from productivity for you or your department.

jargon

Productivity bonus: A raise that isn't technically a raise but still rewards you financially above your base salary. If your employer cannot approve a raise but is responsive to this idea, you should reach an understanding on what the bonus will be based on before you embark on a project.

Market value: Here, the current salary range for a person working in a comparable position in your industry, fulfilling comparable responsibilities. You can determine your market value based on salary surveys published for your profession, conversations with peers, or salary ranges in posted job listings. The important thing is that you be aware of your current market value before you approach an employer for a raise.

warning

Demanding a raise or promotion can backfire. Unless you are fully prepared to change employers, make no absolute demands until you are ready to accept the alternatives. And don't base your request for a raise or promotion on what a coworker may or may not be earning. Your request and discussion should focus on you, your strengths, and the contributions you've made and can continue to make as a valued employee.

Want to increase your chances of winning a raise or promotion? Timing is important. Put in your request as soon as a position is listed or right after you complete a successful project, save your employer money, develop a new revenue stream, increase efficiency, or receive a professional honor or award. When you schedule a meeting with your superior, try to make it in midweek, preferably in early afternoon, when he or she may be most relaxed. On Mondays and Fridays your supervisor may be preoccupied with other matters and unable to devote sufficient attention to your request.

resources •

24 Hours to Your Next Job, Raise or Promotion by Robin Ryan (John Wiley & Sons, 1997): A career coach's guide to getting your career on track and keeping it there.

Beyond Performance: What Employees Really Need to Know to Climb the Success Ladder by Roland D. Nolen (New Perspectives, 1999): Straightforward advice on how business management thinks and works, providing insight on how to fit in and move up.

1. Know the company's salary review policy and opportunities for advancement before you accept a position.

2. Read and understand your job description and responsibilities.

3. Fulfill all your responsibilities.

12. If the company does not conduct an annual review, request a meeting with your superior soon after a significant accomplishment or based on a calendar milestone (six months or one year since the last review).

11. For a raise: in preparation of your annual salary review, prepare a memo to your boss detailing all you've done over the past year above and beyond what's called for in your job description.

10. Throughout the year document your achievements, projects completed, cost savings, new revenue streams, and departmental successes.

13. Determine beforehand how much of a raise you want and find out whether or not a company "cap" is in place.

14. Present your boss with the memo highlighting your accomplishments before your meeting.

15. In the ensuing discussion, highlight what you have contributed to the company.

24. Apply as soon as any job you're interested in is posted.

23. Continually track all job postings.

22. Find out the company policy on promoting from within.

25. Determine if your immediate supervisor will be an ally or foe in your request for a promotion.

26. If an ally, alert him or her to your interest.

27. If you fear he or she will oppose your move, arrange to meet with the person doing the hiring so your immediate supervisor will not immediately be aware of your interest.

35. If you are turned down for inadequate reasons, seriously consider changing your job or employer.

34. If the explanation is not satisfactory, ask that your request be reconsidered.

4. Look for ways to do your job more efficiently and reduce costs.

5. Look for new revenue streams for your employer. If you uncover any, discuss with your superior how to pursue them.

6. Concentrate on developing skills that improve your performance and enhance your value to your employer.

9. Annually determine the salary range for a person in your position, holding your level of responsibility.

8. Dress appropriately.

7. Make a point of getting to know people at all levels of your company. Make sure they know who you are and what you do.

16. If your salary is out of line with the industry average, present proof to your supervisor.

17. After discussing your strengths, contributions, and additional responsibilities assumed, present your request for a raise.

18. If your employer balks, inquire about some alternative form of compensation, such as a bonus based on productivity, meeting a deadline, or realizing a goal.

21. For a promotion: learn how your company posts position openings.

20. If you're not satisfied with the response you receive, begin thinking about changing jobs.

19. If you feel your employer is unreasonable in refusing the above, do not take the refusal personally. Ask what it would take to earn the additional amount you seek.

28. Compile the same documentation used for securing a raise.

29. Update your résumé. Attach a document highlighting your accomplishments and contributions as an employee of the company.

30. In anticipation of your interview for the promotion, rehearse what you need to say about why you want this promotion and how it will benefit the company.

33. Ask when the company will consider your request again. Mark the date on your calendar.

32. If your request for a promotion is refused, ask the person making the decision why. Learn how you must improve to merit such a promotion in the future.

31. Be prepared to present a plan or strategy for your transition to the promotion that will have minimal impact on productivity for your present department or boss.

how to fight age, sex, and race discrimination

15

Most of us never fully grasp the necessity or wisdom of antidiscrimination laws until we need them. Unfortunately, such protection is most needed in situations of forced contact with others: in the workplace, at school, out in public. Insensitivity to others and lack of understanding of antidiscrimination laws can introduce turmoil into the workplace. If you feel that you are the victim of unfair discrimination and you cannot resolve your complaint with your employer, the next step in seeking justice is to register your complaint with the Equal Employment Opportunity Commission.

inside information

Discrimination takes many forms but always involves unfair treatment of an individual simply because of that person's race, sex, age, religious beliefs, sexual orientation, physical disabilities, or even appearance. When prejudices contribute to or guide unfair treatment of an individual in the workplace, a series of federal antidiscrimination laws applies.

State and local municipalities may have their own antidiscrimination laws in place, as well. If you feel you are the victim of discrimination in the workplace, you must formally file a complaint with the EEOC or the local agency responsible for enforcing local anti-discrimination regulation. Agencies at the local and national levels will work together to resolve a case of discrimination. This can include a formal investigation, meetings with you and the accused, an attempt to mediate a resolution, the imposition of fines, and guidance to develop policies so such behavior does not occur again. The EEOC will also determine if you have a right to proceed with a private lawsuit against the person(s) or company you feel has discriminated against you.

jargon

Equal Employment Opportunities Commission (EEOC): A federal commission responsible for the enforcement of antidiscrimination laws pertaining to the workplace, including the Civil Rights Acts of 1963 and 1991, the Equal Pay Act, the Age Discrimination and Employment Act, the Americans with Disabilities Act, and the Rehabilitation Act of 1973.

Fair Employment Practices Agency (FEPA): A local agency that works in concert with the EEOC to ensure that local laws pertaining to on-the-job discrimination are enforced and complied with.

warning

Discrimination tends to escalate until checked and is often an entrenched pattern of behavior. If you feel you are the victim of discrimination, waste no time in making your charge. But the proof you can produce is as important as the charges you bring. Document that younger workers are being hired to replace older workers; that women are being passed over for promotions and not represented in management positions; that despite the number of applicants the company has a poor history of hiring members of your racial group. Be aware of the time limits involved for filing a complaint. You have 180 days from the date a violation occurs to file your charge with the EEOC.

fyi

The EEOC and FEPAs work with all parties to resolve a discrimination dispute and ensure that all applicable laws are complied with in the future. When these agencies determine that discrimination has occurred, the remedies can include reinstatement or hiring, back pay, attorney's fees, and court and related fees, as well as compensatory and punitive damages. The resolution may also include educational programs to ensure that discrimination does not occur again.

Job Discrimination II: How to Fight . . . How to Win! by Jeffrey M. Bernbach (Voir Dire Press, 1998): An experienced attorney offers a frank discussion of job discrimination; what does and does not constitute it; how to deal with it and file a claim; and all its implications.

Every Employee's Guide to the Law: What You Need to Know About Your Rights in the Workplace—and What to Do if They Are Violated, 3d edition, by Joel G. Lewin (Pantheon Books, 2001): A complete guide to laws pertaining to the workplace, including different forms of on-the-job discrimination.

Equal Opportunity Employment Commission: For information on antidiscrimination lawsuits, filing a complaint, or the nearest EEOC office, call (800) 669-4000.

1. Familiarize yourself with the company employee handbook or union bylaws sections relating to on-the-job discrimination.

2. Familiarize yourself with all applicable local, state, and federal laws protecting you against discrimination.

3. Recognize that these laws protect individuals against discrimination based on age, sex, race, religion, physical handicap, and, in some areas, sexual orientation.

6. If discriminatory patterns toward you persist, express your concerns to a superior.

5. Employers and supervisors need to be sensitive to how actions or statements by staff and management could be interpreted by some as evidence of discrimination, and they need to take steps to eliminate such attitudes and behavior.

4. When someone offends you with a comment or behavior in the workplace, express your disappointment and describe the offense to the perpetrator.

7. If you feel you are working in a hostile environment, document that hostility: write down behavior you interpret as evidence of discrimination.

8. If you feel you have been the victim of discrimination, raise your concerns to a superior immediately, in writing. Send a copy to Personnel and keep a copy for your files.

9. File your grievance or complaint as directed in your company handbook or union bylaws.

12. Simultaneously arrange a meeting with an attorney who specializes in cases involving the workplace and/or on-the-job discrimination.

11. Formally file a complaint.

10. If your situation is not resolved to your satisfaction, consider filing a complaint with the EEOC or the appropriate FEPA.

13. Explain your case to the attorney and present your proof.

14. Discuss your options.

15. Await mediation efforts by EEOC/FEPA, and determination of your right to sue.

18. Since filing a a lawsuit can make for uncomfortable relations on the job, decide whether or not you want to remain in your present job, if that is an option, while your case is in court.

17. If a lawsuit is recommended, proceed according to your attorney's advice.

16. If, after mediation efforts, it is determined that you do have the right to sue under the tenets of applicable local or federal law, discuss the matter with your attorney.

how to propose new
workplace options

16

the basics •

If your job centers around computers and information processing, your productivity is no longer entirely dependent on your location. Over the last decade some forward-thinking corporations and a few assertive employees have taken this as the starting point for creating new working arrangements. Once-revolutionary concepts such as telecommuting, working from home, and the virtual office are now standard options for a small but significant portion of the working population. These trends are constantly being fed by advances in technology on several fronts, including computers, communications, and the Internet. But as familiar as such concepts now seem, there are still many employees for whom they hold more promise than practical advantage. Often it takes persistent lobbying by one or two people to convince management to at least experiment with these concepts.

Most employers fail to recognize the potential advantage of options such as telecommuting, working from home, or job sharing until they are shown they can and do work. That responsibility often falls on a single employee who is willing to push for these options. If you want to be that individual, you must first realize that you can't force an organization to revise its policies and procedures overnight. You have to move slowly, at least initially, to make management comfortable with a new concept. Experiment first on a small scale. Begin with an assessment of your job and responsibilities and how they are met. How dependent are they on your physical presence? If they aren't, it's likely you could perform at least part of your tasks from some remote location, including your home. If you want to work fewer hours but hold on to your position, sharing your job and responsibilities with another employee with similar goals may be feasible. In either case, or when proposing any other new type of working arrangement, you need to start slowly, experimenting with the concept for only a day each week or a couple of days each month. Once you have demonstrated that it works, sit down with your manager to discuss ways in which you could formalize these arrangements. Prepare to demonstrate how such a move will benefit the company as well as employees. Use the market studies published in academic and trade journals that show that employee productivity can actually increase under such arrangements to make your case.

Telecommuting: Working from a remote location, sending and receiving work electronically by modem or over the Internet. Telecommuters may work from home full-time or combine days at home with days spent in the office.

Virtual office: Literally, an office without walls. Because of advances in computer and communications technology, it is now possible to send and receive work, e-mail, faxes, and telephone calls wherever one can be reached: in a spare room at home, in the car, on a park bench, even in a telephone booth or airport terminal.

Before you present your case for a new working arrangement, familiarize yourself with success stories and the gains other companies have realized through such programs. It will be easier to convince management to experiment with a concept such as telecommuting if there are no up-front costs. Use your equipment and connections to make your case. Later, when your employer is sold on the idea, it may spring for the costs. If you ask it to do so up front, it may nix the experiment.

warning •

Managers, particularly those entrenched in their positions, may prove particularly resistant to new working arrangements. Often they equate your physical presence with the sense of control that goes with their own responsibility. If you are sensitive to their needs, involve them in the planning and proposal, and present regular reports and meetings as part of the arrangements, they may prove more willing to experiment. Working at home may sound great, but it's not for everyone. It's especially important that you experiment with this concept before making a commitment. Feeling isolated can be a problem for anyone who enjoys the camaraderie of the office. Also, make sure you have the motivation to start work and follow it through without someone looking over your shoulder.

resources •

101 Tips for Telecommuters: Successfully Manage Your Work, Team, Technology and Family by Debra D. Dinnocenzo (Berrett-Koehler Publishing, 1999): Tips, insights, and advice for both employers and employees on how to make telecommuting work in all types of businesses.

Telecommute!: Go to Work Without Leaving Home by Lisa Angowski Shaw (John Wiley & Sons, 1996): A handbook on telecommuting for the employee, with thorough discussions of both the opportunities it offers and the challenges it presents.

1. Evaluate your job and how you fulfill your responsibilities.

2. What are your primary responsibilities?

3. How much of your work requires physical presence at your office?

6. Do you have the equipment and connections that would allow you to work from home?

5. Are they accessible?

4. If you could work elsewhere, what resources would you require?

7. If you are considering proposing job sharing, compile a list of responsibilities and the skills required to fulfill them.

8. Is your position easily filled?

9. Is there some individual who shares your goals and skills?

12. Does it matter when in the day your work is completed?

11. If you are looking for a flexible work schedule, are there any deadlines that must be met on a daily basis?

10. Approach that person to gauge his or her interest before you discuss this option with your supervisor.

13. Outline the type of working arrangement you would like.

14. Search online or in business trade journals for case studies of companies that have launched similar programs or experiments.

15. Read up on the studies, focusing on both the pros and cons of such arrangements.

18. Ask to try an arrangement on an experimental basis, for one day or a couple of days per week.

17. Arrange a meeting with your manager or immediate superior to discuss the possibility of experimenting with new working arrangements.

16. Anticipate any concerns your employer may have and decide on your response.

19. Explain how your supervisor will be able to monitor your activity and productivity and communicate with you.

20. Cite examples of how such an arrangement has worked for other companies.

21. If refused, ask for an explanation of what company policies would preclude this.

24. Schedule a meeting with your superior after the initial experiment or trial period.

23. If your request is approved, set specific goals and procedures for how this arrangement will work and be managed.

22. If necessary, request an opportunity to discuss this with superiors or the human resources department.

25. Review the experiment and the results.

26. Be prepared to demonstrate how this experiment has benefited the company, management, and you.

27. If you are able to demonstrate benefits, ask to formalize the arrangement as part of your regular schedule, or as a component of the terms of your employment.

29. If this is to be a permanent arrangement, ask the company to reimburse you for the costs related to your use of technology and related services.

28. Include in your plans periodic reviews of the arrangement and its impact on productivity.

how to develop a business plan

17

the basics

A business plan is the defining document of any business. Typically used as a tool for attracting outside financing and investment to a business start-up, it also provides the business owner with an operator's manual for running the business and assessing progress. For this document—a multipage booklet, at least—to succeed, it must define the business in terms of its management, purpose, products and/or services, target audience, and marketplace. And it should include realistic financial projections that demonstrate the profit potential of the business and the promise of a return on investment.

inside information

There are companies that offer services for developing a business plan. While they may be able to offer invaluable insight into how to prepare the actual document, it is how you, the visionary behind the business, present your plans that will sell others on your idea. Ideally the business plan should be a document that you (and your partners) produce to define your business goals and strategy for success. What does that entail? Although no two businesses or owner/operators share exactly the same vision, all should be able to define their venture within the context of a traditional business plan. First, the business, its purpose, products and/or services, and target customers should be described in a few sentences. Next, the plan should present, in an "executive summary," a basic explanation of the business, the market you are entering, the distinguishing points of your products and/or service, and what benefits or advantages your company brings to the market. With these points laid out, the rest of the plan should fill in the details, demonstrating your knowledge of the market, the experience you and other members of your team bring to this endeavor, the opportunities you plan to pursue, and how you plan to realize your goals through your marketing efforts. For a business owner, the theory and strategy contained in the plan will prove invaluable in running the business over the long run. Outsiders who are asked for financial support or investment, however, will base their decisions on the financial figures and projections provided in the plan. These numbers will be critical to attracting investment.

jargon

Mission statement: Also called a "statement of purpose," a summary statement that concisely describes the business purpose, products and/or services offered, and its target audience.

Executive summary: A summary, running several pages if necessary, of the details of the rest of the plan, giving readers a quick insight into the business, the opportunity it represents, and its market and business strategy.

warning

The most challenging and critical aspect of completing a business plan is coming up with numbers to support the plan. The numbers should be based on realistic estimates of start-up costs and the operating capital required until the business reaches the break-even point and begins to support itself. The difficulties arise when the numbers reveal that your planned business poses more of a financial challenge than you are willing to admit. The numbers do not lie, and if they indicate that your plan is doomed to fail, it's better to modify your plans or look for another opportunity before you take the business beyond the planning stage.

Investors expect a business plan that demonstrates your professionalism. It should effectively communicate the merits of your business in a format that is easy to digest and appealing to the eye. Draft the details of the plan on your own. When that work is complete, decide if you want to turn production of the plan over to someone else.

Anatomy of a Business Plan: A Step-by-Step Guide to Starting Smart, Building the Business, and Securing Your Company's Future by Linda Pinson and Jerry Jinnett (Dearborn, 1999): A thorough look at effective business plans and what they should contain, with advice and insight on producing an effective document.

Your First Business Plan: A Simple Question and Answer Format Designed to Help You Write Your Own Plan, 3d edition, by Joseph Covello and Brian J. Hazelgren (Sourcebooks, 1998): A simplified approach to producing a business plan that literally steps you through the process.

SBA Online (www.sba.gov/starting/indexbusplans.html): On its Web site, the Small Business Administration offers a variety of useful resources for the itinerant entrepreneur, including a template for drafting a business plan.

1. Decide on a name for the business.

2. Decide on the business structure: sole proprietorship, partnership, or corporation.

3. Begin formulating a plan.

12. What will your method of production and delivery be?

11. What are the advantages and distinguishing characteristics of your product and/or services?

10. Who is your target audience?

13. Define your market in terms of your product and/or services.

14. What is the health of the market?

15. Who are your target consumers?

24. How will you reach your target audience?

23. Define your marketing plans.

22. Are their needs changing?

25. What are your promotional plans?

26. What are your proposed advertising budget and spending plans?

27. What will your start-up costs be?

36. How much are you investing?

35. How much will you need to spend on all items related to operating expenses through the first year?

34. What will your operating costs be?

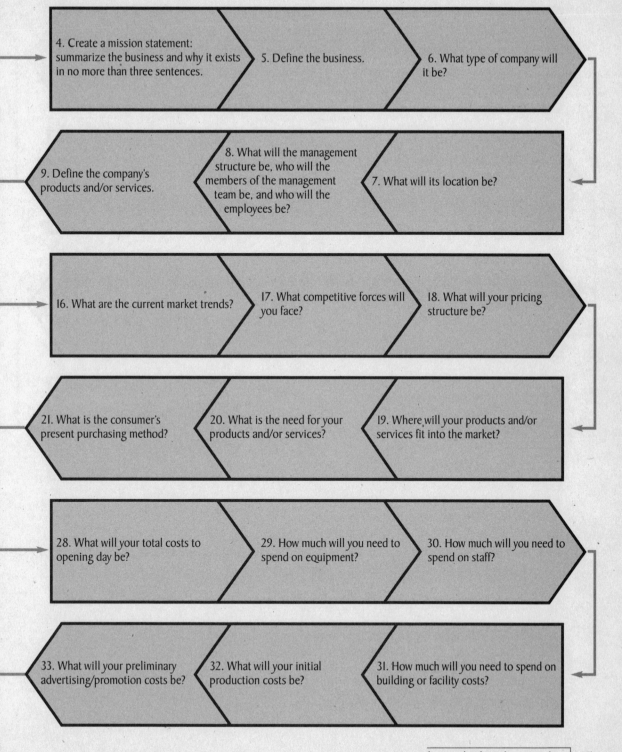

4. Create a mission statement: summarize the business and why it exists in no more than three sentences.

5. Define the business.

6. What type of company will it be?

9. Define the company's products and/or services.

8. What will the management structure be, who will the members of the management team be, and who will the employees be?

7. What will its location be?

16. What are the current market trends?

17. What competitive forces will you face?

18. What will your pricing structure be?

21. What is the consumer's present purchasing method?

20. What is the need for your products and/or services?

19. Where will your products and/or services fit into the market?

28. What will your total costs to opening day be?

29. How much will you need to spend on equipment?

30. How much will you need to spend on staff?

33. What will your preliminary advertising/promotion costs be?

32. What will your initial production costs be?

31. How much will you need to spend on building or facility costs?

37. How much outside financing will be required?

38. What do you expect your return on investment to be?

39. Prepare a break-even analysis.

42. Based on its content, prepare an executive summary, summarizing the key points in each section.

41. Review, revise, and edit all aspects of the business plan.

40. Project the return on investment for your investors and/or backers.

43. Prepare the layout.

44. Proofread the document.

45. Have the plan printed, bound, and prepared for distribution.

46. Periodically assess your progress in realizing your goals. Revise your plan as needed.

how to raise start-up funds
for your business

18

Unless you have an especially deep financial well from which to draw or are planning a very inexpensive business, you're going to require some outside funding to get your business up and running. Typical expenses faced by most entrepreneurs include start-up costs and at least a year's worth of operating capital—whatever is required to carry the business to its break-even point. When figuring these costs, the business's long-term interests will be better served if you overestimate your needs and have too much of a reserve on hand. The other extreme—underestimating your expenses and being caught short during the critical first year—can put the entire venture at risk and introduce unwanted stress in a period when it is the last thing you need.

Banks, investors, and venture capitalists all want to help entrepreneurs with their great ideas—after they have been proven in the marketplace. Unless you and your management team have impeccable credentials in the field you're entering and a product or service that simply cannot lose, they'll be glad to talk to you *after* you've proven your idea, guided it past the break-even point, and weathered a downturn or two. Raising start-up funding is almost always an endeavor in creative financing. And as the principal promoter of a great idea, you should be willing to demonstrate your confidence by supplying at least 50 percent of the funding needed for start-up. Dip into your savings or your retirement fund, sell off valuable possessions, take out a home equity loan. Only when you've exhausted your own options should you turn for outside assistance to family and friends with the resources to fuel your dream. If you still come up short, consider taking on a partner or some form of equity financing to give your business financial wings.

jargon

Breakeven: The point when a business's sales exceed expenses and it begins to show a profit.

Debt financing: A loan to the business; a debt that must be repaid to the institution or individual granting it. Excessive debt financing can drag a good idea down.

Equity financing: A form of financing in which an investor grants a certain amount of money in return for a share, or equity, in the business.

Seed capital: The amount of money required to get a business started. The seed capital should be sufficient to cover start-up expenses and at least a year of operating expenses.

warning

There are two ways to tilt the balance against your business: underestimate the amount of start-up financing it requires, or lean too heavily on debt for seed money. Underestimating costs can undercut your chances of success or introduce significant financial challenges when your attention needs to be focused on the business. Too much debt can overburden the business and make it more difficult to reach the break-even point. Should the business fail, you'll still be responsible for those debts. When borrowing from family, friends, or other outside sources, make sure you have a written agreement that describes the amount and terms of the loan and a repayment schedule. Always treat such a loan as a business transaction.

Only after you've exhausted your personal sources of financing should you turn to friends and family for financial assistance in starting a business. Present it as an opportunity to help you, and consider offering them equity in the business in return for financial assistance. You may also want to consider entering into a partnership with someone who has the resources to get the business off the ground but lacks your management experience and market knowledge. Again, always define all agreements in writing, leaving no room for debate about who agreed to what.

resources •

Financing Your Business Dreams with Other People's Money: How and Where to Find Money for Start-up and Growing Businesses by Harold R. Lacy (Sage Creek Press, 1998): Straightforward advice for new and established entrepreneurs on how to finance a venture.

Where to Go When the Bank Says No: Alternatives for Financing Your Business by David R. Evanson (Bloomberg Press, 1998): A comprehensive guide for those seeking outside financing, with insights from those who have done it, lists to help you weigh your options, and lists of resources to help you in the search.

1. Complete your business plan.

2. Closely analyze your estimated start-up costs and required operating capital projections. Set the total as your target.

3. Tap your personal resources.

6. Determine how much debt you are willing to assume in order to get the business started.

5. Sell off valuable possessions or collections.

4. Turn savings and investments into cash on hand.

7. Determine the amount of money available to you through refinancing your home mortgage or taking out a home equity or personal loan.

8. Tally the above and subtract from the total determined in step 2. Are the costs covered? If so, proceed with your plans. If not, determine the amount still required and prepare to approach other sources of financing.

11. Identify likely candidates for financial assistance among family and friends. Consider only those for whom financially assisting your business start-up will not result in financial risk.

10. Determine the size of the loan you need, the amount of equity you are willing to offer, or the amount of control you are willing to relinquish to a partner(s).

9. Decide if you want to secure additional debt to start the business, trade equity for financing, or take on one or more partners.

12. Decide in what order you will approach these candidates.

13. Approach each, explain your business, and present each with a copy of your business plan. Reveal what you are personally contributing financially to this venture.

14. Present this as an opportunity to help you. Explain your need and how they will be repaid for their assistance.

16. Have an attorney review all points in the document with the other party before signing.

15. Draw up a written agreement with anybody who agrees to assist you. Make sure it spells out the terms of their loan or investment and the expected return or interest in the business.

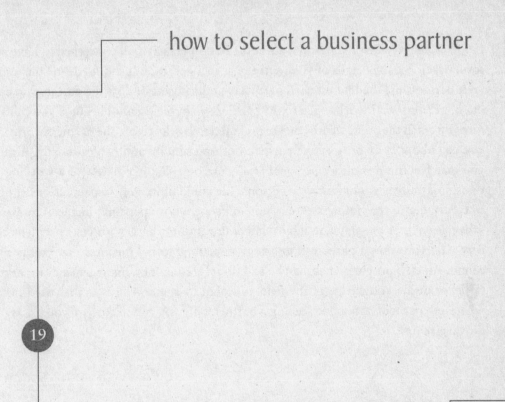

how to select a business partner

the basics

Often partners conceive a business together, but sometimes an entrepreneur approaches a partnership as a way to put a business start-up onto the fast track or relieve him- or herself of overwhelming responsibilities in an already successful operation. Whatever the reason, taking on a partner can prove the wisest step for your business or a misstep that will ultimately doom your venture. Partnerships work when the talents, commitment, and ambitions of the individuals involved complement one another. They fail when one takes more than he or she gives the business; when personalities, goals, and work ethics clash; or when a partner's personal problems encroach on what should be strictly a professional relationship. Considering all the opportunities and risks a partnership can introduce to a business venture, taking on a partner is a decision that should be carefully weighed and thoroughly investigated before transforming an informal relationship into a working one.

If you decide to take on a partner, it's in the best interests of all concerned to have an attorney spell out the details of your agreement in a contract. It should define the terms of your partnership, the interest each party has in the business; how the partnership can be dissolved; and what will happen to the partnership in the event of death or disability. Before you reach the point where you are prepared to legally create the partnership, learn all you can about your prospective partner, both personally and professionally. Although you may feel that his or her personal affairs are outside the purview of a working relationship, trouble in your partner's personal life could ultimately impact his or her ability to contribute to the business. You want someone whose personal financial house is in order, as well, or one day you might find yourself in business with your partner's creditors. And you want a partner who brings something to the business that you need but cannot yourself provide. That may be additional seed money, management or marketing skills, or inside knowledge of the field you plan to enter. Whatever that need may be, whatever your motivation for seeking a partner, only you can make sure you get as much as you give up.

Limited partnership: A partnership agreement that specifically limits the involvement of partners in the business. For example, a limited partner may contribute a percentage of seed money solely in return for a share of the business profits.

Uniform Partnership Law: A law, adopted in most states, that governs the structure and operation of a partnership. It applies when there is no other written agreement defining the terms of a partnership.

A partnership must be legally established with an agreement in writing that spells out all the details of the relationship. Such an agreement is your best protection against future misunderstandings that could imperil the business. It's important that this agreement stipulate the partners' roles in setting up the business, as well as their options if there comes a day when one or more wants out of the business. You may feel your partner is your friend, but a partnership is a legal business relationship and should always be defined and regarded as such.

Before you look outside for a potential partner, consider those in your inner circle as candidates. Spouses, living companions, siblings, children, close friends, and associates are people you already get along with, which is one of the determining factors in the success of any partnership. That said, these candidates must also meet the same criteria you would use in evaluating any partner: they should have a real interest in the business you are entering; have skills or resources that complement your own; and share your ambition to make the venture a success.

resources •

The Partnership Book: How to Write a Partnership Agreement, 6th edition, by Denis Clifford and Ralph E. Warner (Nolo.com, 2001): Legal publisher's comprehensive guide to partnership agreements, start to finish. Includes CD-ROM.

1. Complete a preliminary draft of your business plan.

2. Evaluate your own skills. Compile a list of everything you plan to contribute to your planned business in terms of financial resources, skills and experience, knowledge of the market, etc.

3. Based on the above, identify areas of need. Compile these into a list that you will use in evaluating potential partners.

12. If you're both still interested, present the person with a copy of your business plan and ask him or her to review it. Schedule a follow-up meeting for further discussion.

11. Explain your concerns, your expectations of any potential partner, and what you expect the partner to contribute professionally and financially.

10. If the person is interested, explain your business and the market you are entering.

13. At the follow-up meeting, review the business plan. Discuss your strategic plans thoroughly, evaluating the possible partner's insights, enthusiasm, understanding, and interest. Listen to his or her ideas.

14. Discuss the potential partnership, defining expectations, areas of need, division of responsibilities, amount of investment required, and the corresponding share in the business.

21. Fulfill any local requirements for registering the business or partnership and secure any required licenses.

20. When the agreement is mutually acceptable, sign it.

4. Decide if you want to take on a full or a limited partner.

5. If you decide on a limited partnership, define the extent to which you are willing to relinquish some control or interest in the business and what you expect in return.

6. Identify likely candidates. Look first within your immediate sphere, then outside, matching individuals to your needs.

9. If not, move on to the next best candidate.

8. Approach your leading candidate, explain that you are considering taking on a partner, and ask if he or she would be interested.

7. Consider what you know or can determine about a prospective partner's personality, personal life, financial situation, and professional skills and experience.

15. Inquire about the possible partner's skills and experience, personal finances, and any potential conflicts in his or her personal life.

16. If you're both still interested and want to pursue the partnership, arrange a meeting with the attorney you plan to use as a business attorney.

17. Work with the attorney and partner to draw up an agreement that formalizes the relationship.

19. All partners should review the final document and revise it as needed.

18. Make sure this agreement spells out the terms of the partnership: specific responsibilities; investment and return; percentage interest in the business; method of dissolving partnership; and course of action should a partner become disabled or die.

how to investigate a franchise or business that's for sale

20

If you're eager to be your own boss, you can eliminate some of the risks of a start-up by purchasing an existing business or investing in a franchise. Although no two businesses are entirely alike and franchises can be a different breed entirely, much of the work required to make a smart investment with real profit potential is the same. You want to make sure that you get all you pay for, that the business or franchise offers real promise of a livable return on investment, and that you're not going to assume any hidden financial, tax, or legal liability. You can't do all this all alone; you're going to require the services of a qualified attorney and accountant.

inside information

There's always a reason why a business or franchise is up for sale. Sometimes it's simply that the owner wants to pursue other interests or is ready for retirement. It may be that the franchiser is looking to take a great idea into a new market area. On the other hand, a business might be so overwhelmed with competition or plagued with increasing costs that the owner's best option is to unload the company as soon as possible. Or the franchise company may be more interested in selling franchises than in seeing its franchise owners prosper. Why a business or franchise is for sale is the most important piece of information you can learn. It will help you determine if it is a good investment and what kinds of risks you are taking on, and give you leverage in negotiating the best sale price. The answers may lie in the business's location, in its financial records, in the fact that there is a wave of new competitors rolling into town, or in the news on the financial pages. You need to educate yourself about the market a business or franchise serves before you buy it. Evaluate its location; talk to suppliers; read up on industry trends. With franchises, especially, review all the fine print of the franchise contract with your attorney early on. You want someone else's proven opportunity, not his or her problems. Determining the difference is entirely your responsibility.

jargon

Business broker: A professional who handles the sale of businesses in return for a commission on the final sale price; a good source for learning what types of businesses are available for sale in a market area.

Goodwill: One of the factors business owners often use to determine the value of their business. It is hard to measure and usually not as critical a factor in determining fair market value as the seller may suggest.

Market value: The price of a business, based on current market conditions. Sellers can use a variety of methods to determine this price. Buyers must understand what the market value or asking price is based on in order to determine the real worth of the business.

warning

Business owners can "cook" their books to make their numbers look good; conversely, some may use creative accounting to hide the business's profit potential. Unless you have a financial background, it's unlikely that you'll be able to discern a business's real value and profit potential. With a franchise, everything depends on the terms of the franchise agreement, and there's usually little if any room for negotiation. Let your attorney interpret the fine print and determine just how real an opportunity it represents.

An entrepreneur's chances of success always increase when he or she enters a familiar business, or a field he or she is already interested in. Whether you're thinking of buying an existing business or a franchise, look first for those that already hold some interest for you. If you lack experience and skills but still want to be your own boss, a franchise may be a better bet. Not only will you get a business with a proven name, but the package usually includes management and marketing training and support.

Buying and Selling a Business: A Step-by-Step Guide by Robert F. Klueger (John Wiley & Sons, 1988): Everything a buyer or seller needs to know to negotiate a smart deal. Explains the different approaches used to determine value, the factors to consider, and how to research the real value of a business.

How to Buy a Franchise: An Experienced Franchise Lawyer Shows How to Find, Evaluate and Negotiate for the Right Franchise by James A. Meaney (Pilot Books, 1999): An attorney's in-depth advice for those considering investing in a franchise, with information on evaluating the business and the franchise agreement.

1. Make a realistic assessment of your skills and experience.

2. Compile a list of businesses in which you already have experience or an interest.

3. Determine the amount of cash you have on hand available for investing in a business.

6. Identify the type of business or franchise you would like to own.

5. Decide if you would like to invest in a franchise or an existing business.

4. Read up on franchises, as opposed to independent businesses.

7. Track business-for-sale and franchise listings in your local paper.

8. If you are interested in purchasing an independent business, contact a business broker(s) working in your area and explain the type of business you are interested in purchasing.

11. Once you identify a business or franchise opportunity, alert your attorney and accountant or financial adviser that you will need their help.

10. If interested in a franchise, contact a franchise company and see if one is available in your area, or where franchises are available.

9. If you have a substantial amount of money to invest, contact owners of existing businesses and see if they are interested in selling.

12. Contact the owner or franchise company. Ask why it is selling or expanding into your area. Get a pledge from the owner not to compete with you or from the franchiser that it is selling an exclusive franchise in your area.

13. Start your investigation with the asking price for a business or franchise: determine how the price was determined and what method was used to determine the business's value.

14. Determine what is included in the price: facilities, assets, location, equipment and/or fixtures, vehicles, inventory, business name and logo, etc.

17. Contact key suppliers: Are they willing to extend the same terms to a new owner? Inquire about business trends.

16. Contact the landlord and leaseholders about any equipment. Can you renew their contracts under the same terms as the existing owner's?

15. Visually inspect the business and its location. Are the building, facilities, and location well maintained and in good working order?

18. Contact key accounts: Are they willing to continue trading with the business under new ownership? Have there been any problems dealing with the business or within this market?

19. Have your attorney check to see if there are any liens against the business or any recent or pending lawsuits against the business.

20. Have your accountant thoroughly review the business's financial records, including gross and net sales, taxes paid, payments to suppliers and creditors, and outstanding debt.

29. Must you purchase inventory through the franchisor?

28. What other fees are involved?

27. After the initial investment, what must you pay to the franchisor each year?

30. What are the terms of the agreement?

31. What training and marketing support is available to you?

32. What is the term of the agreement, and under what conditions can the franchise company void your franchise?

41. Also review the demographic profile supplied by the franchise company.

40. What are the terms of any loans to franchisees for facilities or equipment?

39. What is the average return on investment? How long has it taken franchisees to realize a full return on their initial investment?

42. Make sure your prospective customers live in the surrounding area and that there is a large enough trading volume to support a typical franchise.

43. Take any concerns raised by your attorney or account to the franchise company. If the answers are adequate and your concerns are addressed, proceed with the purchase.

44. Have your attorney review any final business purchase contract or franchise agreement before you sign.

21. Have your accountant review payroll records.

22. Have your accountant and attorney review any employment contracts with the business's key personnel.

23. If possible, meet with the key personnel to see if they are willing to retain their positions under new ownership. Listen closely to any concerns expressed.

26. In the case of a franchise, review the terms of the franchise agreement with your attorney.

25. Sit down with the owner and negotiate an acceptable sales agreement.

24. Review all points and determine if the business is worth the asking price.

33. What legal rights do you have if the franchise company fails to provide adequate inventory or management and marketing support?

34. Will the franchise company guarantee that it will not set up other franchises in direct competition with yours?

35. What are the terms for renewing the franchise agreement?

38. How many franchises are in existence? For how long? What are their average gross sales and net sales?

37. Simultaneously, have your accountant thoroughly review all financial statements supplied by the franchise company.

36. Can this franchise be transferred to other family members or heirs?

how to incorporate your business

21

the basics

Incorporating your business may seem like an intimidating process, but it's actually a straightforward procedure. While you can do it yourself with an incorporation "kit" or software, you may want to entrust the responsibility to an attorney. Corporations are approved by individual states and are subject to state regulations. There may be slight differences in state regulations and the application procedure. Incorporating has distinct advantages over operating as a sole proprietorship or partnership. For example, many people don't consider a business legitimate until it is incorporated. By incorporating, you create a new legal entity separate from yourself that is responsible for its own taxes and any legal liability resulting from delivery of its products or services.

inside information

Although you can incorporate a business yourself, in most states it's advisable to seek the assistance of an attorney who is familiar with local regulations and requirements.

The money spent will prove an wise investment in the future. An attorney should also be able to advise you on the tax and legal responsibilities of a corporation and how they will affect you. Incorporating a business introduces several new roles into a business, and you may assume any combination or all of them. These include the incorporator(s), or principals, who actually file the articles of incorporation; the shareholders, who hold a financial interest in the business; a board of directors, who make the operating decisions for the business; and officers—employees—who are responsible for the actual day-to-day operations of the business. Often, the entrepreneur is the principal stockholder and assumes many or all of these roles. Be aware that if you plan to incorporate and sell stock in the business to a significant number of shareholders outside the business, it can complicate matters and bring the business under the jurisdiction of securities laws and regulators.

jargon

Articles of incorporation: A legal document, filed with the state, to establish the corporation. Includes the corporation's name, its purpose, the names of incorporators and the business agent, and the number of shares to be issued. Depending on where you live, this may be called a certificate of incorporation or articles of association.

S corporation: Form of incorporation in which the owners enjoy limited liability for business debts yet treat the business's income as their own and are taxed accordingly.

warning

While most entrepreneurs decide to incorporate in order to protect their personal assets from business liability, the decision to incorporate can actually add to the financial burden put on a business. As a separate entity, a corporation pays tax on its earnings.

fyi

Incorporating is not the only way to go if you are starting a new business. A sole proprietorship is the simplest form of business structure, typically used by an individual who *is* his or her business. Under this business structure, business and personal income are treated as one and the same and taxed as personal income. An S corporation combines this simplified financial responsibility with some of the benefits of incorporating: the business's income is treated and taxed as the owners' personal income, yet they have the same protection from legal liability as if they had incorporated.

resources

How to Form Your Own Corporation Without a Lawyer for Under $75.00: Complete with Tear-Out Forms, Certificate of Incorporation, Minutes, Bylaws by Ted Nicholas and Sean P. Melvin (Dearborn, 1999): A do-it-yourself guide to incorporating your business, complete with model documents you can use to prepare and file articles of incorporation.

How to Incorporate: A Handbook for Entrepreneurs and Professionals by Michael R. Diamond and Julie L. Williams (John Wiley & Sons, 2000): A guide that helps business owners compare different ways to incorporate, understand the ramifications of each, and select the right type of incorporation, then steps you through the process.

1. Investigate all options for structuring your business: sole proprietorship, partnership, limited-liability company, and corporation. If you decide to incorporate, continue.

2. Contact the state office responsible for incorporations, usually the secretary of state or the corporation commissioner's office.

3. Inquire about procedures for filing articles of incorporation and the process for creating a corporation, including appointment of directors and officers, adoption of bylaws, and stock issuance.

4. Decide if this is something you can do yourself or if you must rely on an attorney for help. If doing it yourself, read up on what's required and what's available to you. If using outside help, contact your attorney. Explain that you are considering forming a corporation and would like him to help you handle the required paperwork.

5. Meet with your attorney and explain your plans for the business.

6. Have your attorney explain the pros and cons of incorporating and whether you would benefit from creating an S corporation.

7. Create a record book to record all activity related to your corporation.

8. Name your business or corporation.

9. Check with the state regulatory office to make sure that the name is available.

10. Determine if you need to name a board of directors before or after incorporating.

11. Elect a board of directors.

12. Work with your attorney to prepare and file the articles of incorporation.

13. If you plan to issue large amounts of stock, contact the Securities and Exchange Commission and the relevant state regulatory agency for information on compliance with federal and state securities laws.

14. Review the articles of incorporation and file them with the appropriate state agency.

15. Upon approval, set up a corporate bank account.

16. Draw up corporate bylaws specifying the rights and powers of directors, corporate officers, and shareholders, and how the corporation's business is to be conducted.

17. Hold a directors' meeting.

18. Revise the bylaws if needed and adopt them.

19. Name and approve officers of the corporation.

20. Issue stock to shareholders in the corporation.

23. If any outstanding requirements remain, complete them.

22. Contact your attorney to see if all requirements for incorporating have been met.

21. Deposit any payments in the corporate bank account.

24. Conduct the business as a corporation and comply with all applicable federal and state tax laws.

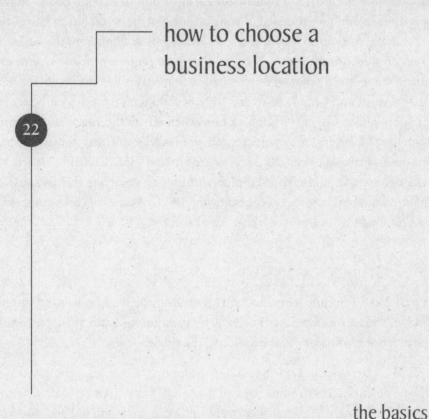

how to choose a
business location

22

Location is a determining factor in the success of many businesses. For enterprises such as a retail store or service center, which are entirely dependent on walk-in traffic, location is a make-or-break factor. Providers of professional services can shape their prospects more by situating themselves where the people they want to serve gather, such as in the business district. In the manufacturing sector, accessibility to major transportation routes is more the concern than visibility. For consultants and the growing legions of entrepreneurs trading in the virtual market of the Internet, location may not be critical to success at all, as long as the business can deliver its good or services.

inside information

What's the right location for your business? There's no simple answer. Rather, your business should be located where it's easiest for your customers to find or reach you. So the search for a home really begins with an assessment of who your customers are, their buying habits, and how it's most convenient for them to purchase your goods or services. This information should be contained in your business plan; if you haven't already completed it, it's advisable to do so before you start investigating a home for the business. The work you do on the business plan will reveal the space requirements needed to give the business an adequate start; what will be needed in that space; whether visibility or accessibility matters most; and what kind of growth you should plan for. It's far better to start with extra space and grow into it than to quickly outgrow the space and be forced to move into a new location. Once you compile your needs, identify the areas that best match your needs. Contact commercial real estate brokers specializing in that area to help you find the right space. Allow yourself plenty of time to complete this process—if you impose an unreasonable deadline on yourself, you may make a dangerous compromise in location, undermining your business's chances of success.

jargon

Cost per square foot: Typically, commercial real estate is defined and priced in terms of square footage. Square footage describes the actual amount of space available for use, excluding the exterior dimensions of the building, the sidewalk, etc.

Trading area: The surrounding area that actually supports a business, entirely dependent on the type of business. The trading area of a grocery store may be limited to the surrounding neighborhood, while a software publishing company will sell and ship its products nationwide.

Traffic: When discussing a business location, you are really speaking of two types of "traffic." First there's the traffic along surrounding roadways. Where traffic is especially congested, it can actually discourage potential customers from visiting a business. Then there's the "traffic" in the business location, the actual number of people who pass by and/or step into that location.

warning

With commercial real estate, especially, the burden is on you to determine a location's worth before you commit to it. Assess the space and facilities in terms of your present and anticipated needs. Track traffic patterns in terms of both the number of consumers passing that location and road congestion. If a location seems too good a bargain, exercise caution and investigate why it's priced so low. Location is one factor where it's rarely worth compromising. When you do find the "right" location, work with your attorney to negotiate a lease that leaves you an easy out if the business fails, yet allows a long-term option to renew the lease should you succeed.

fyi •

A good location commands top dollar because it can fuel a business's success. Until your business is up and running, though, it's usually in your best interest to lease the space rather than buy. The cost of constructing a new facility or completely renovating existing space can overburden a business start-up during its critical first year.

resources •

The Field Guide to Starting a Business by Stephen M. Pollan and Mark Levine (Fireside, 1990): A comprehensive guide including detailed advice on choosing a location for several types of businesses.

The McGraw-Hill Guide to Starting Your Own Business: A Step-by-Step Blueprint for the First-Time Entrepreneur by Stephen C. Harper (McGraw-Hill, 1992): Advice for those planning a business on how to beat the odds and launch a successful business, including information on choosing a location.

1. Complete a draft of the business plan. This will help identify search criteria for a location.

2. Compile a list of what you need in a facility: square footage, number of offices, utility connections, expandability, storage, etc.

3. Compile a profile of your target customers: Who are they? How will they purchase your product or service? What are their shopping patterns?

12. Evaluate the condition and appearance of the building in which you are considering locating.

11. Use Lifemap 47 to evaluate a neighborhood and for guidance in evaluating the surrounding area.

10. Explain your needs and the type of business. Arrange for a tour of area properties.

13. Is the building easy to find, secure, and well maintained? Does it have ample parking? Does it have well-lit stairs, hallways, and elevators? Is it clean?

14. Evaluate the space in terms of your needs.

15. Is the space adequate for offices, parking, storage, etc.? Will it allow for expansion? Does it have ample utility connections?

23. Also contact your attorney for help in negotiating a lease.

22. If all factors meet your needs, get in touch with the landlord to discuss a lease.

4. Compile a list of ways location will help or shape your business. Consider such factors as accessibility; walk-in traffic; types of surrounding businesses that can "feed" traffic to you; transportation needs.

5. Define your trading area: the surrounding geographic region from which you will draw customers.

6. Based on all of the above, compose a checklist of your location needs.

9. Contact commercial real estate brokers working in the area.

8. Visit these, and identify those that offer the best match.

7. Using this information, begin searching for a location. Identify areas, neighborhoods, even streets or malls that match your location needs.

16. How much of the cost of required renovation or remodeling is the landlord willing to assume?

17. What kind of lease is the landlord offering: cost of the space, length of the lease, and opportunity to renew?

18. When you decide you are interested in a particular location, visit it again without the broker.

21. Visit the area at night. Does it seem to be safe and secure?

20. If walk-in traffic is important, visit the area at different times of day to monitor consumer traffic and area road congestion.

19. Consider the building and environs as if you were a customer. Would you bring your trade to this location?

how to set up a home office

23

the basics

Once a novelty, the home office is now an increasingly common feature in the modern house or apartment. For some people, it is the primary home of their business; for others, an office away from the office; for some, merely a place to escape to spend hours on a computer. Whatever its intent, all home offices share the same purpose: to provide the physical and psychological space that will enable you to make productive use of your time. Ideally, a home office is somehow removed from the rest of household activity. That may require something as simple as a room divider or door, or significant remodeling or renovation. To create the right space, devote time to anticipating how it will be used before you start knocking down walls or buying furniture. Do you prefer working by natural or artificial light? How important is a window to your peace of mind? Will you be inviting clients to your office? If so, do you need a separate entrance? Consciously monitor household activity and think of how it might impact the way you want to work. Make a list of all your present and potential equipment needs, and make sure you have the required electrical outlets and phone connections. It's much easier to take care of them while the space is unoccupied. When you know your equipment needs, consider what you'll want in shelving, cabinets and a desk. Carefully planned, a home office can be an asset to both your home and your career.

inside information

Setting up a home office may entitle you to help or benefits you aren't aware of. Over the past decade, many companies have experimented with telecommuting and virtual workforces. The fact that you have a home office may make you eligible to participate in such a program. If your employer has such a program, it may be willing to help set up your office by loaning equipment or paying for the phone line that links your computer with headquarters. A home office may also entitle you to certain tax breaks, provided it is used exclusively for business purposes. If so, you may be able to deduct the cost of equipment and utilities as they relate to business. Note, however, that this is an area that can also invite tax trouble. You must be able to prove that the space and equipment are used exclusively for business. Read up on the latest tax laws before you assume or claim anything related to working at home.

jargon

Home business: Any business run from the home. Always requires some form of home office, which may qualify the owner of the business for certain tax deductions, if properly documented.

MFM: Multifunction machine: An all-in-one piece of equipment that can be especially useful in a home office where space is limited. Typically, an MFM includes any or all of the following: telephone, answering machine, fax machine, scanner, computer printer, and copier.

Telecommuting: Working remotely for an employer, usually at home, sending and receiving work electronically. Telecommuters usually do their work at a computer and are in constant touch with the main office by modem and telephone.

warning

A home office can prove an unwelcome guest if you don't take the needs of others who live there into account before your work "moves in." Your office should adapt to the other occupants of the household; don't expect them to adapt to you. If you're planning to spend a significant share of your workday in your home office, you will want to define the boundary between professional and personal life. Make it an office you can "leave" at the end of the day. Get a separate business telephone line, and make sure there's a door that shuts your work out of your home life whenever you close up shop. One final note: depending on where you live, there may be some restrictions on what you can do in your home office, especially if you're running a home-based business. Contact your local zoning board if you have any doubts.

resources

Home Office Design: Everything You Need to Know About Planning, Organizing, and Furnishing Your Work Space by Neal Zimmerman (John Wiley & Sons, 1996): An architect's advice on how to plan, create, and achieve the home office that's right for you, with many diagrams, photographs, and floor plans.

A Portfolio of Home Office Ideas (Creative Publishing International, 1998): A guide for planning the ideal home office with photographs and information about materials, furnishings, and machines to guide you to the right decisions.

Home Office Mall (www.homeofficemall.com): The Home Office Mall is a source of information on all aspects of the home office with a product search engine and many links to other Web resources, including home office furniture and equipment manufacturers.

1. Determine the type of office you'll need.

2. Identify your equipment needs.

3. Consider how the space will be used.

6. Establish requirements in terms of space, lighting, and accessibility.

5. Find out if there are any local restrictions against setting up a home office (check with the local zoning board).

4. Determine your space needs.

7. Consider the potential tax implications of a home office.

8. Decide if you will need separate telephone and utility services.

9. Can you use space in your home, or will you require separate, removed office space?

12. Determine how much renovation or remodeling is required.

11. Draft preliminary plans.

10. Match your available space to your priorities.

13. Can you do the required work yourself, or should you hire a professional (see Lifemap 6)?

14. If hiring an expert, see Lifemap 59.

15. If doing it yourself, see Lifemap 58.

18. Set up a business e-mail account.

17. Arrange for a new telephone line(s).

16. Arrange for necessary business utility accounts.

19. Use the equipment needs determined above to calculate furniture and shelving needs.

20. Purchase, install, and/or build required furniture.

21. Purchase required reference materials.

24. Get the word out (see Lifemap 27).

23. Prepare letterhead, business cards, signage, etc., with business name.

22. Lease or purchase required equipment.

how to make your home business more professional

24

The world need never know you're running a business from home until you're ready to announce it—if ever. Why wouldn't you want it known? Well, despite the prevalence of home businesses and the many success stories fueling this trend, there are still individuals who regard a home business as something less than professional. Right or wrong, such perceptions can impact your business, stall its growth, or make a difference in whether or not your company wins a critical contract. Over time, in a virtual world, where a business is situated will become an insignificant issue. It still matters to some people, though, and it's surprisingly easy to shape perceptions that your business is so professional that potential clients won't be asking "Where can I find you?" but "How can I reach you?"

What are the issues that raise questions about the professionalism of a home-based business? How about these for starters: telephone calls with kids screaming and dogs barking in the background; an answering machine message that obviously serves both private and professional life; lack of response to voice or e-mail messages; a post office box address; poorly typed correspondence; an amateurish name or logo that conveys nothing about why the business exists. To make a home business appear more professional, start by giving it its own identity. That means its own telephone number, Web site, e-mail address, and mailing address. And you have to be a spokesperson for the business, dealing with everyone from unhappy customers to the local chamber of commerce. A Web site, well done, can prove especially useful in creating a professional identity and selling products and services. All that matters online is the quality of information you can provide about your company, products, and services, not where it is located. Advertising can be important for building the image of a home-based business, but it's what you do on a more fundamental level that will create a perception of professionalism. Make no compromises in what you do that impacts your business's reputation. Develop a distinctive name and logo; invest in good-quality stationery, business cards, and literature; always respond to customer queries or complaints as quickly as possible. The same rules of professionalism apply whether a business is headquartered at home or in a local industrial park. Run the type of company you'd want to deal with, and live up to those expectations.

jargon

E-commerce: Business conducted over the Internet. An ideal opportunity for a home business, but you'll need a Web site and e-mail account before you can participate.

Logo: The graphic identity that serves as a symbol of a business. Together, a catchy name and professionally produced logo can be critical to promoting a business and establishing its identity.

Public relations: Everything you do to promote a business, short of buying advertising. Public relations generates publicity and can include everything from press announcements of your latest product to appearances on a local talk show.

warning

A professional public relations and advertising campaign can eat up a budget pretty quickly and have a questionable impact. You need a Web site and e-mail address for promotion and online sales, but your site need not be a dazzling display of graphics. Have your Web designer focus on its content and making it easy for people to find you with search engines before investing heavily in design. Before you spend any money on outside help, spend internally on all the elements that create a professional identity. And no matter what else you do, remember that word of mouth will make or break your business. Keep your customers satisfied, and they'll help establish you in the marketplace.

fyi

There are companies that specialize in making businesses appear more professional. For a modest fee they can supply you with services such as a mailing address that reads like a suite in a downtown high-rise; an answering service to take calls when you're unavailable, as if answered by the receptionist in your own front office; and an e-mail address that reads as if you already have your own Web domain. Some of these companies even have suites you can rent by the day when you want to impress a potential client. Check the yellow pages under professional services, telephone answering services, or office rentals.

resources

How to Start a Home Business: A Savvy, Step-by-Step Guide to Becoming Your Own Employer by Michael Antoniak (Avon Books, 1995): How-to guide on all aspects of setting up and running a successful home business, with sections on promotion and advertising.

Business Know-How: An Operational Guide for Home-Based and Micro-Sized Businesses with Limited Budgets by Janet Attard (Adams Media Corporation, 1999): A complete guide to the decisions you must make and continue to make once you've decided to launch your business.

SOHO America (www.soho.org): A Web site that serves as a online community for those pursuing a home-based business venture. Tips on all the issues that face owners of home-based businesses, news forums, and useful links.

1. Develop a mission statement.

2. Develop a business plan (see Lifemap 18).

3. Enroll in relevant professional organizations and the local chamber of commerce.

12. Create a Web site or home page or hire someone to set one up.

11. Get the business its own e-mail address, using the business's name.

10. Get the business its own phone number and, if needed, a toll-free number.

13. Buy a good-quality answering machine, hire a professional answering service, or set up a voice mail account to take telephone calls when you're not available.

14. If necessary, rent a professional-sounding mailing address from a mail-drop business.

15. Order business stationery, business cards, order sheets, product lists, signage for yard or vehicles featuring the business's name and logo, phone numbers, e-mail address, and Web site URL.

23. Resolve customer complaints immediately.

22. Answer all telephone messages the same day, all e-mail within twenty-four hours, and all printed letters within five days.

4. Name the business, based on something that is easily remembered and that connotes the business's core purpose.

5. Have a graphic artist develop a logo that represents the business and its products or services.

6. Set up a home office—if you are a home owner, preferably one that has a separate address and a separate entrance from the rest of house (see Lifemap 24).

9. Establish a credit card account in the business's name.

8. Set up bank accounts in the business's name.

7. Learn your neighborhood's restrictions on signage, if any.

16. Prepare and mail out a press release announcing the business's grand opening (see Lifemap 27).

17. Explain your expertise and make yourself available to local media.

18. Determine your advertising budget, and spend it to keep your name before your target audience.

21. Donate time, products, or services to area charities.

20. Participate in area events and activities.

19. Sponsor local youth league teams.

how much should you charge for your service or product?

25

the basics

Pricing is one of the key components in any business strategy. It will also be a key element in your business finances. It must take your competition into account as well as address the cost of goods, operating expenses, and the need for the business to generate a livelihood and support your lifestyle. But pricing is a marketing issue as well. What you charge for your product or service conveys the type of business you run, defines your target customers, and helps establish your customers' expectations of service after the sale. Because of its impact on so much of your business, pricing can be the determining factor in your success or failure.

inside information

Some customers simply want the lowest possible price; others believe that you get more when you pay more, in terms of support and service. More and more of today's consumers want the best of both worlds: the lowest possible price and a hassle-free transaction. If there's a problem, they want to be able to return goods without a question and to have extended warranty protection. Basing your price structure solely on such customer expectations, though, can undermine your business. The price you set should respond to competition and the realities of running a profitable business. It should also account for special skills, expertise, seasonal demands, and exclusivity of the product or service. And it should always allow room to lower the price or to strike a better deal with a customer, should an appropriate situation arise.

Loss leader: An item or service package offered at an attractive price, perhaps at or below cost, as an enticement to attract customers. Used in the hope that once customers are dealing with the business they will purchase other, more profitable goods or services.

Profit margin: The percentage of a sale price that represents actual profit on the sale. Subtract the cost of goods and operating expenses from the selling price. If it costs $5 to bring an item to market and it sells for $6, the profit is $1 and the margin is 20 percent.

Suggested retail price (SRP): Also called manufacturer's suggested retail price (MSRP). Pricing recommendation on a product as suggested by the manufacturer or vendor.

Lowballing your competition on price is one of the surest ways to undermine the stability of your business. If all you can offer is the lowest price around, rest assured that someone else will eventually come along and undersell you. The pricing strategy you adapt should always allow room to lower your price without squeezing the lifeblood out of your business.

Use every resource available to you when setting prices. Most trade groups or leading trade publications conduct annual surveys of sales, profit margins, and prevailing pricing trends. A good hard look at competitors' prices will alert you to what people are willing to pay for a product or service and what support they expect from a vendor. Special offers and sales announcements reveal what level of pricing you have to deal with in order to remain competitive. Vendors, suppliers, and distributors all have broad insight into pricing trends at the consumer level.

resources

The Complete Idiot's Guide to Starting Your Own Business by Edward Paulson (Macmillan, 2000): Business basics for the aspiring entrepreneur.

Trade associations and trade publications: Both may conduct pricing and profitability surveys. Trade magazines continually track marketing and sales trends as part of their editorial cycle.

1. Review your business plan's sections on market trends, start-up costs, and operating expenses.

2. Review your sales strategy and forecasts to determine your projected break-even point in terms of goods or services sold.

3. Translate that figure into an amount of products or services sold, or annual sales volume.

6. Conduct an online search of what similar businesses in other parts of the country are charging for goods or services.

5. Study your competitors' pricing policies and note their pricing on any goods or services you will also be selling.

4. Decide on a pricing strategy: Are you going to be a deep discounter, emphasize service, or fall somewhere in between?

7. Contact relevant trade associations and inquire if any pricing surveys have been conducted recently. Read the relevant reports.

8. Review trade magazines for articles pertaining to pricing and profitability in your industry. Read the relevant articles on pricing.

9. Ask vendors' sales representatives for insight into pricing, both locally and in other regions of the country.

12. Apply this formula, as a percentage over the cost of delivery of goods or services, as an indicator of price range.

11. Use operating expenses, start-up costs (if relevant), and income projections to determine the amount of profit you must make per sale in order to realize your income needs.

10. Contact distributors and ask for insights into prevailing pricing trends.

13. Compare this range with the prevailing pricing among your potential competitors.

14. If your result falls below your competitors', raise your price to the prevailing norm.

15. Make sure your price is high enough to lower it while still allowing for ample profit on special sales or special offers.

18. If it will, proceed with plans and promotion of your product or service.

17. Use each pricing strategy as a test to examine the feasibility of your business. Will the price allow you to meet costs and make this a profitable venture?

16. If there is no direct competition or you have an exclusive product or expertise, set a price that allows sufficient room for profit margin and reinvestment in your business.

19. If not, reconsider pricing at a higher level.

20. If you still cannot make a profitable sale or transaction, consider dropping the product or service.

21. If your pricing model does not demonstrate profitability with a number of products or service approaches, reconsider the whole premise of your business.

how to get publicity

26

the basics

Publicity is the best form of advertising. It's often a third-party endorsement, perceived as being unbiased. Even better, it's free! In fact, some people believe there's no such thing as bad publicity, that as long as your name is in the news it will build awareness of your business or other activities. True or not, few of us welcome bad publicity; rather, we want to promote our accomplishments, our achievements, or our ideas for a better mousetrap. Drawing attention to yourself and creating awareness about whatever it is you want to promote can prove surprisingly easy. All it takes is having something to say, knowing the appropriate media vehicle, getting your message to the right person in the proper format, and following up to make sure your message has been heard.

inside information

The people who can help you publicize whatever it is you want to promote would love to hear from you. Reporters, editors, and producers are always looking for story ideas. At times they are even strapped for "news." Before you can address their needs, you need to know their audience. Then you can figure out if they can help you and how you can help them. For instance, a local television station won't feature your latest promotion on their noon news, but the business editor at a local newspaper may work it into the Sunday section. Most publicity is generated by submitting something in writing, preferably a press release: an announcement about your accomplishment, breakthrough, or new product. Every press release should answer the questions who, what, when, where, and why the subject is newsworthy, as well as provide contact information. A photograph included with the release, or a photo opportunity, can improve your chances of making the news, especially on a slow news day. Long term, you can reap the benefits of ongoing publicity by making it known to the media that you are available as a source, with demonstrated expertise, on issues related to your profession or areas of interest.

jargon

Editorial calendar: A schedule of planned articles, usually for the year ahead, put together by a magazine publisher. An editorial calendar alerts you to special features or sections that might prove a source of additional publicity.

Press kit: A set of documents used to generate publicity. Typically includes press releases, background information pertaining to the announcement, and photos in a self-contained folder.

Public relations: A broad term describing activity used to generate publicity. It can range from a basic press release to a specially sponsored event that promotes awareness of an individual, product, brand, or company.

warning

People in media are usually working against deadlines. Make sure they have the information you want publicized well before a deadline falls. If someone from the media calls, be ready to handle his or her request for more information or an interview, as soon as possible. If you put that person off once, he or she may never call back.

It will help your cause to send your announcement to the appropriate editor or producer. If you don't know who that person is, call the newspaper, magazine, or station and ask. You can increase the likelihood of success by following up a few days after your announcement or release has been sent out. Explain that you're calling to make sure the right person received it and to see if he or she needs any additional information.

resources

The New Publicity Kit by Jeanette Smith (John Wiley & Sons, 1995): A seasoned pro explains how to go about generating publicity, with samples to show readers just how to do it properly.

Bulletproof News Releases: Practical, No-Holds-Barred Advice for Small Business from 135 American Newspaper Editors by Kay Borden (Franklin-Sarrett Publishers, 1994): How-to advice on creating press releases that stand out from the crowd and attract the attention you seek.

www.free-publicity.com: Online resource center for information on publicity, promotion, and marketing. Advice on all aspects of generating publicity, promotional tips, and links to other resources.

1. Define what you want to publicize and whom you want to know about it.

2. Decide if this can be handled through a onetime news release or if it requires an ongoing publicity or public relations campaign.

3. If this is an ongoing effort, decide if you can handle it yourself or if you will require the services of a public relations professional.

6. Also include information establishing your (or your company's) credentials at the end of the release, such as name, years in business, areas of specialization, etc.

5. Edit and revise the release. Make sure the final version has correct information on how to reach you by telephone and e-mail.

4. If doing it yourself, draft a news announcement or press release that answers who, what, when, where, and why the subject is newsworthy.

7. Identify the best media vehicles for the announcement. Take into account the type of medium and its audience.

8. Consider print options: local weekly or daily newspapers; consumer magazines; business, trade, and professional magazines and journals.

9. Consider broadcast options: local and regional radio and television stations; local affiliates of national networks.

12. If appropriate, follow up with a call to the media contacts. Ask if they will be able to use the information or if they need more information.

11. Prepare and send the release to the appropriate contact. Do not distribute your announcement by e-mail unless you have been requested to submit it this way.

10. Identify the appropriate contact at each company.

13. Whether they do or do not use this announcement, let them know that you will be available in the future should they need a source on this particular topic.

14. If a media contact calls you, answer any questions he or she poses in as timely a fashion as possible.

15. When your announcement is used, call or write a brief note to thank the media contact.

16. Continually track media for trends, events, and opportunities that you can use to generate additional publicity.

how to evaluate advertising and promotional media

27

Lucky are the few who run businesses so successful that they've no need to spend anything on advertising or promotion. For most business owners, deciding how and where to promote their business can prove one of the more vexing challenges in transforming a great idea into a success. There are no simple answers; more often than not, business owners arrive at a successful advertising mix through a calculated process of trial and error. Until you know what works for you, spend cautiously and build into your plans some means for measuring the effectiveness of every advertising medium and promotional vehicle you choose.

inside information

Before you can evaluate any vehicle for promoting your business, you need a clear understanding of who your customers are and where you can reach them. First, turn to your business plan and review all the information you've compiled there about your customers: who they are, how they buy your goods or services, and where you can reach them. Then consider what you want to tell them. When you're trying to create name recognition, a billboard or fancy signage for your store may work best. For a sale or special, print or one of the broadcast media may prove more effective. Coupons are also an effective way to promote some special deal and actually measure the results of the promotion. Before you begin buying, though, take a hard look at your budget. Repetition is one of the keys to effective advertising; the more often or the longer your message appears, the more likely it will sow a seed with your target customers. Don't blow your budget on one big splash. And before you spend for advertising, make sure you've taking advantage of every promotional opportunity: stationery, business cards, signs for vehicles and the business, premium giveaways, even bags and packaging should all be used to continually remind the public you are there and what you offer.

jargon

Co-operative advertising: A program in which suppliers or vendors underwrite a share of advertising costs in exchange for featuring their products. Using co-op funds can effectively stretch an advertising budget.

Exposures/impressions: The number of times an ad will be seen by a consumer. Media salespeople use this as one way to measure the potential effectiveness of their advertising or promotional vehicle.

Media kit: A folder containing several support documents detailing the cost of advertising and who you will reach. A media kit should include information on the advertising vehicle, such as a print publication; a demographic profile of its audience; estimates of the number of impressions for an ad placed there; and a rate card providing details on the cost of advertising.

warning

You'll find advertising sales reps always eager to put you on a "schedule." And for a commitment to run your ad repeatedly over a set period of time, they'll offer you significant savings. That's great and worth pursuing once you've established that the medium or vehicle reaches the consumers you want to reach. But never make a long-term commitment until you know what you're getting for your money, no matter how great a package the rep puts together for you.

Marketing involves much more than the advertising space or time you buy in print or on radio or TV. Consider everything that leaves your business as a potential billboard for your business. Broadcast the name on packaging, give out T-shirts and shopping bags, sponsor local sports teams. Such spending can build goodwill and keep the company name before the public. When spending on advertising, include some way to measure your success: tell readers or viewers to ask for a specific sales rep; offer a special, but don't promote it at your business so that customers must ask for it; distribute coupons for specific products in specific media so you get an idea of where your message is being heard. Keep track of everything, and over time you'll have proof of which advertising and promotional media are reaching your target customers.

resources

Advertising Without an Agency: A Comprehensive Guide to Radio, Television, Print, Direct Mail and Outdoor Advertising for Small Business by Kathy J. Kobliski (Oasis Press, 1998): A guide written for the small-business owner who wants to maximize the reach of an ad budget by taking care of advertising in-house. Insights into using all kinds of media to advertise and promote a business.

Entrepreneur Magazine: Successful Advertising for Small Businesses by Conrad Berke (John Wiley & Sons, 1996): A straightforward, hands-on guide to the effective use of advertising for the small-business owner or entrepreneur.

1. Review the information about your target customers in your business plan.

2. Create a profile of your target customers, their buying habits, and how you might reach them.

3. Define your trading area.

12. For name building and awareness, start with the area telephone and business directories.

11. For business introduction and targeted promotions, consider direct mail and telemarketing.

10. Investigate your options.

13. Also consider billboard advertising in all its forms: along roadways and sidewalks, on buildings, on or in public transportation facilities.

14. For name building and specific promotions, consider broadcast and print media.

15. Consider distributing a coupon either as a handout by the business, included in ads, or included in a package of coupons distributed to homes.

21. Plan into your ad some means of measuring its impact: special offer, coupon, discount for mentioning ad. Run the ad and track the results.

20. Explain that you want to run a limited campaign first so you can test the effectiveness of the medium or vehicle. Plan for at least three appearances in print, a week of appearances for broadcast media, a month for billboard advertising, etc.

22. Experiment with other media as well, as your budget allows.

23. Track and compare results, based on business activity generated as a direct result of advertising.

24. Identify the best advertising and promotional vehicles and commit to a schedule, but leave enough money aside to continue experimenting with other modes of promotion.

4. Determine and review your advertising or promotional budget.

5. Decide if advertising is something you want to handle in-house or turn over to an advertising agency, provided its services are within budget.

6. Cover the basics; make sure you are taking advantage of every opportunity to keep your name before the public: signs on business and vehicles, stationery and packaging, etc.

9. Determine a budget for the effort.

8. Begin developing a campaign strategy: who you want to reach, what you want to tell them, and how and where you can reach them.

7. Identify your promotional needs: Are you trying to create brand or name recognition, increase sales, or promote a special offer?

16. Decide which of these options offers the best match for reaching the previously determined target audience. Contact salespeople for that medium or promotional vehicle. Request a copy of their media kit or sales literature describing their services and the audience they can reach.

17. Review this information, and check to see whether the demographic profile of their audience closely matches your description of your target audience.

19. Explain your product and service, what you plan to say, and who you need to reach. Ask what the best times or opportunities to reach this audience are.

18. Consider the exposures and expense: What will it cost to reach how many of these consumers? If this is within your budget, arrange to meet with the ad rep.

how to launch or promote your business online

28

the basics

Want to test a business concept before making a full-scale commitment? Looking for a way to reach more customers and make it as convenient as possible for them to trade with you? Either way, the Internet is one of the most valuable resources for promotion, positioning, and new profit opportunities. E-commerce is the wave of the future, no matter what business you're in. A company Web site is now as basic a marketing necessity as a business card and telephone number. Setting up and maintaining a Web site is an investment that can pay for itself. It makes it easy for people to find you, explore what you have to offer, and initiate a contact that can translate into a long-term relationship.

inside information

People have embraced the Internet so quickly, and in such numbers, because it offers them the most convenient way to gather information. They may be surfing to see who's offering the best price on the digital camera they are thinking of buying; what grocery store in their area combines the convenience of online ordering and home delivery; which local attorney has the expertise to protect their elderly parents' assets as the cost of their medical care climbs. If you're not on the Internet, they're not likely to find you. With increasing frequency, the growing legions of Internet-savvy consumers turn first to the Web. And they are looking for useful information that can make them smarter consumers, whatever their needs. Using the Internet to make it easy for them to find you begins with setting up a Web site, preferably with your own domain name (www.nameofbusiness.com). It should include a home page, which serves as an introduction to and directory of everything else on your site. If you plan to use the site as a virtual storefront to take orders or sell products, the site should also include an electronic shopping cart with online ordering forms; the ability to accept and process credit card orders in a secure environment; and an e-mail link so customers can contact you with questions or request additional information. A mere presence on the Internet is not likely to have any impact on your business. You need to let people know you're there and make it easy to find you. Use every opportunity: include your Web site and e-mail address on anything that promotes the company, such as business cards, letterhead, brochures, and billboards. Online, your site needs to be listed with all the major search engines and directories. Make sure your business pops up whenever a user conducts a keyword search using terms that describe your business, services, or goods. You also want to use links from other appropriate sites to draw potential customers to yours. Every business's site should be linked with those of the local chamber of commerce, city guide sites, or member directories of national trade organizations, for example. To help you determine what's working or not working for the business online, how customers are finding you, and what interests them most, the site should be equipped with tracking features. The information gleaned from these will help you to gauge the success of your efforts, refine the contents of your Web site, and determine if there's real potential for a business concept you're exploring.

jargon

Links: Connections to and from other Web sites. Links can be a useful tool for attracting potential customers, as well as providing site visitors with access to additional relevant content.

Tracking software/utilities: Tools that monitor activity on a Web site as a way of letting the site owner know what about the site is or isn't working. These are available as commercial software or services provided by Internet companies. The information provided may include the number of visitors, or "hits," where they arrived from, what information they viewed on the site, and how long they spent on each page.

Webmaster: The person who sets up and maintains a Web site. Since properly running a site can be a time-consuming process, many businesses turn to an outside provider or webmaster for these services.

fyi

The best place to begin planning a Web site for your company is with a local Internet service provider (ISP). Customer Service should be able to advise you regarding fees for maintaining your site, what tools it offers for building and maintaining the site, and who in the area offers Web development services. There are a number of commercial software programs that can help you build a Web site and upload it to the Internet. It's a relatively simple process but requires a time commitment to do it right. Weigh these requirements against your other responsibilities. Your business may be better served by turning the entire process over to someone who specializes in Web services. Make your site a resource of relevant information and add to it regularly, and you'll give visitors a reason to return.

warning

Many customers use e-mail for their initial contact. Customers who send you an e-mail message expect a prompt response. If you don't get back to them within twenty-four hours, they are likely to lose interest. A business should have its own domain name (www.name of business.com) rather than a Web address that is too long and complicated to remember (www.localsp.com/local/directory/business/yourcompany). It's worth the extra expense. If you use a lot of links to other sites to enhance your own site's content, make sure it's easy for visitors to return to your site. Otherwise, you may lose them permanently once they follow your links elsewhere. Don't forget to include your mailing address, telephone number, and e-mail address on your Web site wherever it makes sense. You want to make it easy for potential customers to contact you.

The Internet Marketing Plan: The Complete Guide to Instant Web Presence, 2nd edition, by Kim M. Bayne (John Wiley & Sons, 2000): A comprehensive resource for the Web-minded entrepreneur, with forms, templates, and other valuable tools for planning and implementing a Web-based marketing plan. Includes CD-ROM.

Marketing Resource Center (www.marketingsource.com): Provides resources to businesses with traditional and Internet marketing efforts, including a marketing forum; a Web site development company; and free and for-fee links to registering a Web site with the top one hundred Web search engines, directories, and indexes.

1. Contact your Internet service provider to see what kind of Web hosting, development, and maintenance services are available and their costs.

2. Decide if you want to develop and maintain the site yourself or turn to an outside webmaster.

3. If doing it yourself, purchase a Web site development application.

12. Once your site is created and uploaded, register it with all major search engines and directories.

11. Utilize tracking software or utilities to help you determine what is or isn't working about your site.

10. Establish links to and from other sites with relevant information.

13. Include your Web site URL and e-mail address on all promotions for the business.

14. Once the site is up and running, visit it regularly to make sure everything is working properly.

15. Use a variety of keywords on search engines to make sure your site appears on relevant searches.

4. If using a webmaster, visit Web sites of area businesses and organizations.

5. Note sites that appeal to you, and contact the site developers.

6. Discuss your needs in terms of site content.

9. Other site content should include pages devoted to individual products or services, electronic order forms, etc.

8. There should be a table of contents on the home page, including basic business information and graphics.

7. You need your own easily remembered domain name and site address.

16. Update the site's content and appearance on a regular basis to encourage consumers to return.

17. Answer e-mail as soon as it is received—within twenty-four hours at the latest.

18. Ship any orders received through the site within your stated turnaround time.

20. Monitor site-tracking information on a weekly basis for insight into ways you can improve your site.

19. If you cannot meet this deadline, contact customers by e-mail immediately.

lifemaps for personal finance

part three

how to obtain a lower-rate or no-fee credit card

29

Credit cards are a fact of modern life. While many people might wish they could survive without plastic and the bills they represent, most of us depend on credit cards as a purchasing tool. Used wisely, these cards can provide convenience and purchase protection. Of course, you must pay for these advantages in annual fees and interest rates. Surprisingly, many people who aggressively shop around for the best deals on the products they buy don't demonstrate the same smart consumerism about their credit cards. There are better deals out there—no annual fees and lower interest rates—for those who seek them out and qualify.

inside information

Want the best deal on a credit card? You have to prove you deserve it by building a credit history that demonstrates you are conscientious about making your monthly payments. Credit card companies offer their best deals to proven credit card customers. If you've had credit card problems or any debt issues, you won't begin to qualify until you've taken all necessary steps to repair your credit history. Before you start looking for a better deal, make sure you know and understand what it's costing you to use your cards now. What's the annual fee on your current credit cards? You should know that as well as the finance charges and how they are applied to purchases. How much of a grace period do you have on purchases before the interest rate kicks in? Are you being charged an additional fee for cash withdrawals made with your cards? All the information you need to assess how good a deal you're getting can be found in your monthly statement. If you can't understand the fine print, call the credit card company's toll-free number and have the customer service representative explain what it's costing you to hold and use that card. Scrutinize new credit card offers the same way. Look beyond your mailbox for better deals. Many newspapers regularly publish comparative lists of credit card rates and fees.

jargon

Debit card: An alternative to the credit card that automatically deducts the costs of purchases from a checking account whenever it is used.

Finance charge: The interest charged on the outstanding balance on your credit card. The interest rate alone doesn't tell you the real finance charge. You must also know how the credit card company determines that balance and when interest starts to accrue.

Truth in Lending Act: Federal legislation that requires prospective lenders to explain to consumers the real cost of obtaining credit from them and the terms of repayment. All they have to do is inform you; it's up to you to read and understand the details.

warning

If you've been responsible in meeting your credit card obligations, your mailbox is brimming with all types of incredible offers for new credit cards. Don't let the low interest rates fool you. Most are offered as an enticement to get you to switch; after the introductory period, a much higher rate kicks in. If you're thinking about switching cards, look for a lower locked-in rate. Always read the fine print. Everything you need to know to make an informed decision is there. It's the law. Don't let a card company's offer of "preferred member" status lure you into carrying a special card that really represents little more than a higher annual fee.

When you find a better deal, call your present card company and ask it to match it. If you've been a responsible customer, it doesn't want to lose you and may be willing to drop its annual fee and/or lower its interest rate. You won't know until you ask. Credit card representatives often call cardholders to let them know they qualify for "free" offers on things such as credit insurance, travel programs, and so on. Never agree until you see a proposal in writing. Often these are veiled attempts to hook you into a program that will actually cost you money and add to the cost of holding the card. You can actually use no-annual-fee credit cards for free if you pay for purchases within the grace period, before interest charges start accruing.

resources

The Wall Street Journal Guide to Understanding Personal Finance by Kenneth M. Morris and Alan M. Siegel (Simon & Schuster, 2000): Thorough guide to all aspects of personal finance, with detailed section on credit cards and how to read your monthly statement.

Lists: Several sources provide comparative ratings of credit card offers. If you can't find them in the local paper, you can view lists online at the CardTrak Web site, www.cardtrak.com.

1. Clean up your credit report (see Lifemap 31).

2. Make regular payments on outstanding debt to build a solid payment history.

3. If necessary, consolidate debt to make it easier to manage.

5. If you can't understand the statement, call the card company and have a customer service rep explain it to you, line by line.

4. Scrutinize your agreement and monthly statement with current credit card companies: What are the annual fees? What are the annual and effective interest rates? How are finance charges determined? What grace period do you have on purchases? What charges apply to cash withdrawals?

6. If you've been a responsible cardholder, ask the customer service rep if the company will waive the annual fee or lower the effective interest rate.

7. When looking for a better deal, scrutinize all offers as you did your present credit card contracts and monthly statements.

8. Avoid store- and company-branded credit cards, as these usually charge the highest interest rate.

11. Also consider any incentives offered with the card, such as credit or travel insurance, extended warranty program, frequent-flyer miles, etc.

10. Scrutinize all appealing offers to determine the real cost of these cards in terms of annual fees, interest rates, how interest accrues, etc.

9. Check in newspapers and online for comparative listings of credit card offers.

12. Request details of the offer in writing.

13. When you find a better deal, call your present credit card company and ask if it will match it.

14. If it won't, transfer your outstanding balance to the new card company.

16. Realize that mistakes are occasionally made on credit card statements. It's your responsibility to catch them when they first appear.

15. Regularly review your credit card statement to make sure the credit card company hasn't changed any of the terms of its agreement, that all charges are accurate, and that it hasn't added fees you have not approved.

how to repair your credit rating

the basics

It's far easier to get into debt than get out of it. Assume more debt than you can afford, and it will eventually catch up with you and overwhelm you. Miss payments, and you start adding black marks to your credit history. What's written in credit bureau reports will ultimately determine what you're able to borrow in the future. For an unfortunate few, mistakes by credit bureaus, or the companies reporting to them, can result in an undeserved negative report and a bad credit history. If you fall into either group, only you can take the steps to repair your credit history and restore your good name as a borrower.

inside information

Repairing and rebuilding your credit history takes time. That's why the easiest strategy to adopt is to prevent problems before they occur. Taking responsibility for your personal financial obligations is certainly a key, but it's not enough to protect even the most astute borrower from a poor credit report. Everyone who borrows money from lending institutions, uses credit cards, or purchases goods or services on installment needs to review his or her credit report at least once a year to verify that all the information it contains is both accurate and current. The credit bureaus must supply you with a copy of it. If your problems are of your own making, the most important step you can take to repair your credit history is to take responsibility for your debts *now.* Look at the total picture of what you owe, compared to your available assets and income. Develop a strategy to pay down your debt. Determine what you can afford to pay each month, and present your creditors with a plan. If you can, consolidate your debt to make it easier to manage. Determine the minimum monthly payment you can make, and never waver from the plan until your outstanding debts are satisfied. If you don't feel you can extricate yourself from your debt alone, consider turning to a credit counselor to help you sort through your obligations and develop a plan acceptable to your creditors. Consider declaring bankruptcy only as a final desperate option, as it will do irreparable damage to your credit rating for years.

jargon

Credit bureau: A company that collects data and compiles payment profiles on individual consumer borrowing and repayment, then sells this information to banks, credit card companies, and other lending institutions.

Credit report: A document that lists all information the credit bureau has been able to gather on an individual consumer's current debt and payment history. This includes information on institutions you've borrowed from and the amounts, outstanding balance, and payment history for each account.

warning

There are a number of firms and schemes aimed at consumers anxious to clear up a bad credit history. Most do little more for you than you can do for yourself. Be wary of any company that charges a fee to repair or erase your credit history or wants a percentage of your outstanding debt to help pay down what you owe. The only way to repair your credit history is to reinvent yourself as a responsible borrower who pays debts in a responsible, timely fashion. If you feel you can't do so alone, contact the local office of the National Foundation for Credit Counseling.

You can't begin to repair your credit history until you know what yours contains. Once a year, and any time you're turned down for a loan based on a bad credit report, you are entitled to review a copy for free. Contact the credit bureaus and request a copy of your report. Read it. When you find a mistake, correct it immediately and request a copy of your amended report. You have the most to gain—or lose—based on what's in that report.

resources

The New Century Family Money Book by Jonathan Pond (Dell Publishing, 1995): A complete guide to personal finance, with a detailed explanation of credit bureau reports and how to decipher the information they contain.

National Foundation for Credit Counseling (www.nfcc.org): A national nonprofit organization that helps consumers get control of their debt by devising a debt strategy and intervening with creditors on their behalf; call (301) 589-5600.

Credit bureaus: There are three major national credit bureaus that gather, prepare, and distribute credit reports: TRW Credit Data, (800) 392-1122; Equifax Credit Information Services, (800) 685-1111; and TransUnion Corporation, (312) 408-1050. Contact each and request a copy of your credit report once a year and anytime you are denied a loan or credit card.

1. Don't allow yourself to get into credit trouble; manage your debt and meet your payment obligations responsibly.

2. Annually, request and review copies of credit bureau reports for yourself and your spouse.

3. Verify that all information is accurate and up to date.

12. Consider a home equity loan or a credit card consolidation at a more manageable payment level.

11. If you don't have sufficient funds to pay off your debt, consider ways to consolidate your loans to make them more manageable.

10. Determine the amount of your monthly income or other resources available to pay off these debts.

13. Cut up, cancel, and discard extra and unused credit cards.

14. Contact your creditors and explain your intention to pay off the debts.

15. Present your payment plan.

4. Correct any inaccuracies immediately by contacting the credit bureau and reporting institutions or company by telephone and in writing.

5. Request an amended copy of your report and verify that corrections have been made.

6. If there were special instances that resulted in lapsed payments detailed in your report, prepare and submit a document explaining the circumstances to the credit bureau.

9. Compile a list of all monthly payment requirements.

8. If you are overwhelmed by debt, tally up all outstanding debt.

7. Request and verify that your report has been appropriately amended.

16. If they are unwilling to work with you or threaten to turn your account over to a collection agency, contact the local affiliate of the National Foundation for Credit Counseling.

17. Work with a counselor to develop a repayment plan acceptable to you and your creditors.

18. Make a commitment not to assume additional debt until you have met all outstanding responsibilities.

21. Always review an amended report.

20. Continue to review your credit report annually and ask that information several years old be purged from your records.

19. Meet your payment obligations on your new predetermined schedule.

how to launch an investment program

31

the basics

Money doesn't grow on trees, but it can certainly grow when properly invested. Over time, the investments you make and how you manage them can make or break your retirement plans. In fact, your investments may determine how soon you can retire or how fully you can realize some basic financial goal, such as purchasing a home or financing a college education. Often the hardest part of launching an investment plan is taking the first steps. You need money to invest, so you must learn to live on less than you make. Once you know you can save, begin investigating ways to put that money to work for you and your future financial goals. It's never too soon—or too late—to begin this process.

inside information

Any investment plan should be based on your present financial situation, your long-term goals, and the amount of risk you are willing to assume. Once you have established these parameters, you can begin to evaluate your options. Today's investor faces a myriad of choices and can easily feel overwhelmed. You may want to manage your investments yourself or, if you have sufficient resources, entrust your investments to a professional. In general, financial advisers recommend that the typical investor diversify or divide his or her money among several different types of investments, such as stocks, bonds, and real estate. At the very minimum, your investment goal should be to earn an annual return at least 3 percent above the inflation rate. One of the keys to your investment plan is to continually invest more and reinvest your return, so you can reach your financial goals.

jargon

Liquidity: The ability or ease with which you can turn assets or investments into cash. Your investments should allow for a certain amount of liquidity in the event of unforeseen financial emergency.

Portfolio: The sum total of your investments in terms of both the different types of investments you hold and the amount you have invested.

Yield: The return on an investment, expressed as a percentage of the amount invested. As a rule, the higher the potential yield, the riskier the investment.

warning

In recent years the news has been filled with stories about those who have made a killing in the stock market by day trading. What's usually absent from these accounts is the fact that for every winner, there are hundreds if not thousands of losers. When investing, there's a direct link between risk and return. The higher the risk, the greater the potential for a significant return; conversely, the more modest your possible gain, the more secure your investment. Even professional investors get burned from time to time; it's unlikely you'll be the one to buck the trend. Always equate your investments with your future and proceed with caution. It's okay, even prudent, to take some risks. But don't risk everything.

fyi

Inflation is an often overlooked factor in deciding which investments to make. In fact, if it's ignored, you can actually end up losing purchasing power over time. You may feel safe with a savings account that's paying 4 percent interest, but if the inflation rate reaches

5 percent, you're actually losing spending power each year. What's the right mix of investments for you? It depends on where you are in life, what your goals are, how much time you have to realize them, and whether or not you'll need to tap your investments quickly in the event of an emergency. Low-risk investments, such as savings accounts, CDs, and money market funds, can be easily accessed in the event of an emergency. At the other extreme, stocks and bonds can prove more difficult to turn into quick cash without risking your investment or taking a loss.

resources ●

The Wall Street Journal Guide to Understanding Money & Investing by Kenneth M. Morris, Virginia B. Morris, and Alan M. Siegel (Fireside, 1999): Easy-to-read and -understand guide to the basics of personal finance and investing, with many charts, graphs, and illustrations to help readers understand the key points.

Online Investing: Become a Successful Internet Investor by Dave Pettit and Rich Jaroslovsky (Crown Publishing, 2000): Timely guide to online investing, its pros and cons, and how you can get started using this invaluable resource.

InvestorGuide.com (www.investorguide.com): A comprehensive guide for the new investor: includes a discussion of different options, definitions of terms, news, and advice on how to manage and assess your investments. Just one of several Web sites providing information on investing. Also sample the information available at Quicken (www.quicken.com) or E*TRADE (www.etrade.com) to get an idea of the types of resources available.

1. Assess your financial situation.

2. Complete Lifemaps 33 and 36.

3. Will your pensions, assets, and income enable you to realize your retirement goals?

4. What other long-term financial goals do you have, such as funding an education or purchasing a home or business?

5. How much money will you need to realize these goals?

6. How close are you today to reaching those goals?

7. Based on your financial assessment and budget, how much money do you have available for launching an investment plan?

8. How much can you realistically plan to regularly invest over time?

9. Assess your willingness to take risks with this money; remember, the greater the return, the higher the risk, and the longer you have to recoup from a loss, the more risk you can assume.

10. Decide if you want to manage your investments yourself or, if you have sufficient resources, entrust your investments to a professional.

11. If you will turn your investments over to a professional, see Lifemap 34.

12. If you plan to do it yourself, read up on the different types of investments available to you.

13. Before you launch your plan, remember that you should have access to a certain level of cash reserves, optimally six months' worth of expenses, in the event of an emergency.

14. Decide how you initially want to diversify your investments among such options as stocks, bonds, and money market funds.

15. Decide how best to further diversify though the use of mutual funds.

16. Base these decisions on to your ability to take financial risks and the desired rate of return to meet your financial goals.

17. Continually track and monitor the performance of your investments. With high-risk investments, especially, you may find it necessary to revise your strategy quickly to avoid substantial losses.

18. Continually reinvest your returns and add more to your investments as your financial situation allows.

how to establish household and personal budgets

the basics

Personal finance is all about managing your money wisely and planning for the future. While it's easy to set goals for savings and investments, determining the best course can prove a bit more elusive. And it's nearly impossible to accomplish unless you know where you're starting and what financial resources are available to you. That's why financial planning should always be based on a budget. Unless you've already accrued more than you could ever hope to spend, you have to get a handle on your expenses to know where your money is going and where and how you can reduce costs so as to set aside more for tomorrow.

inside information

Planning a budget is a two-part process. It involves first looking back at where your income has been going, then devising a strategy to control your spending in the future. Most of the details of your financial picture are already on hand: pay stubs and income tax statements; checkbook register; credit card statements; utility bills; insurance premiums; outstanding loan and mortgage balances. Compiling and reviewing all these records and receipts should give you a good idea of where your money has been going. It's only a partial picture, though. What's missing are your out-of-pocket expenses. Spend an average of just $10 cash per day, and over the course of a year that's $3,650. You may be spending even more! Try recording all the cash you spend in a week or month. Expect to be surprised to see where the money has been going. Once you've determined how you've been spending, you can begin to plan your budget. Most people require separate budgets for household and personal expenses. Use the details of your spending profile to anticipate all expenses and available income. Budget an amount for expenses by the month or week, and stick with the plan. Look for areas where you can reduce spending by changing habits or doing without or less often. Set a goal for regular saving or investment. The more details you can add to your budget, the better it will guide you.

jargon

Household expenses: Everything you spend on running your home and caring for your family. This includes regular monthly bills and basic provisions, as well as cyclical spending for gifts, repairs, taxes, etc.

Personal expenses: Money you spend for your own personal needs: work-related items, transportation and commuting, clothes, grooming, meals away from home, pursuit of hobbies or other interests, etc.

warning

Unless you are committed to following it, preparing a budget will prove an exercise in futility. As you compile your expenses, take a careful look at all the debt you are carrying. If you can increase your regular payments even slightly each month, you'll end up with significant savings over the long haul. Debt, especially at the exorbitant interest rates some credit card companies charge, is a financial burden best shed sooner rather than later. If the details of your financial profile reveal that you've been outspending your income, it's time to seek professional advice.

fyi •

There is an abundance of books and forms available to take the pain out of budget planning. Personal finance software, in particular, has greatly simplified the process of tracking expenses and developing a livable budget. But these tools are valuable only if you use them. Assessing your spending and living on a budget depend on recording and reviewing your spending data to ensure that you live within your means.

resources •

The Budget Kit: The Common Cents Money Management Workbook by Judy Lawrence (Dearborn Trade Publishing, 2000): Guide to planning a budget and living within it, with helpful hints and charts to help you map and measure your progress.

Bonnie's Household Budget Book: The Essential Guide for Getting Control of Your Money by Bonnie Runyan McCullough (St. Martin's Press, 2001): Guide to setting up a monthly budget, tracking expenses, and cutting costs, with work sheets, checklists, and charts to help you live within your means.

Quicken: Intuit's Quicken software simplifies the process of managing your finances, tracking your expenses, and living on a budget. The related Web site, www.quicken.com, offers an abundance of information on personal finance and financial management. Well worth a visit.

1. Compile a list of all your income sources. Calculate the amount of income available to you by the month and week.

2. If you also rely on irregular income sources or payments, estimate the average received per month over the course of a year. Add to the amounts in step 1.

4. Compile a second list of all regular annual expenses, such as property taxes, insurance premiums, tuition, holiday and birthday spending, home and auto repairs, etc.

3. Compile a list of all regular monthly household expenses for the past year or most recent period possible, based on your financial records and receipts: checking account register, utility bills, credit card statements, store receipts, etc.

5. Figure a monthly average for each expense, and add these averages to determine your typical monthly spending.

6. Determine monthly out-of-pocket cash expenses. If you have no record or idea, keep a list of when, where, and the amount of all cash spent over the course of a month.

7. Determine your monthly personal expenses: work-related expenses, transportation, hobbies, entertainment, etc.

10. Is there enough income to cover monthly expenses?

9. Compare this total to the total income calculated in step 2.

8. Tally the monthly totals in each spending category in steps 3, 5, 6, and 7.

11. If there is a surplus, are you saving or investing that difference?

12. If not, set a monthly savings goal.

13. Is there not enough income to cover expenses?

16. Include savings and/or investing as a budget category and set a goal for the monthly minimum you will contribute.

15. Based on all of the above, prepare budgets to cover your household and personal expenses, using the monthly averages and available income as guides.

14. If not, how much is the shortfall?

17. If you must reduce spending, first look for areas where you can eliminate or postpone spending.

18. Next, identify budget categories where you can slightly reduce the amount you spend.

19. Set up a budget allocating specific amounts of money for each spending category for the next three months. Start living on this budget at the beginning of your next pay period.

22. After three months, reevaluate your budget model and make any necessary adjustments.

21. At the end of each month, compare your expenses to the budgeted amounts. Where have you saved, where have you overspent? What adjustments are necessary?

20. Regularly record all spending activity in appropriate categories. Make adjustments as needed to cover basic expenses.

23. Set up a one-year budget for spending, saving, and investing.

24. Continually record and review all activity to see how well you are following your plan.

how to select a financial adviser

33

the basics

At some point, you'll probably require the services of a professional adviser concerning your finances. It may be the attorney you turn to to review your sales contract and handle the closing on your house; the tax preparer who completes your Form 1040; or the financial planner you entrust to transform your inheritance into the nest egg you'll need to retire early. No matter whose services you need and when, it's always best to begin with known entities. Ask around and secure recommendations from friends, family, and business associates. Then the same basic rules apply as with any other professionals: thoroughly interview the candidates about their background and experience, how they are compensated for their work, and their familiarity with the needs of clients like you.

inside information

Financial advisers can help you in a number of ways, but you should never entirely surrender responsibility for your personal finances to someone else. Financial advisers are there to advise you; you, however, are responsible and have most at stake in all your financial decisions. So whose help do you need? At varied stages of your life you may need a different cast of advisers. With some financial advisers you'll want to develop a long-term relationship, others you may turn to only a few times in your life. For instance, you may not need an attorney on a regular basis, but over time you will depend on his or her services for reviewing contracts, closing the purchase or sale of your home, drafting a will, and perhaps incorporating a business. An insurance agent is someone you'll turn to year after year for new policies or to look for better deals. Depending on your income situation and whether or not you run your own business, you may also require the services of an accountant or CPA to set up your books and prepare your tax filings. Whether or not you require the services of other advisers—financial planners, stockbrokers, money managers—depends largely on your financial situation. You may have enough resources to require their ongoing services, or you may need their advice only when you come into a windfall. No matter whose advice you need or when, the more you know about your personal finances and the more clearly you can articulate your goals, the better you'll be able to determine whose advice is worth taking.

jargon

Compensation: Compensation—how an adviser earns his or her salary—should be an important consideration when considering any professional, as it may indicate that person's ultimate interests and loyalty. The options include fee only, commission only, and fee plus commission, a combination of the two.

Risk tolerance: The amount of risk you can or are willing to take when investing. Generally, the higher the potential return, the higher the risk. Risk tolerance should dictate the type of investments you make.

warning

Be aware of potential conflicts and resolve them before entering into a long-term relationship. Such concerns are created primarily by fees and by how advisers are compensated. You turn to people such as insurance agents, financial planners, stockbrokers, and money mangers for advice on products or strategies that will make you the most money at the lowest cost. The livelihood of these individuals may, however, depend on a commission based on sales of specific products. In the case of a stockbroker, that fee is based on transactions, and the more often you buy and sell, the larger that commission. The alternative: advisers who are compensated by a predetermined fee or hourly rate, or those who rely on a combination of fees and commission. Always inquire about how an adviser is compensated, then use your judgment and ongoing evaluation to determine whose interests he or she really has at heart.

fyi

Computers and the Internet have made it much easier to go it alone when it comes to managing your finances. Software options include applications for managing your money and investments, and templates for wills and other legal documents. Online, there's an abundance of unbiased information on everything related to personal finance, as well as Web sites where you can purchase all types of financial services, products, and insurance. To gain the most from these resources, you have to invest time as well as money. One caveat: often, the most important service an adviser provides is questioning strategies objectively, forcing the consideration of alternatives. Such counsel simply doesn't carry the same imperative when it appears as text queries on your monitor.

resources

The Money Book of Personal Finance by Richard Eisenberg (Money Magazine, 1995): Detailed guide to personal finance, including a thorough discussion of different types of financial advisers and how to find and evaluate them.

Online: The Internet provides access to an abundance of resources on all matters related to personal finances. A good place to start: www.quicken.com, the Web counterpart of the popular financial management software Quicken and a virtual clearinghouse of information on personal finance issues. For legal matters, try publisher Nolo Press's site, www.nolopress.com, where you'll find various resources concerning legal topics.

1. Assess your financial situation: income, net worth, investments.

2. Are you satisfied with how you are managing your money, or could you use professional advice?

3. Would you prefer to develop your own expertise using software, books, and Internet resources, or would you prefer to rely on a professional's advice?

12. Depending on your financial situation, you may require the services of a certified public accountant throughout the year or only at tax time.

11. You should also be aware of how a broker or agent is compensated, to determine his or her primary loyalties.

10. When shopping for insurance, you are best served by getting quotes from more than one broker or agent.

13. When evaluating accountants, ask about their professional licenses and certification, years of experience, and familiarity with the needs of individuals or business owners in a comparable financial situation to yours.

14. If you need assistance only at tax time, you may also turn to a tax preparer or enrolled agent. Be aware that some preparers cannot represent you in hearings with the IRS. Enrolled agents can.

15. Financial planners can provide long-term advice on how to manage and invest your money. If you don't yet have money to invest, you don't need their services.

21. Accept that it is your responsibility to review and track any professional's performance on an ongoing basis to determine if you want to continue to rely on his or her advice.

4. Determine which of the following professionals you may need.

5. Unless you are an attorney, you will need an attorney's counsel and advice in certain situations, such as negotiating contracts, closing on a home, and incorporating a business.

6. An attorney is someone you may turn to for advice repeatedly over your lifetime.

9. An independent insurance broker can shop around for the best deals on insurance; exclusive or captured agents may represent only one insurance company.

8. If you get into serious trouble with the IRS, you may require the services of a tax attorney to represent you.

7. Look for one experienced in the types of general legal issues that concern you.

16. Be aware that anyone can describe him- or herself as a financial planner.

17. Look for a planner who specializes in helping people in a comparable situation and can demonstrate that with at least three references.

18. A stockbroker can provide advice on investments in the stock market and is usually compensated by commissions based on transactions.

20. With professionals who will be handling your investments, you want to evaluate them based on how responsive they are to your particular needs and goals, the types of investments they specialize in, their professional expertise and certifications, and their track record.

19. Money managers can assist with managing substantial investments, on average at least $50,000, and are paid by commission, based on the amount you invest.

how to select a pension plan

34

Self-employed people and small-business owners are often so focused on day-to-day concerns that they don't stop to think long term and adequately plan for retirement. It's not enough to count on selling off your business and spending your golden years living off the proceeds. For some self-employed people, especially providers of professional services, there is really nothing to sell: the flow of business revenue ceases the day they stop working and they have no tangible assets they can cash in. For other entrepreneurs, a business may not bring all the owner hopes for when it's sold. Unless you are independently wealthy, some form of pension must be a component of your long-term financial plans, whether or not you plan to retire in the traditional sense. It can defer tax liability on the money you invest today and, with regular contributions, grow into a vital source of unearned income for your older years, when your earned income will be lower or nonexistent.

You can count on some contribution from Social Security for your senior years, but don't look to it as a sole source of income. Most people will need more that just that to support what they consider a comfortable lifestyle. Employees of large companies usually enjoy some form of pension benefits. The self-employed and small-business owners aren't so fortunate. Decades ago, legislators recognized the special needs of these independent professionals and have instituted a number of plans to encourage all those who work for themselves to squirrel away money for their future. Before you can even begin to investigate the best pension plan for you, assess where you are now financially and where you want to be when you reach retirement age. On average, retirees require anywhere from 60 to 80 percent of their working income to sustain their current lifestyle. That need is increased if you plan on retiring earlier than your parents, since you are likely to live longer. There are a number of charts and calculators to help determine how much you should save each year between now and retirement to realize that goal. Once you have a financial goal in mind, you can begin to assess different approaches to building a pension fund. Options for the self-employed include Individual Retirement Accounts (IRAs), Simplified Employee Pensions (SEPs), and Keogh accounts. For business owners with employees, the programs are more complex and may include some form of profit sharing, money purchase and defined-benefit Keogh accounts, 401(k) plans, stock options, and alternative investment plans. Before entering into any of these arrangements, it's advisable to discuss these options with a financial adviser and tax expert. Once you determine what you need to be saving, don't let the amount scare you if it seems unrealistic. Set up a pension account and do whatever you can to make it grow. The important thing is to start now; the longer and more you contribute to a pension, the more there will be for you when you need it.

jargon

Annuitized distribution: A plan in which the pension funds are to be distributed upon retirement at a set rate, monthly or annually over a set period of time or for a lifetime.

Lump-sum distribution: A single, onetime payment of the value of your pension, for which you assume responsibility for managing and investing.

warning

What's the best pension plan for you? Unless you have or are about to develop financial planning expertise, your interests will probably be best served by turning to a professional for advice. Most banks and financial institutions that handle pension and retirement planning options have someone on staff who specializes in these programs. When you're ready to actually set up a pension plan, be aware that some advisers work for a commission based on the pension products they sell and manage, while others will consult with you for a flat fee. Ask about any fees and how they are paid before making your decision.

fyi

If you're a small-business owner considering setting up a pension plan, there's much more to consider than simply what you'll need upon retirement. A pension plan for a business must be available to all employees. Offering such a plan can help attract and retain employees. It can also introduce another expense as well as additional paperwork required to prove that your plan and how it is managed are in compliance with all applicable regulations. All this can divert your attention from where it needs to be focused—on your business.

resources

Ernst & Young's Retirement Planning Guide: Take Care of Your Finances Now . . . and They'll Take Care of You Later by Robert J. Garner (John Wiley & Sons, 1997): A comprehensive guide to help build your nest egg, including insight into and assessment of different plans, and suggestions for implementing a strategy that will guarantee the income you'll need for retirement.

Baby Boomer Retirement: 65 Simple Ways to Protect Your Future by Don Silver (Adams Hall Publishing, 1998): A baby boomer's guide on how to adequately prepare and plan for the future, whatever your income level and retirement income needs.

1. Set a retirement goal: When would you like to retire? How many years from now?

2. Average out your income over the last five years.

3. Consider whether you would like to remain living in your present locale or move to another, less expensive location on retirement.

5. Identify all reliable sources of retirement income: savings, investments, property you intend to sell, existing pension funds, and any other assets.

4. Use a retirement income planner or online retirement income calculator to determine what you will need in retirement income each year. (On average, retirees require between 60 and 80 percent of their working income to support their present lifestyle.)

6. Contact the local Social Security office for a projection of the amount of benefits you will receive when you retire.

7. Combine the above figures. Does the amount meet, exceed, or fall short of your projected income needs?

8. Use retirement calculators in books or online to determine how much you will need to save to create an adequate pension fund.

11. If doing it yourself, begin researching the different options available to you, where they are offered, and the costs involved in setting them up.

10. Decide if this is something you want to pursue yourself or entrust to an expert.

9. Whether or not you can afford to save this amount, commit yourself to setting up some form of pension fund.

12. If entrusting it to an expert, contact your financial adviser or a specialist at your bank or other financial institution to discuss your needs and options.

13. Before considering individual plan options, write down the amount of income and pension you will need, the number of years between now and your target retirement date, and the number of years—based on averages—you and your spouse will rely on this fund.

16. Do you require flexibility in how much and/or when you can contribute to it?

15. Can you determine how much money you can contribute to the pension plan weekly, monthly, annually?

14. Are you looking for a pension plan for yourself and your spouse as a self-employed person, or as the owner of a small business with employees?

17. Do you look forward to a lump-sum payment on retirement, or would you prefer an annuity?

18. Based on all of the above, investigate the merits of different pension plans and programs.

19. Investigate each pension plan option: the cost of the plan; its present and future tax liability; income and payment projections; any and all applicable fees; and the paperwork and reporting involved.

20. Also decide how the money will be invested; any risks in the plan; your rights and any applicable penalties if you change your mind or want to redirect the investment in the future; how the funds will be distributed to you and your spouse or heirs.

21. When satisfied, set up a plan and make regular contributions to it.

how to set and reach your retirement goals

35

Retirement is an event ingrained in our social consciousness. In reality, it is only a concept shaped by our culture and our own aspirations about life, growing older, and the meaning we extract from it. Some look forward to "retirement" as the final freedom from the day-to-day obligations that go with a job or career. For others, retirement is a foreign idea; they neither want nor look forward to the prospect of giving up the work they enjoy or suddenly withdrawing from an active lifestyle. Whichever view you hold, you must accept that the term "retirement" is synonymous with the golden years. Whether they be decades of continued work or unrestricted play, you owe it to yourself to plan ahead to make them a meaningful time in your life. That plan should encompass income considerations, home and lifestyle, and the unique health and emotional concerns that confront the elderly.

The modern notion of retiring at age sixty-five is actually a concept our government created back when the Social Security system was established. In recent years, there have been moves to push the retirement age back further, to sixty-seven by 2027. At the same time, many successful baby boomers, and those with lucrative pensions, look forward to retiring in their fifties. Retiring from and for what? Those are the real issues to confront. While one's financial situation certainly determines when one will be free to leave the workplace, it alone does not determine how much satisfaction one will glean from growing older. We've all heard stories of people who die soon after leaving their jobs; of retirees who embarked on new lives and realized lifelong interests upon retirement; and of others who happily pursued their careers well into their eighties, even beyond. Planning for retirement means assessing what's important to you and preparing for a lifestyle that you will find rewarding. Economics and health are certainly determining factors, but the rest is entirely a matter of individual choice. Where would you like to live and what would you like to do when you reach retirement age? The answers are personal, and planning adequately for retirement is entirely a matter of personal choice.

Early retirement: To cease working prior to reaching retirement age. Taking early retirement can impact the long-term value of pension and Social Security benefits and should be weighed cautiously.

Retirement age: A term tied to the age at which one is eligible to receive full Social Security benefits, currently sixty-five but set to increase gradually. Reaching "retirement age" is considered a milestone that, some believe, should herald the end of the need or desire to be gainfully employed.

You can postpone many choices until retirement is imminent, but if you neglect financial planning until then, everything else you do will be dictated by what you can—or perhaps more accurately cannot—afford and what resources are available to you. Therefore the most important long-term component of preparing for retirement involves financial planning. No matter where you are in your career, it's never too early—or too late—to take steps to ensure that there will be more than just a Social Security check to carry you through your twilight years. The other factor, your health, is one you have less control over. Nevertheless, you can take steps now to minimize potential health risks: you can give up smoking; lose weight; exercise regularly; don't allow minor injuries or ailments to progress into major debilities.

fyi

While health and economics will shape your ability to enjoy your retirement years, ultimately it is your outlook on life that will determine your personal satisfaction in old age. Rich or poor, healthy or sick, it's the way you approach life, at all stages, that shapes what you give to and get from it. These factors depend on issues that should guide other considerations as your retirement looms. Do you cherish being independent and want to remain that way as long as you can? Is it important that you be surrounded by family and friends? Will you keep your home, or will it be the major source of your nest egg? Where would you like to live, and what do you want to do? Whatever else they bring, the retirement years represent your last opportunity to get those things out of life that you value and to give back to those who matter to you. No one knows what the future holds, but we owe it to ourselves to do all we can to make it a future without regrets.

resources

The New Century Family Money Book: Your Comprehensive Guide to a Lifetime of Financial Security by Jonathan Pond (Dell Publishing, 1993): A comprehensive guide to personal finance, including detailed advice on all aspects of retirement planning.

How to Retire Early and Live Well with Less Than a Million Dollars by Gillette Edmunds (Adams Media Corporation, 2000): A guide to developing a retirement strategy that will allow you to take advantage of early retirement.

1. Make a personal assessment of where you are in life today. What's important to you? What would you give up if you could? How many years are you from retirement age?

2. Is "retirement" something you look forward to or something you hope never to experience?

3. Accept that whatever you want from your retirement years, aging presents unique challenges and you must plan in advance to deal with them.

11. What lifestyle changes can you make today that will positively impact your health in the future?

10. Are there health issues or ailments you've been ignoring that could progress into serious ailments in the future?

9. What other supplemental insurance may you need?

12. Accept that housing can impose special challenges for those living on a fixed income and who are no longer physically able to maintain it.

13. Do you own your home, condo, or co-op?

14. Will you use the proceeds from selling it as a retirement nest egg?

22. What special skills can you develop, and what actions can you take now, to make it easier for you to achieve these goals?

21. What would you like to accomplish in retirement: Complete or further your education? Devote more time to a hobby? Launch a new business? See the world?

20. Who are the people you want to remain closest to in your retirement years, physically and emotionally?

23. Consider your answers to all of the above and any other issues that matter to you, as you plan and prepare yourself for retirement.

4. Assess your present financial situation in light of retirement needs. What income can you expect from all sources? What assets will you sell off to raise additional funds?

5. Use Lifemap 35 as a guide to determining your retirement income needs and investigating your pension options in building a nest egg for the future.

8. What can you look forward to in terms of Medicare coverage?

7. Will this same coverage be available to you on retirement?

6. What kind of health insurance coverage do you have today?

15. Are you considering a reverse mortgage as a way to remain in your present home after retirement?

16. Is it important that you live near other family members or friends?

17. If you're planning to relocate, use Lifemap 37 to help plan your destination.

19. What matters most to you: Family? Continuing your career? Giving back through charitable acts? A carefree lifestyle?

18. Satisfaction in retirement depends largely on the personal goals and aspirations that have guided you throughout your life, or that you have deferred until retirement. As you plan for retirement, you need to revisit these goals and prioritize your objectives for a more satisfactory life.

how to select a
retirement location

the basics

Where will you live when you retire? Your destination should take into account what will matter most to you in retirement, your financial situation, and how you would like to spend your golden years. Your preference may be to remain in the home or apartment where you already dwell, among familiar surroundings. Or your retirement dreams may be based on the sale of your home, your most valuable asset. Many people equate retirement with the launch of a new stage in life, and they look for a fresh location. Whatever your plans, deciding where to retire should be a decision based on affordability, access to health care and other amenities, and the level of independence you seek.

inside information

Choosing a retirement location is not as imperative as other aspects of retirement planning. Nevertheless, you should investigate your options with increased urgency as retirement looms ever closer. The overwhelming consideration for most seniors is affordability.

Unless you plan to continue working or have a substantial nest egg, you'll probably need to make do with less in retirement. Your expenses will likely drop, too, and there are many local and national programs to assist seniors with living expenses that may actually help you stretch your budget. But what you can afford may well dictate where and how you live and whether you relocate to a more modest home or apartment or to another part of the country entirely. Your next home should not cut you off from what matters in your life but allow you to maintain ties with all that you value and need. For retirees intent on retaining their independence until their last day, a home they can call their own is a compelling consideration. Others may seek relief in retirement from many of the responsibilities and day-to-day concerns of running a home. For these, a retirement community may be the best option.

jargon

Retirement communities: Communities designed and developed from the ground up, based on the unique and specific needs of retirees. Certain qualifications may apply to membership, and members of these communities may pay for their living facilities as well as additional monthly fees.

Reverse mortgage: A loan plan in which a lending institution, usually a bank, issues a loan based on the amount of equity you have in a home, which the home owner receives as regular monthly or annual payments. Reverse mortgages are often used by retirees as a way to generate cash flow to cover expenses. Also called home equity conversion plans.

warning

The patterns and preferences that will determine how much you enjoy retirement are already set. A happy, optimistic person can make the most of any situation, whereas a change in scenery will do nothing to benefit a miserable one. Choosing a home for your retirement should be a decision you and your spouse make without undue influence by children, friends, or peers. Retirement is your last opportunity to pursue what you enjoy in life, to live your dreams. If you're happiest where you are, find a way to stay there; if you've always dreamed of living in a small town, start searching for the ideal location. If you're always wanted to tour the country, get out the maps. Retirement is not a time to compromise your dreams. Where you live will have much to do with how happy you are. Let others make that choice for you, and you'll end up surrendering some of that happiness.

When it comes to deciding where and how to retire, today's seniors enjoy more options than any previous generation. Reverse mortgages can be used to generate an income stream for those who want to stay in their homes. Retirement communities surround you with peers and the amenities you require. Many also include assisted living facilities for those who can still live on their own but require periodic care and attention. Today's manufactured homes can be an instant solution for those looking to set up an affordable house in a new locale.

Retirement Places Rated by David Savageau (Hungry Minds, Inc., 1999): A guide to help evaluate what you want in retirement, with information on more than two hundred areas and ratings based on cost of living, available housing, climate, employment, services, and leisure activities.

50 Fabulous Planned Retirement Communities for Active Adults: A Comprehensive Directory of Outstanding Master-Planned Residential Developments by Robert Greenwald (Career Press, 1998): A guide to fifty of the largest planned retirement communities in the United States, with comparative information on what they offer and their costs and requirements.

1. Determine what matters most to you in selecting a retirement location. Then consider the following factors.

2. Affordability: What income, from all sources, will be available to you in retirement?

3. Access: What are your needs in terms of access to doctors and medical facilities, shopping, community center or educational facilities, friends, and family?

4. Independence: Do you want to live on your own? In a community with other seniors? With friends or family members?

5. Do you want to remain in your present home?

6. If yes, can you afford to?

7. If you can't afford to, investigate possible solutions, such as taking out a reverse mortgage, taking in a roommate or boarders, or having family members move in with you to share expenses.

8. Or consider selling your home and buying or renting a more modest home or apartment in the same area.

9. Do you plan to relocate?

10. If yes, consider what you want in terms of:

11. Climate.

12. Cost of living.

13. Employment opportunities.

14. Taxes.

15. Transportation.

16. Access to medical care.

17. Entertainment options.

18. Hobbies and other interests.

19. Based on the above considerations and the lifestyle you want to pursue, consult a ratings guide to identify your best options.

20. Contact a real estate agent in the area to learn about your options in home or land purchase, rentals, or retirement communities.

21. Procure copies of an area newspaper and read it for a sense of the community.

23. If it does, work with a real estate agent or on your own to identify an affordable housing solution.

22. Before making a final decision, visit any area you are considering and spend a few weeks there to make sure it lives up to your expectations.

how to determine your insurance needs

37

What if something were to happen to either you or your spouse? Would the survivor and any dependents have the financial resources to gradually adjust to their new circumstances, or would they need to make instant, monumental decisions? A life insurance policy is a way to guarantee them the time to make savvy choices. Before you think about that, though, you should make sure your health insurance needs are covered. And what else do you need? As a home owner, you have a lot at stake in your house and possessions. Home owner's insurance protects against loss and against liability if someone is hurt on your property. Renter's insurance offers comparable protection to apartment dwellers. As a car owner, you are protected by auto insurance against the catastrophic costs of even the mildest fender bender, as are other drivers. Business owners may want special liability insurance, as well as coverage in the event business is disrupted. To determine where and what insurance you need, look at your total lifestyle and consider all the areas where insurance offers a guarantee and protection that your financial well-being will not be disrupted, whatever happens. Whatever risks exist in your life, you're likely to find insurance policies to protect against them.

No matter what type of insurance you're considering, apart from life insurance, the cost is usually a product of the amount of coverage you seek and the amount of deductible you are willing to assume. The larger your coverage, the higher the premium; conversely, the larger the deductible, the more affordable the policy. The final cost may also depend on the type of policy you choose, and there is an abundance of options. When you're ready to shop for insurance, you must decide if you want to investigate your choices yourself or rely on the services of a professional insurance broker. It's a broker's job to know, understand, and explain your options. Understand that many are paid by commission, based on the cost of your policy, so their interests and yours are not necessarily the same. No matter which approach you choose, it's prudent to estimate your coverage needs before shopping on your own or through an agent. Also, research the different types of policies available to you. That way you won't be oversold or underprotected.

Deductible: An initial amount for which the insurer is not required to provide compensation, as spelled out in the policy. Depending on the policy, there may be an annual deductible for each family group, for each family member, for certain areas of treatment, and/or for each specified deductible per claim.

Fee-for-service providers: Less common than agents or brokers, fee-for-service providers work for a flat fee, based on time spent counseling you or per policy, to put together the insurance coverage you need.

Insurance agent: A sales representative of one insurance company or a number of noncompeting insurers. Agents are paid a commission based on the premium you pay for the insurance policy.

Insurance broker: A professional whose specialty is selling insurance policies. Brokers aren't tied to any single insurer and are free to shop around to find the policy that meets your needs. Brokers are also paid on commission based on the premium you pay.

It may seem a gargantuan task, but you really must read the fine print before you sign your name to an insurance policy. The language and terms can be extremely confusing for the novice, so you may want to consult your broker. If you want a specific type of coverage—against fire damage or theft on a home owner's policy, for example—make sure it's included in the policy. Review the terms and language of a policy anytime it's renewed. Realize, too, that it can be as important to ask what isn't covered and under what circumstances a policy won't pay. Finally, you should be as concerned about the company writing the policy as what the policy does not cover. The coverage you pay for so diligently is worth nothing if the insurance company goes bankrupt or lacks the resources to cover claims.

You may find the best deal on any type of insurance coverage by eliminating the middleman and purchasing your insurance directly from the company. Many companies now sell directly to consumers by telephone or the Internet.

The Complete Book of Insurance: The Consumer's Guide to Insuring Your Life, Health, Property and Income by Ben G. Baldwin (McGraw Hill Professional Publishing, 1996): A complete guide for consumers on all types of insurance and how to shop for and find the policies that best match your income and coverage needs.

Insurance.com (www.insurance.com): Affiliated with Fidelity Investments, this Web site explains your options for all types of insurance; it also provides insurance calculators, a glossary of insurance terms, and free online quotes.

1. Consider the following in terms of existing coverage or need:

2. For you and your dependents: health insurance.

3. Life insurance for you and your spouse.

12. Other needs as they may occur: travel insurance, rental insurance, key man insurance, etc.

11. If a business owner: business property and liability insurance.

10. If an auto owner: car insurance, including damage, theft, medical coverage, and liability coverage for all qualifying drivers and vehicles in the household.

13. For each type of insurance, review your present policies.

14. If they are inadequate or nonexistent, assess your needs or work with an insurance adviser to do so.

15. Decide if investigating and purchasing policies is something you want to do yourself, or if you'd prefer to rely on the services of an insurance broker or adviser.

24. What is the cost?

23. Use the terms of coverage—what is and is not covered—as one basis of comparison.

22. Review all terms of each policy.

25. If the cost seems excessive, look for ways to lower it, such as increasing the deductible.

26. Inquire if the insurance will be renewable after its term—usually one year—expires.

27. If working through a broker paid by commission, ask for a better deal.

4. Accident or disability insurance for work-related injuries.

5. Check with your employer to see what types of coverage you have through employment and how or if you might increase that coverage.

6. For the home owner: house and property insurance.

9. If a landlord: building and liability coverage.

8. If a renter: renter's property insurance.

7. Fire/theft insurance.

16. Determine the amount of coverage you need (see Lifemaps 39 and 40).

17. Investigate the different types of policies available to you.

18. If you plan to work with a broker, request bids from at least two of them.

21. Request bids on the types of policy you seek from at least two brokers in your area or at least two companies by telephone or online.

20. If searching for insurance on your own, look online for policy information.

19. Ask the brokers if they are paid by commission or if they work on a flat-fee basis.

28. Thoroughly read the insurance policy contract to make sure it provides all the coverage you seek.

29. Have the broker or company explain what the policy does not cover.

30. If you are satisfied, endorse policy and pay premium.

31. If you are not satisfied, continue shopping around.

how to buy home and auto insurance

38

While some people debate the need for other types of insurance, few question the merits of adequate insurance on a home or automobile. Both represent expensive investments, and both expose the owner to considerable liability. Consequently, if you own either, it's in your own interest to be adequately insured. Home owner's insurance can be the source of much-needed financial assistance should disaster strike and you need to repair, replace, or rebuild your home. That same coverage can help replace any personal property lost and can provide liability protection if anyone is ever injured on your property. Financial protection against damage or personal liability in an accident is also the primary purpose of an auto insurance policy. The typical policy pays benefits, at different levels, for personal injury to any individual, for all individuals involved in an accident, and for total property damages. As with home insurance, you can greatly expand the scope and terms of coverage, but each enhancement will increase the total cost of your premium.

In order to make a profit, insurance companies need to take in more from premiums than they pay out in claims. Consequently, auto insurance companies closely track and profile which consumers file the most claims, where and how they live, and what they drive. By gathering this data for decades, they have developed statistical profiles that they use to minimize their risks. Factors such as where you live and how your home is constructed have a direct bearing on what you'll pay for home owner's insurance. For drivers, considerations such as the make and model of one's car, as well as one's driving history, determine the final cost. Don't assume that a standard policy is all the insurance you need. You may need to make several amendments to achieve adequate coverage. You can significantly reduce the cost of both home and auto insurance by aggressively shopping around, learning which factors may put you into a higher-risk group, and making the appropriate changes.

jargon •

Collision insurance: Insurance that covers damage to your vehicle, no matter who is at fault or what the cause of an accident is. The cost is directly dependent on the make and value of the car and the cost of repairs.

Floater: An additional policy added to the basic home owner's insurance to provide coverage for a specified valuable. A floater provides a specific amount of coverage for each such valuable, based on a professional appraisal.

Umbrella policy: An insurance policy that supplements the liability coverage in your home owner's and/or automobile insurance with expanded coverage for all family members, whether at home or away, including legal expenses.

warning •

When shopping for insurance, look at both the policy and the company writing it. Along with the insurer's financial health, you need to know how prompt it is in responding to claims. Talk to someone who has actually had to file a claim with that insurer. Was a settlement promptly reached, or did it seem more an exercise in delay and frustration? When reviewing any policy, it's as important to know what's not covered as what is covered, especially with home owner's insurance. Ideally, the policy should provide for adequate compensation in the event of most conceivable circumstances (other than floods and earthquakes, which require separate policies). Auto insurance can be one of the hidden expenses of new-car ownership. Before you purchase a fancy foreign sports car, find out the cost of adequately insuring it. What you learn could redirect your sights to something more modest.

fyi ●

Don't assume that because you rent your home or apartment, you don't need insurance. If you value your furnishings and possessions, you should be carrying some form of renter's insurance. Ask your landlord what type of coverage his or her policy provides for damage to your personal property and then shop for the appropriate renter's insurance. If you own an older car, it doesn't always make sense to carry collision insurance on top of your basic liability coverage. When insurance companies pay out on damage claims, they pay for the cost of repair or the book value of the car, whichever is less. If you consider your older car a classic, you need a special insurance policy and can expect to pay handsomely for it.

resources ●

Smarter Insurance Solutions by Janet Bamford (Bloomberg Press, 1996): A basic guide to all types of insurance, with resources, work sheets, summaries, and self-assessments.

The Complete Book of Insurance: The Consumer's Guide to Insuring Your Life, Health, Property and Income by Ben G. Baldwin (McGraw Hill Professional, 1996): A guide to the basic types of insurance most people need and how to shop for and compare policies to determine your best buy for adequate coverage.

Automobile Insurance Made Simple by Ed Boylan, Mark Swercheck, and Scott Werfel (Upublish.com, 1999): An easy-to-understand consumer's guide to all you need to know when shopping for automobile insurance, with charts, graphs, tips on how to shop, and the types of discounts available.

Insure.com (www.insure.com): Comprehensive Internet resource for information on all aspects of insurance with explanations of types of policies, links to companies, FAQs, and glossaries. A good place to begin your quest for any type of insurance.

HOME: 1. For home insurance, use the current value of your home and possessions to determine the minimum amount of coverage you need.

2. Make an inventory of your household furnishings and possessions to determine the amount of coverage you need on personal property.

3. Familiarize yourself with the terminology related to home insurance and the different types of coverage available to you.

6. When you are offered a policy at an acceptable cost, closely scrutinize it to make sure it adequately covers all your needs.

5. Explain what you need, and inquire about the type of policies available to you and their cost. Be prepared for a representative of the insurance company to request a visit to your home for an appraisal.

4. Start shopping around through local insurance agencies, or conduct a preliminary search online.

7. At minimum, a policy should include adequate coverage for your home, outbuildings, and personal property, as well as personal liability, medical payment for injuries to others on your property, and damage to your property as well as the property of others.

8. Review the types of risks to your home and property that are covered in the policy, such as fire, lightning, wind, etc.

11. Inquire about any discounts you may be entitled to or what you might do to qualify for discounts, such as installing an alarm system.

10. Have the agent or representative explain any exclusions stipulated in this policy.

9. Make sure coverage for your possessions is for the replacement value.

12. Amend or upgrade the basic policy as needed in order to ensure that coverage is adequate.

13. Thoroughly review the terms of the policy every three years and anytime you are informed that your policy has been amended.

AUTO: 14. For auto insurance, familiarize yourself with the terminology used to describe auto insurance.

17. Decide if you need collision, theft, or uninsured motorist coverage as part of your policy.

16. Determine how much liability coverage you need.

15. Investigate whether your state has a minimum package of coverage, and determine whether its minimums are sufficient.

18. Begin shopping around through brokers and online. Get several quotes.

19. Compare the quotes and terms of the policies.

20. Try to learn from others insured by these companies how prompt they have been in handling claims.

23. Before you choose a policy, inquire about any discounts you may be entitled to or what you can do to become eligible for discounts.

22. Amend the coverage as needed.

21. Ask the broker or agent what isn't covered by any policy you are considering.

24. Always review the terms of your policy when it has been amended or you are renewing it.

how to buy life and disability insurance

39

the basics

Disability and life insurance policies are necessities. Both are guarantees that should the worse happen, you and/or your family will be able to cope with the financial realities of an untimely injury or death. Most people recognize the wisdom of an ample life insurance policy, but the merits of disability insurance tend to be overlooked. Life insurance can be relatively inexpensive, depending on the type you buy. Disability insurance, on the other hand, may seem comparatively costly, but it is an assurance that your lifestyle will not be at risk should you ever face a prolonged disruption of your working life. You have a far greater chance of becoming disabled than of dying early.

inside information

Your challenge is to determine how much coverage is sufficient. Both decisions should be based on your present income and lifestyle. What is it costing you to live now, and what resources will be available for your family if your income is stopped? Although insurance brokers will be glad to supply charts and graphs detailing their recommendations for coverage, you'll be better served by making these projections yourself. In the case of life insurance, you'll want to come up with a sum sufficient to carry your family for a set number of years, usually a minimum of three to five years' worth of income. With disability insurance, you should think in terms of annual income. Once you arrive at these figures, review the amount of coverage, if any, that is being provided by your employer as part of your fringe benefits. If it does provide insurance and it's not sufficient for your projected needs, look into increasing your coverage to a desirable level and paying the difference yourself. This could be the cheapest way to go. If you must buy insurance on your own, by all means shop around. Read up on the different types of policies and coverage and familiarize yourself with the terminology you'll be hearing.

jargon

Cash value insurance: A form of life insurance that combines a life insurance policy with a type of savings or investment account. A portion of the premium goes toward the policy, while the rest is invested for your future use. Also called whole life or universal life.

Rider: An attachment to an insurance policy that modifies or enhances the terms of the coverage. Riders add to the premium but are often required to ensure that the policy is adequate for your needs.

Term insurance: A straightforward life insurance policy in which all your premiums, minus commission, apply toward the insurance benefit for a specified number of years.

warning

When deciding how much life insurance you need, take all projected expenses into account. There may be tuition bills to pay more than a decade away, or a sizable mortgage or other major expense you'll want to address. With disability insurance, you'll want to make sure the coverage is for your "own occupation," meaning that if you cannot perform your normal line of work you will be eligible for benefits. Also, pay attention to the "elimination period," the amount of time you must be disabled before you are eligible for benefits. With both life and disability insurance, you want the long-term assurance of a renewable policy.

In the past, for all your insurance needs you went to a company agent, independent broker, or the handful of companies that sold directly by phone. Today, the Internet is an excellent place to shop for all types of insurance, with an abundance of online calculators to help you determine your needs and the costs of all types of insurance. If you are self-employed, you may also want to check with any professional, trade, or business associations for which you qualify. Many offer different types of insurance at attractive group rates.

The New Life Insurance Investment Advisor: Achieving Financial Security for You & Your Family Through Today's Insurance Products by Ben G. Baldwin (McGraw Hill Professional Publishing, 2001): An analysis of different types of life insurance products, with examples and updates on annuity products, to guide you in selecting the right type of coverage.

How to Insure Your Income: A Step by Step Guide to Buying the Coverage You Need at Prices You Can Afford by the Silver Lake Editors (Silver Lake Publishing, 1997): A guide to planning ahead and ensuring you'll be adequately covered in the event of a debilitating injury or disability.

1. Determine your annual income needs: add up all your sources of income and average annual expenditures.

2. Tally your available financial assets in the event of an emergency.

3. Determine your insurance needs.

12. If self-employed and not adequately insured, check with professional organizations to see what types of group policies are available to you.

11. If the coverage is insufficient, see if you can increase coverage to desired levels.

10. Review the policies presently provided by your employer.

13. Before you begin shopping and comparing policies, familiarize yourself with insurance terminology and the different types of policies that are offered.

14. Begin shopping.

15. Use online search engines to find and compare different types of policies.

23. Make sure the policy is renewable before signing.

22. Ask for any riders required to make sure you get the amount and type of coverage you need.

4. For disability insurance, a rough estimate is 60 to 80 percent of present income.

5. Determine how long you would need this coverage and how soon you would need to receive benefits if disabled.

6. For life insurance: determine your household income needs and the number of years the policy will be the source of this income.

9. Review all insurance policies you presently have to see if coverage is adequate.

8. Compare your final tally with figures reached using online calculators or insurance-buying guides.

7. Also, take into account any anticipated major expenses.

16. Contact at least three agents or independent brokers and explain the type of coverage you seek.

17. If possible, ask for a quote by phone or mail to avoid a high-pressure sales meeting.

18. Check into the financial stability of the company writing the policy.

21. If you are uncertain about any of the terminology in or terms of the policy, have a company representative or agent explain it to you.

20. Review any special conditions that would limit your eligibility or void the policy.

19. Thoroughly review policies from all sources.

how to buy long-term care insurance

40

The longer you live, the greater the likelihood you'll require some form of long-term medical care in either a facility or your own home. A debilitating illness, or simply the mere process of aging, can translate into a lengthy hospital or nursing home stay that can deplete a lifetime's worth of savings. It's an unwanted experience too many people may one day face. Estimates are that anywhere from one third to more than half of the people looking toward retirement today can expect to require long-term care at some point in their lives. If you have the resources and motivation to plan ahead, long-term care insurance can prove a buffer against this potential drain on your finances. Despite what many people think, provisions for long-term health care expenses are rarely included in standard medical insurance. If you want that kind of protection, you need to purchase it separately.

One of the common mistakes people make in planning for retirement is assuming that Medicare and Medicaid will provide for all their health care needs. In reality, they may cover only a portion of expenses, and only after you've exhausted your own assets. If you have significant assets you want to pass on to your heirs, you probably have the means to invest in long-term care insurance. At today's rates, a year in a low-cost nursing home can cost as much as $30,000; who can predict how much it will cost in the future? Long-term care insurance is a form of guarantee that serious illness won't prove a major financial burden for you and your family. Like all other forms of insurance, the cost is entirely dependent on the amount of benefits you seek and the length of coverage. Review the details of policies and any and all riders to make sure they deliver the coverage you want, under all foreseeable circumstances.

jargon

Activities of daily living (ADL) triggers: Insurance carriers use the inability to perform normal activities of daily living to determine when a person becomes eligible to receive long-term care benefits.

Custodial care: Long-term care provided by nonmedical personnel to help people with their regular daily activities.

Skilled nursing care: Physician-prescribed care, usually administered in a health care or nursing home facility, for a specific medical condition.

warning

Any insurance policy is only as good as the company writing it. Buy only from an established company with experience writing long-term care policies. And read all the details. Before you purchase any long-term coverage, make sure you understand the amount of coverage you are paying for, the benefit period during which it will cover your expenses, what expenses are excluded, how long you must cover expenses before the policy begins paying, and what type of care it will and won't cover.

Most people don't purchase long-term care insurance until retirement looms, but coverage is available from most insurers from middle age on. As with life insurance, the younger you are when you buy the insurance, the lower your premium will be and the less expensive the policy will be in the long run. You can reduce costs by paring both the amount and the length of coverage. Before you buy, check into the prevailing rates for hospital and nursing home care in your area and use them as a basis for determining the amount of coverage you'll need. Expect your agent to present you with a variety of riders to improve your coverage and address special circumstances. The one rider you will probably want to include, even though it is expensive, is an adjustment for inflation. Medical costs keep rising, and you don't want to be caught short, even with all your careful planning for long-term care.

resources •

Long-Term Care Insurance Made Simple by Les Abromovitz (Health Information Press, 1999): A consumer's guide to a complex product, with practical advice on how to go about buying adequate long-term care insurance.

Long-Term Care: Your Financial Planning Guide by Phyllis R. Shelton (Kensington Publishing, 2001): A guide to anticipating and adequately planning for long-term health care and the importance of adequate insurance, with advice on buying.

1. Review all existing life and health insurance coverage, and see if any provides for long-term care or nursing home coverage.

2. Contact your insurance agent and inquire about what types of long-term insurance coverage are available.

3. Request details on the types of coverage and the costs, or arrange a meeting to have them explained to you.

6. When making this determination, recognize that long-term care insurance is most often purchased by individuals with significant financial assets they want to protect and pass on to their heirs.

5. After reviewing the types of coverage and cost, determine if you need and can afford long-term care insurance.

4. Request additional estimates from other agents or online.

7. If you decide to purchase long-term care, try to determine, based on best estimates, the amount of coverage you will want on an annual basis.

8. Determine the length of time for which you would like to be eligible for benefits.

9. Determine the type of long-term care you want covered, such as in-home, custodial, or nursing home care.

12. Learn when you would become eligible for benefits, the benefit period, the circumstances under which you would be eligible for coverage, and any special circumstances under which you would not be eligible for benefits.

11. Find out about the financial stability of the company writing the policy, including how long it has been in business, how long it has been writing this type of insurance, and its rating.

10. Discuss the cost of this coverage with your insurance agent.

13. Find out if a policy is available that would refund your premiums to your heirs if you do not require payments for long-term coverage.

14. Work with your insurance agent to ensure that any riders to the policy give you the amount of coverage you think you will need.

15. Check into the cost of a rider to cover the impact of inflation on health care costs.

16. Before signing any policy, make sure it will be renewable for the entire period for which you anticipate you may require the coverage.

how to avoid a tax audit

the basics

Everyone dreads a tax audit, especially those who have something to hide. The audit process can be an emotional and financial wringer that ultimately costs you time and, in the worst case, money to cover any additional taxes and penalties levied against you. Although the chances of an audit are remote, it happens to some individuals and businesses each year. If you're a business owner with a large number of vendors and customers, the chances could be higher. If an audit of one of them turns up some discrepancy in their report of dealings with you, the IRS might decide to take a closer look at your tax returns as well. Once the notification of an audit arrives, a period of crisis management sets in as you prepare for the worst and hope for the best. The best way to prepare for an audit is to do all you can to prevent one in the first place. Comply with the tax laws in such a way that if an auditor does come calling, you have absolutely nothing to worry about.

There's nothing you can do to prevent the IRS from scrutinizing your tax return. In past years, a random sampling of all tax returns were given a closer look, simply as a matter of practice. If IRS representatives find or suspect something that seems out of the ordinary, that may prompt an audit. You'll be asked to present supporting documentation for that portion of your tax filing in question. What might prompt that closer look? Any number of things: underreporting your income; outlandish deductions that reduce your taxable income significantly; a thriving business whose owner claims paltry wages; unusual medical expenses; exorbitant business-related entertainment or equipment expenses; even bad math on the filer's part when computing the amount of tax owed or the refund due. The first rule in making your return audit-proof is to prepare and file a tax return that is completely honest, whether you do the work yourself, use tax preparation software, or rely on the services of a financial consultant. Rule two: Have the documentation to support any claim you make. Keep good, accurate records throughout the year and hold on to all checks, bills, and receipts. If you know that something on your tax return will seem out of the ordinary, attach copies of supporting proof to the return and explain yourself. If an IRS agent questions a deduction and the proof is at hand, there will be no need to call you in for an audit. Rule three: Thoroughly review your tax return before it is submitted. Compare your records and receipts against any claims. Verify the math. Check that all answers are correct and in the right place, including Social Security numbers and business identification numbers. Then sign and date the document.

Disclosure Statement Form 8275: A form you can complete and attach to your tax return to explain any deductions that seem excessive, with supporting documentation.

Red flag deductions: Deductions that are likely to catch a tax reviewer's attention and possibly result in a tax audit. Typical red flags include large deductions for home office expenses when a person works outside the home, and significant charitable donations as a share of total income.

Only a small percentage of taxpayers, typically less than 1 percent, are audited each year. If you keep accurate records, hold on to receipts, and can support any claims you make, you have little to worry about even if you are audited. If you are one of the few, ask the investigator handling your case for specifics on what is in question and what supporting documentation you will need. Promptly provide only the support requested with an explanation, and you may avoid a wider investigation of your return.

Business owners, especially, should work year-round to make sure they have a paper trail that can protect them in event of an audit. Pay all taxes due for employees and the business when they are due. Get receipts from all vendors. Hold on to utility bills and keep a log of mileage and maintenance of all company vehicles. Know what is and isn't allowed in deductions for business travel, entertainment, and related expenses. When preparing your tax return, make no assumptions. If you can't find an answer in IRS documents, contact a field office or taxpayer hot line. Be sure to record the name, title, and phone number of the responding representative, and the date and time you got your answers.

How to Beat the I.R.S. at Its Own Game: Strategies to Avoid—and Fight—an Audit by Amir D. Aczel (Four Walls Eight Windows Press, 1995): This guide explains how the IRS selects returns to audit, which parts of a tax return are typically scrutinized, and steps you can take to increase the chances that you won't be audited.

What the IRS Doesn't Want You to Know: A CPA Reveals the Tricks of the Trade by Martin Kaplan and Naomi Weiss (Villard Books, 2000): CPA Kaplan discusses IRS audit strategies and concerns, with advice on ways to minimize the chances of an audit.

Online: The Internal Revenue Service's own Web site (www.irs.gov) is your best source for official tax publications, booklets, and downloadable tax forms.

1. Prepare for an audit-proof return throughout the tax year.

2. Keep accurate records of all business expenses and expense-related items and activity.

3. Log mileage and maintenance expenses for business vehicles.

6. Make estimated tax payments on schedule, as required.

5. Hold on to canceled checks as proof of payment for products and services.

4. Hold on to all receipts.

7. Pay all employee-related taxes on time.

8. Adjust your withholding at work to reduce the amount of your potential refund.

9. Make sure you have accurate business identification numbers for vendors and Social Security numbers for employees.

12. Organize your records and receipts by category, such as business equipment expenses, business travel expenses, capital investments, etc.

11. If you plan to prepare your own taxes, use the final version of tax preparation software for the year.

10. Familiarize yourself with any changes in tax codes, laws, or credits that may impact your tax return.

13. Enter your records into a computer program or turn them over to a professional who will prepare your taxes.

14. Make sure you are entitled to any deductions you plan to claim.

15. If you cannot verify them on your own, contact an IRS field office.

18. Double-check all amounts for income categories.

17. Complete all relevant forms and reports.

16. Record the name of the person who provides you with answers, as well as the date and time of your call.

19. Double-check amounts for any deductions.

20. Review all deductions. If you cannot verify a deduction with documentation, don't claim it, or else anticipate that it might become a target for an audit. If any deduction or claim appears excessive or out of the ordinary, complete and attach Disclosure Statement Form 8275 with copies of supporting documents to your return.

23. Keep a copy of the return for future reference.

22. Sign and date the return.

21. Review the entire return before signing. Double-check the math. Verify that Social Security numbers and business identification numbers are correct.

24. File in time to meet IRS deadlines.

how to handle a tax audit

42

the basics

It's the letter everyone dreads: you're being audited by the Internal Revenue Service. Actually, there's little to worry about as long as you have the records and documentation that make the case for the deductions you've claimed. Anything less, and you have cause for concern. But not panic. Some taxpayers actually walk away from the process with a refund; others must write a check to cover their honest mistakes; and a few—well, life would have been easier had they been honest with themselves, and the IRS, when filing and defending dubious deductions.

inside information

The IRS isn't out to get you, despite what you think. Its representatives, investigators, and auditors are merely doing their job: seeing that our tax laws are obeyed to the letter. When you're contacted for an audit, it's because something in your return seems out of the ordinary. Your deductions may seem disproportionate to the amount of income you've reported, or you may have claimed a loss that you haven't documented. The agency uses a model, based on line-by-line examinations of tens of thousands of returns, to establish norms. Just because your claims fall outside these norms doesn't mean you are wrong. For instance, you may in fact give more to charity than others in your income bracket. But the burden of proof, once the IRS questions your return, is on you. That's why it's so critical to hold on to receipts and keep good records. Depending on the complexity of your return and the issues that triggered the audit, you may be subject to a correspondence audit, which can be handled by mail (the most common type); an office audit, in which you must report to an IRS office to review a portion of your return with an agent; or a field audit, in which an IRS agent meets with you at your home, office, or tax preparer or attorney's office to review your entire return (the rarest type).

jargon

Audit: Here, audit refers to a review of your tax return and supporting records and documents by an IRS representative. An audit almost always means that the IRS is questioning something about your return that indicates that you may actually owe more taxes than you paid.

Criminal audit: The worst type of audit, undertaken by the IRS when it suspects tax fraud, which is a crime. Anyone who is the subject of a criminal audit should retain an attorney, preferably one with experience defending people who are the subject of criminal audits.

Taxpayer Compliance Measurement Program (TCMP): A line-by-line examination of tens of thousands of randomly selected tax returns that the IRS, in the past, conducted every three years to set and revise the statistical models it uses to review tax returns.

warning

If you're the subject of a tax audit, you will only make things more difficult by blaming the IRS representative who handles your case. He or she can be your ally in resolving the dispute fairly and with expediency. Anger or blame on your part can undermine your relationship. The other way to make things worse is by being anything less than honest. Don't volunteer any unrequested information, but at the same time, answer direct questions to the best of your ability and furnish the proof requested. If you don't have proof, admit it. But remember, the IRS doesn't require receipts for deductions of $25 or less. In addition, having excellent documentation of other deductions may compensate, in the examiner's eyes, for not having a couple of receipts.

fyi ●

If you disagree with the ultimate findings of a tax audit, you do have the right to appeal. There are several levels of appeals. First is to the supervisor of the IRS representative who conducted your audit; if you are still not satisfied, you can take your case to the IRS Appeals Office. Usually, because of the pressure to close cases, some mutually acceptable compromise can be reached at the supervisory level. If not, and you believe you are in the right, you can take your case to tax court, a costly and time-consuming process.

resources ●

How to Settle with the IRS—for Pennies on the Dollar by Arnold S. Goldstein (Garrett Publishing, 1997): A consumer's guide to working with the IRS to resolve tax bills, with information on the agency's Offer in Compromise program. Includes sample documents needed to settle with the IRS.

Keys to Surviving a Tax Audit by D. Larry Crumbley and Jack P. Friedman (Barron's Educational Series, 1991): Straightforward advice on what to do, how to prepare, and how to comply with the IRS in the event of a tax audit.

Internal Revenue Service: Through its many publications, the IRS can provides detailed information on how to file tax forms, the types of deductions that are and are not allowed, and how to appeal an audit. Start with IRS Publication 1, "Your Rights as a Taxpayer." Contact your regional IRS office or go to the IRS Web site, www.irs.gov.

1. Before filing your tax return, double-check it line by line.

2. Make sure you have the records, receipts, and other support documents to back up any deductions.

3. If you are informed by the IRS that you are being audited, respond immediately.

12. If you are informed that you are the subject of a criminal audit, retain the services of a lawyer who has experience in cases of this type.

11. If it's to be a field audit, ask the IRS investigator how long it will take and block out the appropriate time on your schedule.

10. If someone else prepared your tax return, it's advisable to consult them and possibly take him or her with you to the hearing.

13. During the audit process, don't volunteer information, but answer any questions completely and to the best of your ability.

14. Provide the IRS investigator with copies of all support documents, and make notes of what proof you provide and when.

15. If you cannot substantiate some part of your claim, admit it.

4. Call or contact the IRS investigator handling your case and inquire how you can comply with the audit.

5. Ask what proof or documentation you need to provide. Take detailed notes.

6. Gather that proof and make copies of it.

9. If it's an office audit, arrange a meeting at a mutually convenient time.

8. If it's a correspondence audit, mail your records (certified, return receipt requested) and any other support documents to the IRS representative. Make sure your case number is marked on all documents.

7. Whether you are to provide proof by mail or in person, hold on to your original documents and records.

16. Work with the representative to resolve any disputes as quickly as possible.

17. If you are not satisfied with the result, consider appealing your case.

18. Before you do, secure and review copies of IRS Publication 1, "Your Rights as a Taxpayer," and Publication 5, "Appeal Rights and Preparation of Protests for Unagreed Cases."

19. If you are still not satisfied after the appeals process, weigh the merits of taking your case to tax court.

how to make a will

43

the basics

Do you need a will? Consider what happens to the estates left by those who don't prepare one and are categorized by the state as dying intestate. When there's no will, state laws stipulating how your property is to be divided will take effect. A judge will appoint an executor, not necessarily of your choosing, who will ensure that the laws are carried out and claim a percentage of your estate as his fee. If minor children survive, the court will also appoint a guardian for them, and it may not be the person you'd want raising them. In fact, without a will, you surrender control over how all you've accrued in life will be distributed. It's highly unlikely that anyone outside your immediate family will get anything to remember you by. And if there are no surviving kin and no will, the state could actually lay claim to your assets. If there's anything you want to pass on to heirs or preserve for their future, you need a will.

In legal terms, a will is merely a document, drawn up by you, that stipulates how you want your property, wealth, and any assets to be divided and distributed after your death. The key contents of a will include a description of all your assets; a list of beneficiaries by name; the name of a guardian for any minor children; and the name of the executor—the person you trust to see that your wishes are carried out. You must sign your will in the presence of impartial witnesses, people not named as beneficiaries. They must sign the will as well, as proof that you knew what you were doing at the time you signed the will and were not coerced into preparing it or its contents. You can have an attorney draw up your will for you, or you can write out your will in your own handwriting. In either case it's critical to keep the original will in a safe place and tell the executor or someone else you trust where it can be found. You may also want that person or your attorney to keep a copy of the will should any questions about its validity arise in the future. Your will can be revised at any time in your life, as often as you feel necessary, by drafting an entirely new document or adding an amendment or codicil to your will. This should be done whenever significant events take place, such as a change in your fortune or marital status or the birth of a child. When you update your will, it's important that it be witnessed, that you destroy the previous document, and that you inform your attorney or trusted friend that you have made changes and give them a copy.

Holographic will: A will written in your own handwriting. It must contain the same elements outlined above and be signed by both you and witnesses.

Intestate: A person who dies without a will is said to die intestate. In such cases the courts intervene and apply state laws on the distribution of property and the appointment of guardians for your minor children.

Living will: A legal document, entirely separate from a will, that stipulates what medical treatment you want in the event of a tragic accident or terminal illness, as well as who has the authority to make medical decisions for you.

Probate: The legal process for orderly distribution of a person's estate, including the appointment of a executor when a person dies intestate.

You don't need an attorney to draw up your will. In fact, there are a number of books with fill-in-the-blank forms, as well as computer software programs that can guide you through the process of drafting and preparing a valid will. It's important to be as specific as possible when stipulating how you want your property divided and who is to get what, so that there can be no confusion about your intentions. If you have any doubt about your need to draft a will, you may want to check what your state laws prescribe for the division of property when there is no will and make sure you can accept those terms.

Your will is your only opportunity to control what will happen to your property after you die. Don't assume that anyone will understand your intentions and carry them out unless you put them into writing. Your will is your final legacy. If you are a parent, even with adult children, who plans an uneven distribution of your estate in favor of one or two, you should explain your decision to all while you are still alive. If you don't, your actions could create an irreparable and permanent rift in the family, and those left out might still find cause to challenge the validity of the will. Your will is only a part, but admittedly a key component, of your estate planning. If you have significant assets, you should consult with a financial adviser on how to minimize the impact of taxes on your estate at the same time you begin to draft your will.

The Complete Will Kit by F. Bruce Gentry and Jens C. Appel (John Wiley & Sons, 1996): An updated edition of a popular do-it-yourself guide to writing your will with step-by-step instructions.

Willmaker8 (Nolo Press, 2001): Easy-to-understand software steps you through the process of completing your will with a series of easily answered questions. Includes worksheets and background information on many of the considerations that should go into making a will. For Macintosh and Windows PCs.

1. Determine the necessity of preparing a will.

2. If you doubts you need one, find out what your state prescribes for the division of property if a person dies intestate.

3. Decide if this is something you want to do yourself or with the advice and assistance of your attorney.

6. If you want everything to go to your surviving spouse, state that in your will.

5. If preparing the will yourself, check the state requirements, in terms of the number of witnesses and how to register the will, if applicable.

4. If you have significant assets, consider consulting an adviser on estate planning at the same time you begin work on your will.

7. Name a guardian and an alternate guardian for any minor children, and explain any provisions you are making for their care.

8. If you are dividing your estate among heirs and beneficiaries, make a list of your financial assets: property, bank accounts, investments, life insurance policies, etc.

9. Where pertinent, gather any documents related to ownership, such as policy or policy number, deed or title, locations of accounts, etc.

12. Also, compile a list of any debtors and what they owe you.

11. Compile a list of all outstanding debts.

10. Compile a list of personal property you want to pass on to heirs or other beneficiaries.

13. Prepare a list of the heirs and beneficiaries of your estate.

14. Stipulate how you want your debts to be cleared up after you die.

15. If you plan to release any debtors from their obligations to your estate, state that in your will.

18. Be as detailed as possible in describing how you want all property distributed.

17. If you plan to leave specific property to a specific beneficiary, say so.

16. Stipulate how you want your property divided among your heirs and beneficiaries.

19. Stipulate what you want done with the remainder of your estate that is not specifically covered in your will.

20. Name an executor and an alternate, in the event that your first-choice executor is not able to fulfill the duties.

21. Thoroughly review the document before signing it.

24. Have them sign it and date it.

23. Sign your will in the presence of impartial witnesses who are not named as beneficiaries.

22. Consider having it reviewed by an attorney, if you are preparing it yourself.

25. Keep the will in a safe place.

26. Tell your attorney and family members where your will is located.

27. Give a sealed copy to your attorney and/or a trusted friend or the executor.

28. Amend your will as needed when your circumstances change.

should you buy or rent your home?

44

Should you purchase or rent your next home or apartment? It's a decision that has to be made whenever you think about relocating. There are pros and cons to either. There's a certain sense of pride that goes with living in a home of your own, and you can do a lot more in a house or condo than in an apartment you rent. Purchasing a home also allows you to invest in your financial future the considerable sum that would otherwise go to rent. Renting, on the other hand, doesn't tie you down the way home ownership does. When you want to move on, it's just a matter of either not renewing or breaking your lease. And a rental doesn't carry the potential for added expenses that home ownership does, such as the necessary costs of repairs and maintenance. Rent or own? It comes down to what you can afford, financially, and what you want, emotionally, in the space you call home.

Whether to rent or purchase may seem to be a question rooted in fiances and affordability, but there are important psychological aspects to consider as well. For some people, living in a home of their own is worth the sacrifice, whatever it entails. Others don't want that commitment or simply don't need the extra space. Whatever your own case, the first factor to consider is what you can afford. Home ownership requires more: not only is there a monthly payment for a mortgage, but there are other expenses, such as insurance, basic maintenance and repairs, taxes, and utility bills, that can increase costs considerably. Most buyers need to come up with a substantial down payment for the right of ownership. On the other hand, the money thus spent isn't lost. In fact, it can yield a significant return when you decide to sell. And the monthly expense can actually cost you less than comparable rent, since you can deduct the interest paid on a mortgage from the income you pay taxes on.

Affordability: What you can afford to pay for housing. To determine affordability, consider what you have available for shelter against the total cost of renting or purchasing.

Down payment: Easily overlooked when quickly comparing the advantages of renting versus purchasing, the down payment represents a substantial amount of money, usually 20 percent of the purchase price, which you must produce before you can obtain a mortgage.

Rent to own: An arrangement whereby a landlord applies the monthly rental against the down payment or purchase price of a home, financed by the landlord.

In their zeal to purchase a home, some potential home owners, especially first-time buyers, overextend themselves financially. Some secure loans from family and friends to make their down payments, on top of the mortgage. Or they structure their mortgage payments so that the loan payments gradually increase, assuming that their income will climb during the same period. If home ownership is a goal of yours, the best strategy is never to assume more debt than you can realistically afford, based on best estimates of the total cost. If it's out of reach now, it's better to admit it and continue renting as you save up to make a larger down payment.

The toughest hurdle for many buyers is coming up with a down payment. A number of programs and financing options are available that make it easier for a first-time buyer to purchase a home. Inquire at local lending institutions if such programs are available in your area. If you are a renter and presently considering purchasing a home as an investment, make sure you look at the total cost of ownership before making a decision. There may be other investment opportunities that could produce a quicker return on the additional amount you'll be spending for home ownership.

resources

Stop Renting Now: Here's How the New National Home Ownership Strategy Can Move You out of a Rental and into Your Own Home by Gary W. Eldred (National Initiative for Home Ownership, 1996): An in-depth look at ways individuals can make the transition from renting to owning a home.

Area lending institutions and mortgage sources: Once you have decided how much you are paying for shelter and what you think you can afford to pay, speak with a loan officer at one of the likely sources of a mortgage. He or she can help you determine if you are ready to purchase and what the difference between purchasing a home and continuing to rent will be.

Online rent/own calculators: A number of Internet sites feature calculators to help you determine affordability and compare the cost of renting versus owning. Try, for example, those at **Financenter** (www.financenter.com).

1. Complete Lifemap 46

2. Calculate the amount you spend for rent in twelve months.

3. Contact a mortgage lending institution, or consult mortgage charts. If your monthly rent were payments on a typical mortgage, how large a mortgage would it entitle you to?

12. Renting: Low monthly expense.

11. Renting: Ability to relocate quickly.

10. Renting: Freedom from responsibility for home maintenance.

13. Renting: Convenient location/transportation/commute.

14. Renting: Limited need for space.

15. Owning: Satisfaction of ownership.

24. If you can afford a home, begin investigating options (see Lifemap 46 and Lifemap 47); if you cannot afford to purchase now but want to, start saving for down payment (see Lifemap 51).

23. If interested in buying, consider ability to purchase, determined above, against prices in your area.

22. Continue renting, if that matches your goals/interests.

4. Ask a lender how big a down payment would be required to secure a mortgage at that level.

5. Combine the mortgage with the down payment for an indication of the type of home you could afford, if spending at your present level.

6. Add to that amount best estimates of any additional expenses, such as higher utility bills, home maintenance, taxes, insurance, etc.

9. Check the family needs that are most important.

8. Check local real estate listings to see what it would cost to rent a home or apartment with these facilities.

7. Compile a list of your family's needs in terms of space: number of bedrooms and bathrooms, parking space, etc.

16. Owning: Freedom to do as you please.

17. Owning: Expand, revise space as needed.

18. Owning: Invest money for shelter in own future.

21. Review above list to determine if you would be happier owning or renting.

20. Owning: Interested in home maintenance and repair or ability to pay for same.

19. Owning: Yard or garden.

how much can you afford
to pay for shelter?

45

the basics

Knowing how much you can afford to spend on a home, and staying within that budget, is fundamental to financial stability. Housing is one of our most basic needs and one of our major expenses, and therefore is always a spending priority. Live beyond your means for housing costs, and the burden will eventually consume you and bring your financial house of cards tumbling down. To avoid doing so, make an honest assessment of your financial obligations and expenses and subtract the total from your monthly income. The difference will give you an idea of what you can afford for housing.

inside information

There are several widely accepted formulas for determining what you can afford to pay for shelter. At one time, the common wisdom held that no more than 25 percent of one's net income should go for shelter. Today, something in the range of 33 percent may be considered more the norm. Others believe a potential home buyer should look for homes in a price range two to two and a half times annual income. While such "rules" are widely accepted, there's a much greater variance in what people can and do pay for shelter. A thrifty few can work miracles on a meager budget; at the other extreme are some who barely get by, no matter what their income level. The moral: only you can really decide what's affordable for you. The typical mortgage finances only 80 percent of the price of a home. Your loan officer may still rely on time-honored formulas to calculate what monthly payments you can afford after the down payment. If you can't convince him or her that you can pay more, that's a challenge to focus on raising a larger down payment so you can get a more affordable mortgage.

jargon

Down payment: The amount of cash you'll need to put down on a house up front to secure a mortgage. It's a major expense that must be considered along with the monthly bills to determine affordability.

Mortgage: Financing you secure for purchase of a home. Having a mortgage usually means there is a monthly payment to be made. What you can afford in a monthly mortgage payment has a direct bearing on what lending institutions consider to be an affordable price range.

Mortgage deduction: The interest on your home mortgage that you are entitled to claim as a tax deduction when you itemize your return. The mortgage deduction can actually lower the cost of ownership and make it more affordable.

warning

Determining affordability requires you to make an honest, thorough assessment of your financial resources, assets, and obligations. Anything less, and you could lull yourself into a false sense of what you can spend for shelter. If you believe you can spend more for shelter than the mortgage provider says you can, try living within such a budget for at least three months to make sure it will support your lifestyle.

fyi

You may be able to borrow more than 80 percent of the home price from a mortgage lender, but the lender will add a monthly premium for additional insurance to your payments. There are programs that make it easier for first-time buyers to afford a home. Contact local mortgage sources for information on all the options available to you.

resources

10 Steps to Home Ownership: A Workbook for First-Time Buyers by Ilyce R. Glink (Times Books, 1996): Guides the first-time buyer—or anyone—through the home-buying process, with pointed advice to help determine just what you can afford for shelter.

LoanPage (www.loanpage.com): A Web site with resources to help home buyers investigate their options in a mortgage. Follow the calculator link to a menu of useful tools, including one to help you determine what you can afford.

Local lenders: Your best resources for information on what types of financing are available to you as well as how much they are willing to lend in a mortgage, based on your income and expenses.

1. Write down your monthly income, after taxes, from all sources.

2. Compile a list of typical monthly expenses.

3. Include a list of regular monthly bills: outstanding loans, credit card bills, insurance, tuition, car payment, investments, etc.

6. Make sure the list accounts for annual or semiannual expenses such as vacation or holiday spending. Divide this annual spending into a monthly amount and add to the expense tally.

5. Include a second list of regular monthly expenses: food, clothing, transportation, entertainment, medicine, savings, etc.

4. Make sure the list accounts for annual or semiannual payments such as insurance premiums, if applicable. Divide each annual payment into a monthly amount and add to the tally of regular monthly bills.

7. Add the monthly tallies for bills and expenses.

8. Subtract this total from the monthly income after taxes.

9. The remainder is what you can afford to spend each month for shelter.

12. Identify any areas where you could reduce spending, such as entertainment, transportation, eating out, etc.

11. Scrutinize your monthly spending.

10. If this is not sufficient, look first to reduce your expenses, then to increase your income.

13. Based on the reduced costs, recalculate the monthly income available for housing.

14. Before you consider this to be what you can afford, try living on a budget based on this level of spending for three months.

15. Contact a local mortgage source. Discuss your goals and determine what type of financing is available to you (see Lifemap 52).

18. Set a savings goal that will allow you to make a larger down payment and secure a smaller, more affordable mortgage.

17. If what you can afford for housing is not sufficient, consider asking for a raise or developing new sources of income, such as a second job or side business, to strengthen your shelter-buying power.

16. Inquire how much of a mortgage you prequalify for. Do you have the resources to make the appropriate down payment?

how to judge a community

the basics

Purchasing a house involves making a commitment to a community. The surrounding neighborhood will help determine the return on investment or quality of life you'll enjoy in your next home. So whether you're purchasing your next home with the intention of eventually selling or looking for the ideal locale in which to sink your family roots, the neighborhood and community should influence your decision. What factors should you consider? That depends entirely on where you are in your life and what you want from your next home. A young couple with children would want to know about schools, parks, and churches. A professional couple might put more weight on such factors as commuting and area restaurants. Retirees' primary concerns might encompass other factors, such as area medical facilities, public transportation, and cost of living. Whether you're in the market for a three-bedroom Colonial or a downtown co-op, you must assess your personal needs and then weigh neighborhoods against the criteria that matter most to you. Ideally, you should shop for a neighborhood before you shop for a home. If you can't, thoroughly investigate the neighborhood and surrounding community before rushing into any purchase. You're planning on moving not only to a new home but to a new neighborhood, as well. Your happiness will depend on how well it matches your needs.

inside information

Much of the research that will help you compare neighborhoods and communities has already been done. There's an ample selection of books and online resources that draw comparisons between neighborhoods and communities. The local chamber of commerce and an experienced real estate broker should be able to provide you with information about an area, its amenities, schools, stores, and so on. But that's only half of what you need to know. Real insight into an area, especially if it's a place you want to call home, comes only through personal experience. When it's time to tour a home, brokers are going to drive you there by the route that makes the best impression. If you want to know what the rest of the area looks like, you'll need to conduct your own tour. The resources, area statistics, and agent's opinions can provide you with a sketch of an area and its potential appeal. To fill in the details, drive around and get a feel for the place. How easy is it to get to schools and hospitals? Where are the supermarkets? What stores are downtown or in the mall? Find the answers to your concerns. Back up your driving tour with a walking tour of the neighborhood(s) that interest(s) you. Stroll around. Is it the kind of place you'd want to consider your own? Only you can answer that.

jargon

Location analysis: A term often used for commercial properties, it also describes what a potential homeowner should consider along with the property: location, surrounding properties, quality of neighborhood, roads and access, nearby stores, etc.

Zoning: The classification of property specifying how it can be used, such as residential or commercial, as determined by the local zoning board. How an area or neighborhood is zoned indicates what type of future development you can expect there.

warning

Here are a few signs that should serve as red flags about an area: a large number of homes offered for sale can indicate flight from the area; vacant stores, especially in the downtown area, speak of a town past its prime; streets and parks empty of children on a Saturday reveal that it may not be a family-friendly place; much graffiti, stores locked behind grilles, and security bars on homes suggest that crime may be a serious concern; empty lots near a subdivision or within a city will eventually fill in and obscure views; properties that aren't well maintained can erode the value of others in the area.

fyi

Like all things in life, neighborhoods ebb and flow. People move in and out; communities prosper and decline, only to be rejuvenated. If you're adventurous and willing to take a risk, you can find real bargains in neighborhoods poised for rejuvenation. But it's a risk that will require the commitment and energy of others like you before it can pay off.

resources

Places Rated Almanac by David Savageau and Ralph B. D'Agostino (Hungry Minds, 1999): An informative resource about cities and towns with populations of at least 50,000, located in a county with a total population of at least 100,000. Ratings by cost of living, job outlook, transportation, education, health care, crime, the arts, recreation, and climate.

iOwn.com (www.iown.com): Among its many resources, this Web site lets you conduct neighborhood comparisons, by zip code, throughout the United States. Enter zip codes for up to five areas and get a quick comparison profile, based on census data on household income, cultural diversity, age of residents, percentage of families, local weather. It's a start.

1. Compile a list of what's important to you about an area.

2. Consider your family's needs in terms of schools, transportation, shopping, social activities, entertainment, medical facilities, parks and recreation, etc.

3. If you are looking to relocate to a new city or state, consult a "places rated" reference for best matches.

6. Search newspapers, home buyers' guides, and online for current listings in those areas.

5. Use online resources, census data, and informal driving tours to narrow your selection to specific neighborhoods, based on the criteria that matter most to you.

4. Write local chambers of commerce and national real estate companies for more information.

7. Contact real estate companies there for more information, based on what's important to you.

8. Arrange meetings with real estate agents in appropriate neighborhoods.

9. When you meet, explain what's important to you and what you want in a home and neighborhood. Obtain whatever written information is available from the agent.

12. Consider the surrounding properties: Do they enhance or detract from the value of individual homes?

11. Consider your first impression as you drive.

10. Have the agent conduct a tour of the area and individual homes. Also, have the agent drive you to those features that matter most to you: train station, schools, church, shopping, etc.

13. Consider the surrounding neighborhood: Is it well maintained, are there good roads and access to shopping, etc.

14. Look for warning signs: many houses up for sale, poorly maintained streets, vacant schools or stores, etc.

15. Ask all the questions that matter to you, including how much area utility rates and property taxes are.

18. Take a walking tour. Note the condition and appearance of homes and the overall "feel" of the neighborhood. Are the people you meet friendly, congenial, abrasive?

17. Take a driving tour of the area on your own. Explore side streets and routes other than how you arrived there with the sales agent.

16. Contact the local zoning board or planning commission to find out how the area is zoned and what future development may take place.

19. Inquire about potential development in any adjacent or nearby properties.

20. Pick up copies of the local newspaper for as long as you are shopping for homes. Read it as if you lived there.

21. Do you like what you learn about what's going on there?

22. Consider all you learn to be factors that will enhance or undermine the appeal of any individual home or apartment.

how to judge an individual apartment, co-op, or condominium

47

the basics •

If you're not planning on purchasing or renting a detached single-family home, your shelter options include renting an apartment, becoming a member of a building co-op, or purchasing an apartment outright as a condominium. Although the legal implications of each method of obtaining shelter are vastly different, each entails some form of multiunit dwelling. No matter which approach you choose—and the pros and cons of each should be carefully weighed—you need to scrutinize the building and its setting along with the space within that building you plan to call home. Only when these prove satisfactory should you explore the legal procedures of obtaining that space.

inside information •

Which option is right for you? That depends entirely on your financial situation and goals. Briefly, when renting an apartment, all your money does is grant you the right to live there. It's your landlord's responsibility to maintain the building and grounds. As a member of a co-op, you own shares equal to the value of your apartment, which is yours as long as you remain a member in good standing. As a co-op member, you must also share the expenses required to maintain the building. As purchaser of a condominium, you own your space, but you don't enjoy the same control over the surrounding space as if you owned a single-family home.

jargon

Condominium: An apartment or building complex in which individuals purchase their apartments or town houses and share equally in the expense of maintaining the complex.

Co-op: A cooperative that owns a building and the apartments it contains. Members of a co-op hold shares in the co-op equal to the value of their apartments. It is ruled by a board of directors who are member/owners residing in the building.

warning

Whether you sign a rental lease, become a member of a co-op, or purchase a condo, you are committing to a legally binding contract. It's your responsibility to know and understand the terms of that contract before signing. In an apartment, whether it's a rental, co-op, or condo, there will be restrictions on what you can do with your space and what is and isn't allowed. Know what you're getting into before you make any commitment: thoroughly review the terms of your lease; read the the bylaws of the co-op and review minutes of its board of directors; scrutinize the purchase agreement of a condo. If you have questions about the terms of any agreement or the governing bylaws, consult the board and/or your attorney.

fyi

There's no better source of inside information on any form of shelter than the people who already live there. They can be both honestly encouraging and brutally frank. Ask prospective neighbors about your concerns: Is the landlord responsive to tenants' needs? Have there been significant unforeseen costs for maintenance? Are other condo purchasers satisfied with their investment?

The Condo and Co-op Handbook: A Comprehensive Guide to Buying and Owning a Condo or Co-op by R. Dodge Woodson (Hungry Minds, 1998): A complete guide for anyone considering these shelter strategies, with advice on what to look for in the building and contract.

Tips and Traps When Buying a Condo, Co-op or Townhouse by Robert Irwin (McGraw-Hill, 1999): Straightforward advice on evaluating whether these are the right options for you and how to identify the best deal once you know which option you want to pursue.

Apartment Renter's Resource (www.aptrentersresource.com): A Web resource for apartment dwellers.

1. Determine your needs and priorities: total living space; number of rooms; distance to commute, schools, shopping; etc.

2. Identify areas or neighborhoods where you would like to live.

3. Complete Lifemap 46.

12. Are the elevators in good working order?

11. Are interior entrances and halls well lit and clean?

10. Are stairways, entrances, and doors secure?

13. Are the rooms well maintained?

14. Is there sufficient closet space?

15. Are there sufficient windows?

24. If you decide to become a member, inquire about joining.

23. Request and review copies of the minutes of recent co-op board meetings. These could reveal any potential problems or unresolved issues facing co-op members.

22. Request a copy of the co-op's bylaws and thoroughly review them.

25. If all of the above points check out and this is a condominium, arrange to meet with the seller.

26. Negotiate the terms of your sale and contract, using Lifemap 50 as your guide.

27. Thoroughly review the terms of any legal agreement.

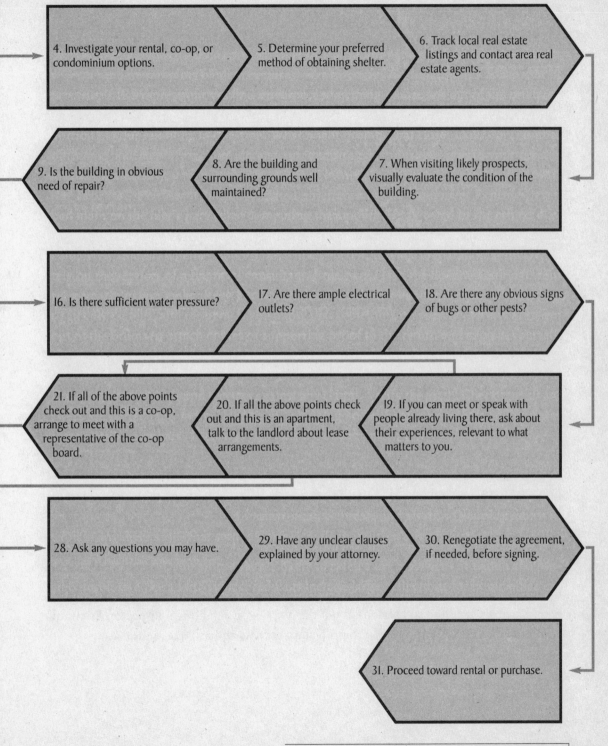

4. Investigate your rental, co-op, or condominium options.

5. Determine your preferred method of obtaining shelter.

6. Track local real estate listings and contact area real estate agents.

9. Is the building in obvious need of repair?

8. Are the building and surrounding grounds well maintained?

7. When visiting likely prospects, visually evaluate the condition of the building.

16. Is there sufficient water pressure?

17. Are there ample electrical outlets?

18. Are there any obvious signs of bugs or other pests?

21. If all of the above points check out and this is a co-op, arrange to meet with a representative of the co-op board.

20. If all the above points check out and this is an apartment, talk to the landlord about lease arrangements.

19. If you can meet or speak with people already living there, ask about their experiences, relevant to what matters to you.

28. Ask any questions you may have.

29. Have any unclear clauses explained by your attorney.

30. Renegotiate the agreement, if needed, before signing.

31. Proceed toward rental or purchase.

how to judge an individual house

48

the basics

Almost every house is unique, so it's one of the few things you'll ever buy for which there's no comprehensive buyer's guide. It's entirely up to you to determine if its features, condition, and setting warrant making an investment you'll live with for years. Your evaluation begins when you drive down the street looking for the address and shouldn't end until you head for the closing. In between it should include everything about the home: the surrounding neighborhood and properties; the look of the house and its interior; its condition and maintenance history; its appliances and utilities; the garage and outbuildings; the yard and landscaping. Forget the real estate agent's advice—you're truly on your own here. Later on, if you're still serious about the home, you can hire an inspector. But until you reach that point, it's up to you to probe into corners and ask questions.

This evaluation is one place where you'll pick up points to use when negotiating the purchase price. Make notes of any concerns. If that requires more than one trip, so be it. On the other hand, if you immediately know you aren't interested, don't waste your time or the agent's. Spend time only on properties that interest you. Initially, give yourself a chance to get a feel for the place with a walk-through. When questions come to mind, ask them. If the agent can't provide answers, insist on getting them from the owner. Often what's not said can be more important than what is. You need to ask as many and as detailed questions as required to get your answers. Look for any signs of hidden or covered damage, decay, or neglect that could make the home more of a liability than an asset.

Comparable: Recently sold homes comparable to the one you are evaluating. The agent should supply you with a list of these on request. They can help determine if the home is realistically priced.

Curb appeal: How a home looks to you when you drive up. You can often decide whether or not you are interested in a home based on curb appeal.

Easement: An agreement that gives another person limited use of the property. An easement could impact the owner's privacy and enjoyment of the property and should be carefully considered when evaluating any property.

Find out why the owner is selling. The reason could provide more leverage in the price negotiation.

If you notice that a lot of homes in the area are up for sale, take it as a red flag. The owners may know something you need to consider in your evaluation of the home and neighborhood. Find out why there is so much sales activity. Pay close attention to any surfaces that show signs of having just been painted. A fresh coat of paint is a common remedy for covering old problems. If you decide to use an inspector, make sure it's one you find, not someone recommended by the agent or owner. Make sure your evaluation includes the heating and cooling, electrical, and plumbing systems. Learn their age and condition and get an idea of how well they've been maintained. Replacing any of these can add significantly to the price of ownership.

resources •

Stephen Pollan's Foolproof Guide to Buying a Home by Stephen Pollan and Mark Levine (Fireside Books, 1997): A step-by-step guide to the home-purchasing process, from determining needs to closing, with a section devoted to evaluating a home.

100 Major Item Home Inspection Checklist for Home Buyers by Stanley Harbruck (Standards and Testing, 1999): A checklist and guide to inspecting a home, written by a professional home inspector.

100 Questions Every First Time Buyer Should Ask: With Answers from Top Brokers from Around the Country by Ilyce R. Glink (Times Books, 2000): A guide for the new-home buyer, based on the experiences of one hundred real estate brokers throughout the country.

Realtor.com (www.realtor.com): Its many resources for home buyers and sellers include information and tips on how to evaluate a home.

1. Consider the neighborhood (see Lifemap 47).

2. How does the house fit in with the surrounding homes? Do they complement one another? Are there any nearby homes that detract from the appeal or value of this home?

3. What is the curb appeal? What's your first impression as you drive past or drive up?

6. In what direction do the house and the dominant windows face? South brings warmth in winter and brightness throughout the year.

5. Do trees and foliage enhance the look and provide ample shade or windbreak?

4. Is the landscaping neat and well maintained?

7. Walk around the house.

8. Check the roof and gutters.

9. Check the condition of the driveway and any walkways.

12. Do the windows and doors have storm windows and screens?

11. Are there an ample number of windows on all sides?

10. Are fences and boundary lines obvious and well defined?

13. Enter through the main entranceway. What's your first impression?

14. Are there any offensive odors?

15. Does the door close tightly?

18. How well are the floors finished? Are they carpeted?

17. Note if and where the floors creak or sag—these could be danger signs.

16. Move through the house room by room, examining the floors, walls, and ceiling. View each room with lights on and off.

19. If carpeted, what type of floor is underneath?

20. Are there any cracks, holes, or noticeable repairs in the walls or ceilings?

21. Is there any separation at the corners of the room or where the walls meet the ceiling?

30. Pay especially close attention to the kitchen and bathroom(s), as these are the most expensive rooms to renovate.

29. How many bathrooms are there, and where are they located?

28. How many bedrooms are there, and where are they located?

31. Does the kitchen provide ample working space?

32. Are the fixtures and appliances in good working condition? Is there any buildup of grime?

33. Is there sufficient cabinet and pantry space? Are the countertops and cabinets in good condition?

42. What types of heating and cooling system and water heater are used? How have they been maintained? How long since they were installed?

41. Look for signs of roof or weather leaks in the attic.

40. Look for signs of water or bug damage in the supports in the basement.

43. What type of plumbing pipes are used throughout the house?

44. Ask about the wiring. Does the electric panel have circuit breakers or fuses? Fuses will probably need to be replaced at some point in the future.

45. Is the garage sufficiently large and well maintained? Are there any other outbuildings? If so, what kind of condition are they in, inside and out?

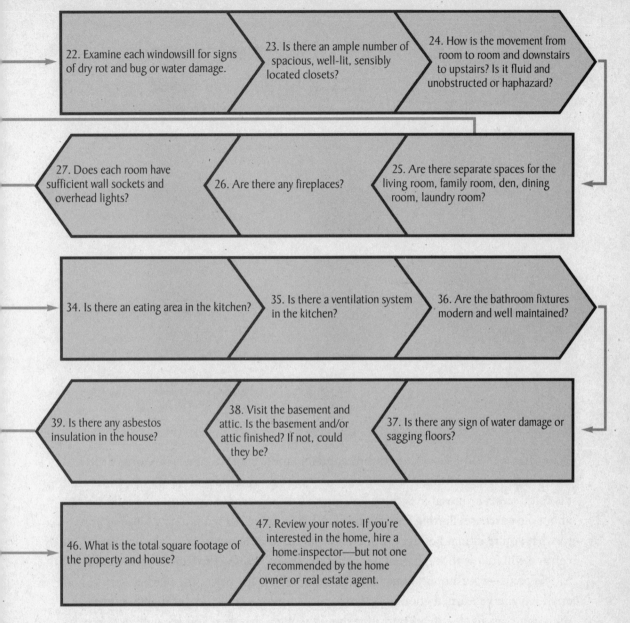

22. Examine each windowsill for signs of dry rot and bug or water damage.

23. Is there an ample number of spacious, well-lit, sensibly located closets?

24. How is the movement from room to room and downstairs to upstairs? Is it fluid and unobstructed or haphazard?

27. Does each room have sufficient wall sockets and overhead lights?

26. Are there any fireplaces?

25. Are there separate spaces for the living room, family room, den, dining room, laundry room?

34. Is there an eating area in the kitchen?

35. Is there a ventilation system in the kitchen?

36. Are the bathroom fixtures modern and well maintained?

39. Is there any asbestos insulation in the house?

38. Visit the basement and attic. Is the basement and/or attic finished? If not, could they be?

37. Is there any sign of water damage or sagging floors?

46. What is the total square footage of the property and house?

47. Review your notes. If you're interested in the home, hire a home inspector—but not one recommended by the home owner or real estate agent.

how to negotiate the price and sales contract of a home

49

the basics

Your offer is the first legal step toward actually purchasing a home. You can ask the real estate broker representing the seller, or your own agent, to pass along an offer, but until the seller sees a proposal in writing you haven't demonstrated that you are really serious about the purchase. Putting your terms of purchase on paper lends a new sense of gravity to what you're doing. Before you submit a purchase offer, make sure it's something you can and will follow through on if it satisfies the seller. Take all the factors you've gathered to this point—your notes about the home, the seller's list price, the market trends, and anything you've learned about why the home is up for sale—and put together what you think is a reasonable offer. Your offer should include the price you are willing to pay, as well as any contingencies that may impact your ability to follow through on the offer. If there's something that may prevent you from purchasing the home, such as an inability to get a mortgage or issues you want addressed before purchasing the home, spell them out. You may decide to make a low initial offer, planning to negotiate a final price between it and the list price. Realize that for as long as you are negotiating, until your offer is accepted, the seller is free to consider and accept other offers as well. If the market is tight and you really like the home, you may want to make a more reasonable offer initially.

A real estate agent is obligated by law to pass along any offer, serious or not. That agent or broker works for the deal, but the commission paid depends on the selling price. To ensure that there's no conflict of interest, you want your interests represented by a buyer's agent, if you have one, or your attorney. You'll know if you want to proceed further by the seller's response to your initial offer. As soon as you know the seller is receptive, your concern is the written proposal. The broker may have a Residential Purchase Agreement you can fill out, or you may need to have your attorney draw up the document. In any event, you want your attorney to review the document before it is submitted. The more you know before you submit an offer, the more leverage you will enjoy in negotiating the best price. Here's where the information you've gathered while investigating the home can help. If the buyer is eager to sell, he's likely to make concessions in order to close the sale. Include in your offer a list of any concerns or issues you want addressed. Also include a list of any extras you expect to be included. An eager seller will make those concessions, or lower the price accordingly, to accommodate a serious buyer. Also allow yourself an easy out in case there's any reason you change your mind or decide against the home. For example, if you aren't already preapproved for a mortgage, the sale should be contingent on your ability to get one. You will want an inspector's report on the condition of the home before you proceed with purchase, as well. It can take a lot of back-and-forth, offers and counteroffers, to hammer out a sale agreement that's mutually acceptable. Once the buyer and seller agree to terms, in writing with their signatures, they have a binding contract. Make it as specific as it needs to be, and once again, have it approved by your attorney before you sign it.

Counteroffer: The seller's response to an offer that he or she has not accepted. In effect it is an alternative proposal, which the potential buyer can either accept or respond to with another counteroffer.

Earnest money or deposit: A percentage of the selling price that demonstrates good faith of your intention to buy after you have negotiated the purchase and conditions of sale with the seller. Earnest money is deposited in an escrow account and later applied to the closing costs.

Ratified sales contract: The final version of the sales contract, outlining all terms and contingencies and carrying the signatures of the buyer(s), the seller(s), and their legal representatives.

Residential Purchase Agreement: A standardized form for specifying the terms of a home purchase between buyer and seller. This form is used by Realtors, members of the National Association of Realtors.

warning

The sales contract, once accepted, must address every concern and contingency about the purchase. Everything must be spelled out. Be as specific as you need to and have the entire document reviewed by an attorney before signing it.

fyi

You can withdraw your offer right up until you receive notification of its acceptance by the seller. While other professionals may be involved in negotiations, the final terms of the agreement are entirely up to the buyer and seller. You can strike any deal that's mutually acceptable. If you are able to offer cash or can enter negotiations already preapproved for a mortgage, you can expedite the sale and possibly win more concessions from a home owner who is eager to sell.

resources

Robert Irwin's Pocket Guide for Home Buyers: 101 Questions and Answers for Every Home Buyer by Robert Irwin (McGraw-Hill, 1998): A guide by a recognized expert on real estate, including tips on negotiating the price and contract.

Stephen Pollan's Foolproof Guide to Buying a Home by Stephen Pollan and Mark Levine (Fireside Books, 1977): A step-by-step guide to the home-purchasing process, including chapters on negotiating the sales price and contract.

1. Get preapproval for a mortgage (see Lifemap 52).

2. Determine your available down payment and the amount of earnest money you can put down (see Lifemap 51).

3. Review your notes on the home, including its features and condition, and the prices of comparable homes on the market.

6. Determine your negotiation strategy: a quick move to close the deal or prolonged negotiations.

5. Consider the market conditions: Is it currently a buyer's or seller's market?

4. Consider this information in light of the list price.

7. Identify your leverage: cash on hand, preapproved mortgage, amount of time the home has been on the market, how desperate the buyer is to sell, etc.

8. Make an initial verbal offer to the owner or through a broker.

9. Review the seller's response.

12. Contact your attorney.

11. If the owner responds positively, begin the preparing a written offer.

10. If your offer is dismissed outright but you are serious, ask the broker what it will take to get a counteroffer and how willing the home owner is to negotiate. Determine if the seller is still interested.

13. If using a Residential Purchase Agreement form, fill it out under the guidance and advice of your attorney.

14. Meet with your attorney and have a prepared list of all concerns and contingencies about the contract.

15. Draw up an offer and review all its terms and conditions, under advice of your attorney.

18. Respond to the counteroffer with your own.

17. Review the counteroffer, if any.

16. Submit your offer to the owner or the owner's representative. Note how much earnest money is included as part of the offer.

19. Negotiate a mutually acceptable contract.

20. Set all final terms, contingencies, and details of contract.

21. Set closing date.

23. Exchange signed contracts with the owner.

22. Have the final version of the offer reviewed by your attorney before closing. This will be your contract.

how to raise a down payment

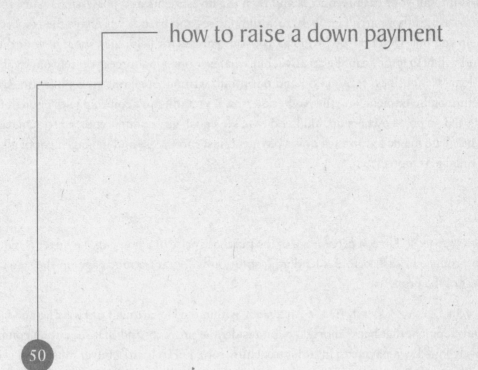

50

the basics

If you're planning to purchase a home with a mortgage, you're going to need cash for a down payment. Although there are programs to ease this burden on first-time and low-income home buyers, most people can still expect to need at least 20 percent of the price of a home in cash in order to complete a purchase. Don't forget that buying a home is a form of financial investment that will grow over time, so the money you put up for the down payment can do as well for you here as anywhere else.

inside information

The only strategy that matters for raising a down payment is the one that works for you. Purchasing a home is such an important step and investment that it's time to pull out all the stops in raising capital. First set a target, based on the amount of mortgage you qualify for and any "breaks" on down payments that may apply to you. First-time buyers, for example, may be able to cash in an IRA for a down payment without penalty. But look first into all your cash resources and then the investments and possessions you can turn into cash. If those aren't enough, turn to relatives and friends who have the resources to help you out. Don't be too proud to ask your parents for help; they share in your dreams and will help if they can. Be creative, but whatever outside sources you rely on, treat such a loan as a business transaction and put it into writing. Spell out your obligations, their return on investment, and the payback terms. If you still can't come up with enough to get started on home ownership, hunker down, set a goal, and commit yourself to achieving it. There's no magic to raising a down payment, just careful use and management of all your available resources.

jargon

Down payment: Here, a percentage of the purchase price of a home that a buyer is required to produce in cash before a lending institution will grant a mortgage on the remaining cost of the property.

Federal Housing Authority (FHA): An agency within the Department of Housing and Urban Development that backs mortgages on residential property and that requires a comparatively low down payment. In order to qualify for an FHA loan, a buyer must meet certain income criteria, and the qualification approval process may take longer.

Promissory note: A written promise to repay a sum of money on specified terms on a certain date or on demand. A simple loan agreement that can be used when borrowing from family or friends.

warning

You'll likely need more than the down payment alone to get through the closing. So when figuring the amount of money you'll need for the purchase, also consider such other factors as points; applicable inspection, filing, and attorney's fees; and any other factors that could add to the amount of cash you'll need on hand.

fyi

Mortgage lending institutions are in the business of helping home buyers make a purchase. They won't let you assume more debt than they think you can handle, but they can offer advice on all options available for getting past the down payment hurdle.

Robert Irwin's Pocket Guide for Home Buyers: 101 Questions and Answers for Every Home Buyer by Robert Irwin (McGraw-Hill, 1998): A guide for the home buyer, including inside advice on raising a down payment and tips on how you may be able to negotiate a lower down payment.

Stephen Pollan's Foolproof Guide to Buying a Home by Stephen Pollan and Mark Levine (Fireside, 1997): Step-by-step guide, with tips on where and how to look for funds to meet your down payment requirements.

Local lenders: It is their business to know and understand the intricacies of all options available to home buyers. A loan officer can be your best source of information on topics from how large a mortgage you prequalify for to the different types of mortgages available to you.

1. Complete Lifemap 46.

2. Identify likely mortgage sources and types of mortgages.

3. Contact mortgage source to see how large a mortgage you presently prequalify for and how large a down payment you would need.

12. Strategy B: Borrow what you need.

11. Strategy A: Work extra hours, take on a second job, or launch a side business to generate income to be saved for a down payment.

10. Consider alternative strategies for raising a down payment.

13. Determine how much you need; whether you will borrow from one or more sources; and how much you will pay in interest.

14. Identify those who are in the best financial position to lend you the money.

15. Approach these sources, starting with those with whom you have the best and closest personal relationships (parents, siblings, etc.).

24. Or you may need to concentrate for the immediate future on selling off possessions and creating new sources of income so you can meet your goal for a down payment for the type of home you want.

23. If all these efforts fail, reconsider your goal for a down payment. You may need to set your sights on a more modest home.

22. If your efforts succeed, put the agreement into writing and proceed with home search and purchase.

4. Inquire about other mortgage and down payment strategies you may qualify for.

5. Determine the minimum amount of down payment cash you will need, including closing costs.

6. Take an inventory of all your available financial assets: savings, bonds, investments, CDs, etc. If they are not sufficient, proceed to the next step.

9. Combine the proceeds from these sales with your available financial assets. If insufficient, proceed to the next step.

8. Sell a portion or all of these possessions until you have enough for the down payment.

7. Inventory your personal possessions, collections, insurance policies, etc., that you could liquidate to help raise money for a down payment.

16. Explain your need and ask for their financial assistance to reach your goal.

17. If their answer is "no" or they cannot lend you the full amount, approach other sources.

18. When you have secured a sufficient down payment, draw up a legally binding promissory note(s) or loan agreement(s) defining the terms of the loan.

21. Identify your best sources and approach them.

20. Before you approach anyone, thoroughly consider if this is a course you want to take. Determine how much control or ownership of the home you are willing to give up.

19. Strategy C: Invite others to join you, as partners in or co-owners of the home, to invest in the property with you.

how to obtain or refinance a mortgage

Unless you have plenty of cash on hand, you'll need a mortgage to finance the purchase of your next home or co-op. A mortgage is the loan you secure to meet the full cost of a property. In return for this loan, the mortgagor, or lending institution, holds the title of the property until the debt is satisfied. Obtaining a mortgage loan is a relatively simple and straightforward process—provided you have good credit history, can demonstrate your ability to meet your mortgage payments, and the home or property is appraised at a value that warrants the loan amount you seek. There are a number of different mortgage sources, and institutions may vary in the amount they are willing to lend you and the terms of the mortgage. As with any purchase, it's in your best interest to shop around. But don't wait until you find the home of your dreams. Your interests will be better served by investigating all finance options before you shop. Knowing how large a mortgage you can prequalify for will steer you toward homes you can afford. Prequalification by a lending institution is not a commitment on its part to lend you money, but it is an accurate indicator of the financing available to you. When you find the right home, obtaining a mortgage is merely a matter of completing an application, paying any fees, and awaiting approval. It can be that simple for those who meet the necessary criteria.

Once they have purchased and lived in a home, some people decide to refinance their mortgage as a way of obtaining an infusion of cash. Some refinance because mortgage rates have fallen significantly, others to raise money to make significant improvements. Should this time ever come, the lending institution will base its decision on the same proof of income, payment, and credit history and the assessed value of the home. Refinancing a mortgage is a step that should be carefully weighed against all other financing options.

Mortgage sources include commercial banks, credit unions, mortgage companies, savings and loans, insurance companies, and even the Veterans Administration, if you qualify. There are almost as many sources of mortgage financing as types of mortgages available. Before you investigate mortgages, get your financial house in order. All lenders want proof of your ability to pay down your debt. The first factor they will consider is household income. But income alone will not grant you a mortgage. They also want to see your credit history, as it's the best indicator available to them about how responsibly you handle your debts. The mortgage approval process can take weeks to months. Credit history problems can disrupt the approval process, even deny you a mortgage, and cause you much emotional stress. Therefore, the first step in obtaining a mortgage is to obtain a copy of your credit report. Make sure everything is in order, make any necessary corrections, and explain any late or missing payments. Then investigate your options. Most newspapers publish information on mortgage rates and types of mortgages available from area institutions each week. Review these and contact the institutions offering the rates or types of mortgage that most interest you to find out how large a mortgage you prequalify for. (If you're thinking of refinancing, it's especially important that you track these rates, compared to the rate you're already paying. Obviously, if you're going to refinance, you want a better deal.) This will steer you toward homes in your price range. You can't apply for a mortgage until you pick out a property. Expect to pay an application fee, a credit report fee, and possibly an appraisal fee. The mortgage lender may want proof of how large a down payment you plan to put toward the property. Mortgagors will lend only a certain percentage of the appraised value. You can request—and pay for—a second appraisal if you disagree with the findings, but more likely you're going to have to make up the difference in your down payment.

Adjustable-rate mortgage (ARM): A type of mortgage loan in which the interest is adjusted periodically, based on market conditions.

Balloon mortgage: A mortgage loan made for a specified period of time—five years, for instance—after which the remaining principal is to be paid in full or the mortgage renewed.

Fixed-rate mortgage (FRM): A mortgage loan in which the interest rate is fixed, or remains constant, for the duration of the loan.

Graduated-payment mortgage (GPM): A mortgage loan set up so that the initial monthly payment gradually increases and then reaches a set rate over a period of time.

Points: The fee the lender charges for granting the mortgage, with each point equal to 1 percent of the total amount being borrowed.

The type of mortgage you choose, as well as the lending institution you borrow it from, can have as much impact on the total cost of the mortgage as the amount you borrow. Carefully weigh the different approaches in light of your own finances and needs, in order to identify the best mortgage strategy for you. Shopping around from institution to institution as well as comparing the types of mortgages available will serve your financial interests both long and short term. For instance, monthly payments on a fifteen-year mortgage may seem higher, but you'll actually spend half as much for the same loan as if you'd secured a thirty-year mortgage. The number of points the institution applies, or penalties for early payment of the loan, can impact its total cost. Investigate the details. It can be a mistake to put yourself in a financial bind to meet monthly mortgage payments now, on the assumption that your income will rise later on.

The process of refinancing a mortgage is largely the same as that of applying for your initial mortgage. Now more than ever, the lending institution will scrutinize your history of meeting your payment obligations on your initial mortgage. Refinancing can add substantially to the real cost of a home, so it's a solution that should be carefully weighed against other options before proceeding.

Buy Your First Home! by Robert Irwin (Dearborn Trade, 2000): A guide to home purchase with advice to help you through the mortgage process.

Century 21 Guide to Choosing Your Mortgage (Real Estate Education, 1996): A guide to mortgage selection, mortgage options, and the application and approval process, prepared under the authority of this leading real estate company.

1. Request a copy of your credit report(s).

2. Review the report(s).

3. Contact the credit-reporting agency about any incorrect information.

12. Gather personal financial data.

11. Investigate the types of mortgages available to you and their likely sources.

10. Investigate online mortgage options.

13. Contact lending institutions and speak with loan officers about their mortgage programs and the types of mortgages available to you.

14. Identity the institution that offers the best mortgage for your needs. Ask about points, terms, prepayment penalties, and any other factors that will contribute to the total cost of a mortgage.

15. Pick up a mortgage application and inquire about prequalifying for a mortgage amount.

24. Clear up any problem immediately. Document your ability to meet loan payments. Inquire about the appeals process.

23. If rejected, find out why and request a written explanation.

22. If approved, take a photocopy of mortgage approval to your attorney and review before signing.

25. Appeal any rejection, but move forward with a loan application at another institution at the same time.

26. Redo the above process, if needed.

27. If you are considering refinancing your mortgage, continually track mortgage rates and investigate other types of mortgages.

4. Attach a statement explaining any late or missed payments.

5. Submit the statement to the credit agency and ask that it be attached to your report.

6. Request and review an updated credit report. Amend again if necessary.

9. Review and track mortgage rates published in the newspaper.

8. Determine affordability: How much can you afford to pay each month?

7. Determine the amount of money you have available for a down payment (see Lifemap 51).

16. Use prequalification and down payment as a guide to how much you can afford to pay.

17. Go home shopping (see Lifemaps 47, 48, and 49).

18. After selecting a home, contact the lending institution and request a mortgage application.

21. Await a decision.

20. Take the completed application, your financial data, and the down payment information to the institution. Be prepared to pay for the application process.

19. After choosing a home and signing the contract, complete the mortgage application.

28. Meet your current bills and address any problems in your credit history.

29. Before applying to refinance a mortgage, carefully calculate the actual costs of this move, versus continuing with your present mortgage.

30. If you decide to refinance, complete the application process as described above.

how to obtain a
home equity loan

52

One of the advantages of home purchase is that you can borrow money against the amount you have invested in the property. Millions of home equity borrowers use this form of loan to finance renovation, fund an education, consolidate debt, or take care of a personal emergency. Your sources are the same lending institutions you considered for your original mortgage. Before you qualify for this type of loan, lenders will want to see the same proof that earned you your original mortgage: good credit history, proof of income, and ability to meet additional payments; proof of your home's value; and proof that you have as much invested in the home as you want to borrow.

inside information

Lenders like home equity loans because they are secured: you put up your home as collateral on the loan. If your credit history demonstrates that you've been meeting your mortgage obligations, you can borrow as much as the full value of your home, minus your outstanding mortgage balance or any other liens on the property. That includes your down payment, along with the principal you've paid back on your original mortgage. One advantage to this form of borrowing is that the interest may be tax-deductible. Although a home equity loan means taking out a second mortgage on your home, there are other ways of "borrowing": if the mortgage rates have changed considerably since you originally purchased the home or the value of the property has significantly increased, you may also want to investigate refinancing your mortgage.

jargon

Equity: The value of your investment in a home, including down payment and realized principal on your loan, minus the outstanding mortgage balance and other liens.

Home equity line of credit: A form of borrowing in which you are approved for a set amount of credit, which you borrow only when and as needed. As you repay the principal, it again becomes available to you

Home equity loan: A lump-sum loan, structured like any other loan, based on the amount of equity you have in the home. You borrow this money for a set term at a set interest rate with a specified repayment schedule.

warning

When you take out a home equity loan, you are borrowing against the value of your home. While this may seem an attractive form of borrowing, you could lose your home if you default on the loan. If you decide to pursue this form of borrowing, carefully weigh the amount you borrow and be sure not to overburden yourself with loan obligations.

fyi

Some companies aggressively promote home equity borrowing, enticing consumers with offers to lend them as much as 150 percent of the value of their home. Proceed with caution! Always read the fine print in a loan agreement, and if you have any questions, consult an attorney.

How to Get the Best Home Loan by W. Frazier Bell (John Wiley & Sons, 2001): Frank advice on the different loan options available to home buyers and owners, with tips on matching a financing option to your needs.

Online: Many Web sites explain and offer different home equity loan plans. At its Web site, the **Better Business Bureau, Inc., Serving Eastern Massachusetts, Maine & Vermont** offers many consumer resources.

1. Determine how much money you need.

2. Contact local lending institutions.

3. Speak with the loan officer for information on all loan options available to you.

6. Tally your down payment and the amount you have paid off on the principal on your mortgage. This is the amount you will be able to borrow.

5. If no other option appeals to you, determine the amount of home equity loan available to you.

4. Shop around: compare rates and terms.

7. If this sum isn't adequate for your needs, also investigate refinancing your original mortgage (see Lifemap 52).

8. Decide if you want a home equity loan or a home equity line of credit.

9. Contact a loan officer at your bank or at the lending institution that offers the most attractive terms.

12. Gather these documents and meet with the loan officer.

11. Ask what documents you should bring when you apply for the loan.

10. Discuss your needs and set up an appointment.

13. Explain the amount of home equity loan or line of credit you seek and how you plan to use it.

14. Again inquire about other loan options available to you.

15. Reconsider these alternatives.

18. Complete and submit your application.

17. Evaluate the payment schedule. Make sure this is a manageable addition to your other debt.

16. Before filling out the application, have the officer explain the terms of the loan, the interest rate, penalties for late or missed payments, applicable fees or penalties for early repayment of the loan, and the loan schedule.

19. If and when the loan is approved, carefully review all terms before signing a final contract or loan agreement.

20. Have your attorney or a financial adviser review the agreement as well.

21. Proceed with your planned use of this money only after you have been approved for the loan or line of credit and the money is actually available to you.

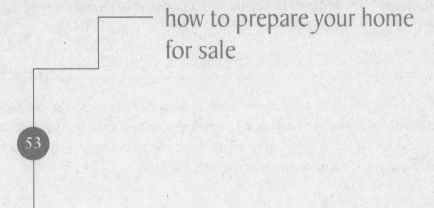

how to prepare your home for sale

53

the basics

The better your home looks, the faster it will sell and the higher the price it may bring. As you ready your home for sale, you want to do all you can to make it look its best, show off its positive features, and downplay any negatives, all the while spending as little as possible. When potential buyers see a home that appears to be well maintained on the surface, they assume that what they don't see is treated with the same care. It's much easier for them to buy a home that conveys that assurance.

inside information

This is not the time to embark on expensive renovation or remodeling because you think it will add to your home's market value. You're not likely to recoup the full cost of the project. Rather, you want to focus on a less costly course, the little things that contribute to an overall favorable impression: things such as a fresh coat of off-white paint, clean windows and floors, new handles on cabinets, and new light switch plates. Clutter makes rooms seem smaller and darker. Get rid of things you don't need or put them in storage. Clean everything! If it's too much of a chore, hire a professional cleaning service. Its work will more than pay for itself in the long run.

warning

Listen to what the real estate brokers say needs to be done to improve the marketability of your home. They are as interested as you in selling your home and will give you honest advice. As you prepare your home, don't try to deceive potential buyers about any major problems. However, mitigate them to the extent possible.

fyi

Nothing speaks as well of a home as cleanliness. It can't be too clean, especially when someone is considering purchasing it. Once it's sparkling, use natural and electric lighting to highlight the cleanliness.

resources

100 Surefire Improvements to Sell Your House Faster by R. Dodge Woodson (John Wiley & Sons, 1993): Advice on how to improve the marketability of your home, from the obvious to the not-so-obvious.

Stephen Pollan's Foolproof Guide to Selling a Home by Stephen Pollan and Mark Levine (Fireside, 1997): A detailed guide for the seller, including information on what you should and shouldn't do to prepare your home for sale.

Realtor.com (www.realtor.com): A Web site for home buyers and sellers, including tips and information on what you should and should not do to improve the chances of selling your home more quickly and for a better price.

1. Determine when you want to sell (late spring to early summer is best). This will let you know how much time you have to prepare.

2. Inspect your home yourself. Focus on curb appeal and the interior. Look for anything that detracts from the appearance or distinguishing features of the home.

3. Clean up and remove clutter. Empty your closets of unwanted clothes.

6. If you have made any significant improvements or renovations to the home without the required local permits, find out what you need to do, who needs to check the work, and what papers need to be filed.

5. Unload unwanted and unused items by giving them away, selling them at a yard sale, or putting them in storage.

4. Determine which furniture can stay, which must go.

7. Take all appropriate actions to ensure that your home is completely legal.

8. Invite someone you trust for his or her candor in to make an assessment of the home. Ask him or her to point out the things that detract from the home.

9. Take care of minor concerns, such as unpruned hedges, clutter in the yard, and overfurnished or dark rooms.

11. Meet with the agents and take them on a tour of the home, asking for suggestions on what you can do to improve the marketability of the home. Take notes of all they tell you, room by room. After these meetings, review your notes. Highlight any suggestions mentioned by all three. Consider these your priorities.

10. Contact three real estate agents or brokers (see Lifemap 55). Explain that you are considering selling your home and would like them to come by and take a look.

12. Take care of any structural repairs or renovations necessary to bring the home into compliance with zoning laws and local codes or to make it legally salable.

13. Give the home a thorough cleaning, sprucing up floors, washing windows, and painting wherever needed.

14. Decorate to sell: bright, airy rooms, exposed floors.

17. When the house is ready, reach an agreement with a broker.

16. Address any remaining concerns.

15. Invite back your leading broker candidates for another tour. Ask for their reassessment.

18. Determine if you want only scheduled appointments for viewing or if the agent can bring potential buyers to the home as needed.

19. If showings are by appointment only, agree on the minimum notification you require. Stress that you always want to be called before someone is brought to the home.

20. If the house will always be open to potential buyers, recognize your responsibility to always keep it looking its best, with prompt cleanup after meals.

23. Inside, open the windows, let in the light, keep fresh flowers on the tables.

22. Outside, Add flowering plants in season.

21. Keep both the inside and outside looking their best.

24. Be available but discreet whenever a tour is under way. Stay in the background and let your broker do his or her job.

how to find a trustworthy real estate broker

54

the basics

Unless you want the hassle of selling your home yourself, you need the services of a real estate broker. Brokers bring a lot to the process: expertise on area home values and market trends; experience in showing homes to prospective buyers; and knowledge of how and where to market your home. In return for their efforts, they receive a commission, based on the final selling price. A real estate salesperson must meet certain qualifications and pass licensing tests before he or she can be called a "broker." Sales agents are licensed too, but only to act under the authority of a broker. Make sure you ask for a broker and speak with him or her before you arrange any appointment with a representative of a real estate office.

inside information

Brokers are paid by sellers, spend time with buyers, but actually represent the deal. They make money only by bringing sellers and buyers together and facilitating sales. Their primary service is providing information: telling sellers how market conditions and other factors affect the market potential of their home and identifying properties that match individual buyers' search criteria. While some individuals may be born with these skills, they are more often a product of training and experience. When you evaluate individual brokers, consider the size of the agency they work for, how long they've worked there, how many years they've worked in real estate, how much experience they have working in your market area, and what their professional affiliations and licenses are.

jargon •

Broker: A person licensed to bring together parties and help negotiate a contract between them, in exchange for a commission or fee.

Comparative market analysis: A document that includes information on "comps"—homes similar to yours, in the same area, that have recently been sold. The quality of this presentation, especially how "comparable" these homes are to yours, is a good indication of local market conditions and a broker's working knowledge of them.

Listing: The assignment of your home to be sold by a broker or agency.

Multiple listing service: A database of available homes in an area, available to all real estate agencies, that assists sales agents in matching buyers to properties.

Realtor: A trademarked term that identifies real estate professionals who qualify for membership in the National Association of Realtors.

Sales agent: A real estate practitioner who is licensed to operate under the authority of a broker but cannot contract his or her services directly with the public. An agent may be the one who actually sells your home, but your contract is with the broker.

warning •

Brokers' skill levels vary widely. The broker and his or her affiliated agents will be your representative. You want someone who is personable, knowledgeable, and experienced in the local market. Resist any pressure to sign a long-term contract for an exclusive listing of your home. You won't really know how good the broker's services are until you've seen him or her in action. Ideally, your best agreement is one month exclusive with the right of renewal, based on performance.

The Internet is becoming increasingly important as a tool for home buyers to prescreen properties before they ever speak with a broker. Today, you want to make sure your home will be on the Internet on the agent's, broker's, or agency's Web site before you sign any agreement.

Stephen Pollan's Foolproof Guide to Selling Your Home by Stephen Pollan and Mark Levine (Fireside, 1997): Includes a section on what to look for in a broker, how to find one, and how to negotiate a contract with him or her.

Buying and Selling a Home by Kiplinger's Personal Finance Staff (Kiplinger's Books, 1999): A complete guide to the home real estate transaction from both sides of the fence, with information on how to list and what to look for in your broker.

Realtor.com (www.realtor.com): Its many services includes a search engine to help you locate members of the National Association of Realtors in your area.

1. Gather a list of candidates.

2. Look around your neighborhood for real estate professionals currently handling homes. They know and understand the area and the unique market forces at play.

3. Ask friends who live in the area and who have recently bought or sold a home for names of brokers.

12. Ask how long each of these homes was on the market.

11. Listen to their market presentation. It should be a well-prepared series of documents of similar homes in your area, with descriptions and selling prices. They should give you an idea of where your home fits in.

10. Write down any suggestions they make on improving the marketability of your home.

13. Have the broker explain market conditions, where your home fits in, and the probable price range.

14. Have the broker explain his or her marketing plan for your property. The range of options includes listings on a multiple listing service and the Internet, flyers, brochures, newspaper ads, cable television spots, open houses, etc.

15. Find out who will be showing your home.

24. If the references don't support your initial choice, call the references of your second or third candidate.

23. If the references support your initial choice, finalize it.

22. Call the references of your preferred candidate. Ask about the quality of service, the quality of potential buyers, and if they would use this broker again.

25. Call the winning candidate and make an appointment to formalize your deal.

26. Negotiate the fee.

27. Give the broker an exclusive listing for one month, with right of renewal.

35. If not, call another candidate.

34. If so, renew the contract.

33. Are you happy with his or her services?

4. Check the telephone directory for brokers working in your area.

5. Identify the three best candidates, based on your knowledge, others' experiences with them, or their familiarity with your neighborhood.

6. Prepare your home for the initial meeting (see Lifemap 54).

9. Accompany them on a tour of the home and let them do the talking. Listen to what they have to say about the house and its appearance.

8. The broker you choose will be representing you. Evaluate candidates on the basis of personality, professional appearance, courtesy, and knowledge of the area.

7. Call the candidates and set up appointments. Invite them to meet you at your home and explain that you are thinking about putting it onto the market.

16. Ask about the broker's fees.

17. Voice any concerns or special conditions you have.

18. Ask for references from recent sellers.

21. After meeting all candidates, evaluate their performance, the quality of information provided, and their willingness to work with you.

20. Explain that you're meeting with other brokers but will make a decision within a week

19. Drop any candidate who cannot or will not provide them.

28. Shake hands and go to work.

29. Call other candidates, thank them for their time, and let them know you have selected someone else to represent you for now, but that if anything changes you will give them a call.

32. Did he or she give you ample warning before tours?

31. Did he or she bring serious buyers, or was your home being used solely for comparison to others?

30. Evaluate the broker's performance over the first month.

how to price your home for sale

55

Setting the list price of your home is one of the most complex challenges in the real estate sales and marketing process. Ask too much, and you could price yourself out of the market; start too low, and you could cheat yourself out of thousands of dollars. You need to set a price that realistically reflects the condition and appeal of your home and the forces at play in the local real estate market. But it's not simply a matter of determining what your home is worth, painting a sign, and posting it in the yard. Since the price you set is the foundation of your sales strategy, it should take other factors into account as well. If you're in a rush to sell, you may want the price to be very attractive to buyers. On the other hand, if there's no need to hurry the sale, you can start in a higher price tier, just to test the waters, and lower the price gradually, if necessary. Wherever you live, there are certain well-defined pricing tiers in real estate you should become aware of before you set your price. Generally these run in $50,000 increments: $150,000 to $200,000, for example. Your home will fit into one of the ranges. Your initial list price, within a given range, sends a message to potential buyers about its appeal, its condition, and how much you may be willing to negotiate.

As with consumer product, the price of homes fluctuates with supply and demand. In every market there are times of year when there are simply more buyers shopping for homes, and that can help drive prices up. Your real estate broker (see Lifemap 55) can be your best ally in obtaining this and other information to help you set the right price for your home. To know what is happening in your market right now, you need to look at "comparables," homes in your area that have recently been sold. The more they are like the one you're about to sell, the more indicative its selling price is of what you can expect. When using a "comp" as a reference, you want to know its original asking price as well as the selling price, along with how long it was on the market. Buyers will be looking at these figures as well. If there's something distinctive about your home that you believe warrants a higher price than that of others in the area, you may want to consider hiring an appraiser to establish this. Most home owners, however, will find themselves adequately served by listening to what real estate brokers can tell them about the local market, current trends, and where their home fits in. Trust their judgment. As they are paid on commission, it's in their best interest to see your home command top dollar.

Comparative market analysis (CMA): A record of homes similar to your own that recently sold in your area, supplied by your real estate broker. This indicates the health of the market and what selling range you should expect for your home.

Days on market (DOM): A key indicator in the CMA is the amount of time homes have spent on the market, as it reveals current trends in the area. The fewer days on market for area homes, the greater the demand and the more you may be able to get.

Incentives: Price concessions you are willing to offer to make your home more attractive to potential buyers. You should decide what incentives, and for how much, you are willing to make before you set your price.

Listing price: The opening price of your home in its initial sales listing. It should reflect what you expect to get, based on what you've learned about area real estate prices and trends.

You alone have the authority to set the price of your home. Your real estate agent or broker is engaged only as a consultant; he or she cannot set the price of your house. That said, it would be foolish not to take brokers' advice into consideration. It is their business to know what's going on in the local real estate market. If you balk at the thought of paying a commission, you can sell your home yourself. Before you do, consider all the work that will be involved in pulling together the information that can guide you to the right listing price. And when you do set the price, however you arrive at it, never present it as an "asking price." That betrays your own lack of confidence.

The market will let you know pretty quickly whether or not you've priced your house appropriately. If no one comes to view your home in an otherwise healthy market or you get no serious offers, it may be the time to consider gradually lowering the price. But the longer your home is on the market and the more you have to come down from your original list price, the stronger the message it sends to potential buyers that something's "not right" about the house. That's why it's so important to enter the market with an appropriate list price.

Stephen Pollan's Foolproof Guide to Selling Your Home by Stephen Pollan and Mark Levine (Fireside Books, 1996): A complete consumer guide to selling a home, with sections devoted to researching the local market and setting the right price.

Century 21 Guide to Selling Your Home (Dearborn Financial Publishing, 1997): A complete guide to home sales, prepared by one of the country's leaders in residential sales.

How to Sell Your Home Fast, for the Highest Price, in Any Market: From a Real Estate Insider Who Knows All the Tricks by Terry Eilers (Hyperion, 1997): An expert's advice on all aspects of selling a home, including pricing it to move at the best price for the owner.

1. Identify why you are selling.

2. Is there some deadline by which you must sell?

3. Decide if you are going to sell your home yourself or hire a real estate broker.

6. Identify local market conditions: Are homes up for sale for prolonged periods of time or are they selling soon after listing?

5. Comparables: homes in your area that have recently sold (if doing it yourself, review the record at the local register of deeds office).

4. If selling the home yourself, gather the following information; if hiring a broker, ask that he or she supply you with the following.

7. Check newspaper listings of homes for sale in your area.

8. Search the Internet for homes currently for sale in your area.

9. Keep notes on homes in your immediate area or most similar to yours. Keep records of list prices.

12. Use this list as a guide to the price range your home fits into.

11. Compile a list of the homes that best match yours and their listing prices.

10. If possible, drive by or visit homes in the area that seem most similar to yours.

13. Realistically assess where your home fits in this range. Is it best in its class, or does it need work to bring it up to par?

14. Determine what you need, net, from the home sale to satisfy all outstanding debt, taxes, etc.

15. Determine any incentives or price concessions you are willing to offer buyers and how they may impact your final price.

16. Determine a price based on all of the above that reflects market conditions, your need to sell, the appropriate price range for your home, where it fits within that range, any concessions you are willing to make, and what you need to walk away from the sale with.

17. Consult with your real estate broker about the price you have determined. Carefully consider any additional advice he or she offers.

19. Track market response, based on the number of people who come to visit your home and the offers submitted, to determine if you need to reconsider your list price after the first month and monthly thereafter.

18. List your home.

how to hire and deal with a moving company

56

the basics

Moving to a new home or apartment is always exciting. But the enthusiasm can be tempered by the moving process. Preparing for a move can be a full-time job. Fortunately, those of us with neither the time nor the inclination can turn the job over to a moving company. Wherever you live or plan to live, local franchises of national moving companies can help make the transition almost painless. These local franchises may be your best choice, since each is held accountable to the national firm. And since these companies move so many people, they have a national network of resources to make sure your possessions arrive when you need them.

inside information

Like most businesses, moving is an industry in which supply and demand determine the cost. When more people are relocating, the demand for services drives prices up. Conversely, in the off-season (the winter months) you can strike a better deal. The moving industry is highly regulated, so any reputable company should be in compliance with all applicable laws and interstate license requirements. Still, it's your responsibility to verify this information, as it could impact your insurance coverage should you need to file a claim.

jargon

Bill of lading: The agreement you sign with the moving company. It should include details on pickup and delivery dates, destination, insurance coverage, type of liability, and all applicable fees.

Binding estimate: An estimate that represents your actual final cost for the move. You may pay a fee for the commitment, but it's well worth it. Nonbinding estimates usually come in lower but are only a guess at the final cost of the move. Many consumers who rely on a nonbinding estimate often discover that the move costs more than anticipated.

Liability: The mover's financial responsibility for your possessions. This is defined before you sign the bill of lading. Limited liability pays for damages to property based on weight, regardless of value. Added valuation covers replacement costs for damaged or lost goods, after depreciation. Full value protection is, as it sounds, insurance coverage for the actual value of your property, although a deductible may apply.

warning

Anyone with a truck and a couple of burly friends can describe himself as a mover. It will seem like a great deal to pay such a crew by the hour—until something is broken. If you aren't handling the move yourself, you will be best served by a company that is licensed, fully insured, and affiliated with one of the national moving companies. You may pay more for its service, but it's worth it. Before you agree to insurance offered by the moving company, check with your own insurance company. Your policy may already offer the coverage you need, or you may be able to purchase what you need more cheaply than that offered by the moving company.

Stephen Pollan's Foolproof Guide to Buying a Home by Stephen Pollan and Mark Levine (Fireside Books, 1997): A step-by-step guide to the home-purchasing process, from determining need to closing, with a section devoted to finding a qualified mover and what to expect in its contract and services.

Moving companies: Movers can furnish you with helpful brochures written by their national affiliates on how to prepare for the move to make things easier for yourself and their staff.

1. Decide if this is a job you want to do yourself or one you'd rather entrust to a professional mover (see Lifemap 6).

2. Determine what property and possessions you want to keep and what you will get rid of.

3. Hold a yard sale or donate unwanted property to charity.

12. Ask about any special needs or requirements that may impact the cost: a piano, large and very valuable antiques, etc.

11. Arrange a meeting so the salesperson can give you a more accurate cost estimate.

10. Give an estimate of the contents.

13. Inquire if the mover is bonded, what type of insurance it has and any applicable deductible, its license, and its affiliation with a national company.

14. Request a binding estimate for your move. This bid should include a total price for the move, a description and estimate of the amount of property to be moved, and pickup and delivery dates.

15. Get information in print about insurance and liability coverage, as well as any warehousing or storage fees.

24. Review the mover's inventory of your possessions. Make sure it is complete, and have the mover explain any special notes about your property or furnishings and its condition.

23. Make sure boxes are properly labeled to make it easy for you to unpack.

22. Be at home when the movers pack and load the truck.

25. If you disagree about the condition of furniture as described, note it on the inventory list before signing.

26. Be at your new home or apartment when the movers arrive for delivery.

27. Be prepared to pay the mover prior to unloading the truck at your new home or property. Also plan to tip those doing the work.

4. If you decide to hire a professional, ask friends or family for references or look in the phone book for three candidates.

5. Select companies that have been in business a long time or are local franchises of national moving companies.

6. Check with the local Better Business Bureau to see if complaints have been lodged against any of these companies, and if so, what type.

9. Contact each candidate and tell the salesperson when and to where you are moving.

8. Estimate the contents of your home—total square footage, number of bedrooms, and living quarters—so you can give the moving company a rough estimate of the amount and type of furnishings to be moved.

7. Eliminate any candidate that has a significant number of complaints against it.

16. Contact your insurance agent to see if you need additional coverage.

17. Choose the lowest reliable bidder.

18. Contact the salesperson and thoroughly review the contract.

21. Consider moving valuables or cherished heirlooms yourself.

20. Inventory the property you plan to have moved.

19. Resolve any questions before signing.

28. Verify the inventory list against what's delivered.

29. Check for any damaged goods or boxes.

30. If you see any damaged goods as they are unloaded, make the moving company foreman immediately aware of them, and make a note of them on the inventory list.

33. Start unpacking.

32. When all your possessions are unloaded to your satisfaction, tip the movers.

31. If you intend to file a claim for damaged property, leave the goods in the mover's packaging until the claims representative has seen it and filed your claim.

how to plan a home renovation project

57

Renovation projects can enhance your living quarters. Properly planned and professionally executed, they can also add value to your home. Some projects can be handled yourself. Others are best left to those who make a career of remodeling. Most people can get by with the services of a contractor who specializes in remodeling. More ambitious and expensive projects may also require the professional vision of an architect and interior designer. Whatever the project, and whomever you choose, a rushed project invites disappointment. Devote time to planning your renovation carefully, and it will serve your needs for years to come.

Home remodeling and renovation are seasonal activities. Prices of materials and labor climb with the temperature. In the winter you'll find contractors eager for work and more than willing to negotiate price with home owners. Licenses and certification are important considerations when deciding who to choose, as are personal references. Make sure contractors are in compliance with the codes that will apply if you ever sell the home. Always check references. Whenever possible, visit the sites of projects similar to yours. Contractors often use the services of subcontractors on larger projects. For your protection, you need to understand who is responsible for their payment before you allow them into your home.

jargon

Contractor: The person with whom you "contract" a project. In home-remodeling projects, the contractor is often involved in the project himself, as well as supervising his crew in the work.

Face-lift: A remodeling project that does not change the physical space but is more focused on improvements in the overall look, including things such as a new coat of paint, flooring, cabinet doors, etc.

Subcontractor: An individual responsible for one aspect of the total project. He may do this work himself or have his or her own crew. He or she is hired by the contractor.

warning

Carefully weigh contracting work with anyone who asks a significant share of the fee up front, in the earliest stages of a project. It is common practice, however, for a home owner to pay for materials as they arrive or are needed. Regularly check on work as it progresses, and address any problems when they first appear. The longer you wait, the larger they will become. Be sure to allow for the time during which your home life will be disrupted when planning a remodeling project. Projects often exceed the projected cost by at least 10 percent. Don't contract out a project for the full amount of your budget, or you could feel a real squeeze later on or be left with an improvement that's only halfway there. Finally, don't make a final payment until you are completely satisfied with the work.

fyi

Some contractors will let you work with them to cut costs. The most likely areas where your labor could save you money are preparing the site before the work begins, picking up and delivering materials, and cleaning up.

Stephen Pollan's Foolproof Guide to Renovating Your Kitchen by Stephen Pollan and Mark Levine (Fireside, 1997): Although it focuses on a kitchen renovation, this book provides a system for planning and completing any renovation project.

Homestore.com (www.remodel.com): A Web site devoted to remodeling and renovation, with useful information and help in finding a local contractor skilled in the type of project you are planning.

Local home improvement chain stores: The staff at the projects desk at major chains such as Home Depot and Lowe's can help you plan, revise, and complete any project, if you have the time. They can supply design plans and a list of materials you'll need for the job, as well as books and tips on how to see it through to completion. All you need to do is ask for the advice.

1. Identify what you like and don't like about your home or the portion of it you're considering renovating. Get input from other household members.

2. Compile a list of improvements you'd like to make, as well as what you presently like about the space.

3. Prepare a rough sketch of what you want to accomplish.

6. If you decided to proceed, determine whether you want to do the job yourself or hire an expert (see Lifemap 6).

5. Decide whether to renovate. Will this project prove an asset or liability to your lifestyle and your bankbook?

4. Determine a budget for the project. How much can you afford or are you willing to spend?

7. If you decide to do it yourself, work up plans and proceed with the work.

8. If you decide to hire an expert, determine if you need an architect, interior designer, or general contractor specializing in home remodeling and renovation.

9. Whomever you decide on, contact at least two candidates. Find them through personal references, telephone listings, and/or referrals from local organizations.

12. Ask that they bid on the project and give them a deadline.

11. Ask about local licenses, accreditation, and certifications; if they are bonded; what type of insurance they carry; what local or state licenses they hold. Ask for references of past customers.

10. Set up a meeting in your home. Show the candidates the space and your plans. Explain what you want done and ask them to review it and make suggestions.

13. While waiting for their bids, check their references.

14. Review the plans and bids.

15. Have them explain what is included in the bid.

18. If they'll be using subcontractors, make sure it's their responsibility to see the subcontractors are paid.

17. Ask who will be doing the work: they and their crew or subcontractors.

16. The bid should include a description of services, as well as any materials to be used, including the types of appliances to be installed if applicable, how materials are to be paid for, and estimated starting and ending dates.

19. Ask who will be responsible for cleanup.

20. If the lowest bid is acceptable and matches your expectations, proceed with the project.

21. If the lowest bid exceeds your budget, ask your preferred contractor to help find ways to cut costs.

24. If you cannot revise within your budget, reconsider doing the project yourself or doing it at all. However, do not increase your budget.

23. If practical, consider working with the contractor in some capacity to cut costs.

22. If necessary, modify your plans.

how to find and choose a
home renovation contractor

58

Unless you have the time, ambition, and tools to take on a major remodeling project yourself (see Lifemap 58), you're going to need professional help. The type of help you need will depend as much on the scope of the project as on where you live. In a rural area where building codes are lax or nonexistent, you may be able to do almost everything yourself. In a major metropolitan area, local codes may require that licensed professionals be involved in all aspects of the work. And there may be additional restrictions if you live in a historic district or in a building that has some sort of historic designation. So before you start looking for candidates, speak with your local building inspector or your building department's code office, whose expertise you must have on board to complete the project. Then you can start your search.

inside information

Most projects can be handled by a general contractor who specializes in renovation and remodeling. But the more ambitious your project, the more professionals you may want to involve. If you are significantly altering the structure of a building or adding to it, you may want to turn to an architect first, to design the space. If it's a major overhaul, you need someone to manage the project and all the subcontractors required to complete the work in compliance with local codes. These professionals work together on a regular basis, and they can be a good source of referrals for other aspects of the project. Be sure to get bids from at least two candidates for any aspect of your project. Prices vary widely among contractors and from season to season. For your best deal on a remodeling project, hold off until winter, when contractors may be willing to make some price concessions in order to stay busy in their slow season.

jargon

Building codes: The local laws that stipulate how a project must be completed. Codes can cover everything about the project from the spacing of wall studs and electrical outlets to the type of plumbing pipes that can be used.

Building inspector: The professional(s) responsible for ensuring that local codes are complied with.

Face-lift: A minor sprucing up, as opposed to complete remodeling, as a less costly solution for giving a space a new look. A kitchen face-lift, for example, might include new paint, light fixtures, appliances, and cabinet doors.

warning

Whatever the project, when hiring the services of any professional you want an agreement in writing. Make sure it spells out the cost; the materials and who will pay for them; estimated starting and ending dates; liability; and who is responsible for paying subcontractors. Pay for services in installments, and never make a final payment until you are completely satisfied with the work. If you are asked to pay for materials, pay only as they are delivered to your site. Stress the importance of completing the work on schedule. Contractors are often guilty of starting many projects, then leaving home owners hanging in order to line up work for the next few months.

A professional who is serious about his or her career is duly licensed, insured, certified, and affiliated with professional organizations. There's no shortage of people who can give you a great deal on work because they don't carry any of that overhead. Let the buyer beware!

resources

Stephen Pollan's Foolproof Guide to Renovating Your Kitchen by Stephen Pollan and Mark Levine (Fireside, 1997): This guide to kitchen renovation, from start to finish, steps the reader through the process with advice that can be applied to any remodeling or renovation project.

Homestore.com (www.remodel.com): A Web site with all sorts of advice and tips for the home owner. Includes a search engine for locating professionals in your area who are licensed and certified to do all types of renovation projects.

Better Business Bureau: Always check with the local BBB to see if there are significant complaints against any professional before you invite a bid.

1. Complete Lifemap 58.

2. Determine the types of professionals required to complete the project.

3. Contact the local building codes department or building inspector and describe your project.

12. For all of these professionals, gather candidates through personal references, referrals from businesses you trust, or local or national professional certification organizations.

11. Tradespeople: carpenters, electricians, roofers, plumbers, etc., who will contract their services directly to you or subcontract their services to a general contractor.

10. A general contractor, who may have the tools, resources, and crew to complete all steps or the experience to complete the project, using subcontractors where necessary.

13. Identify at least two candidates for any work to be done.

14. Check with the Better Business Bureau to see if there are any complaints against them. Drop all candidates with significant complaints against them.

15. Ask all candidates what licenses they hold, what type of insurance they have, what guarantee they offer for their work, and who is is liable for any damage.

23. As work proceeds, when you have any questions or concerns, bring them to the attention of the professional immediately.

22. Include a stipulation of your right to terminate the agreement if the work does not proceed as scheduled or does not meet professional standards.

21. When the bid is submitted, make sure it spells out the cost and how you will be billed; who will pay for materials and how they are to be paid for; estimated starting and ending dates; terms of payment; guarantee of work.

24. Make final payment only after you are completely satisfied with the quality of the work.

4. Inquire what permits, inspections, and other filings are required in order to complete the project, and who must file them. Write this information down.

5. Decide if you will do the job yourself or hire professional help.

6. Identify the professionals you need. These may include the following.

9. An interior designer, if you want the new space professionally decorated after the work is completed.

8. A project manager, if this is an ambitious project involving several different teams of professionals and tradespeople.

7. An architect, if architectural drawings must be filed and/or significant changes are to be made to an existing structure.

16. Explain your project and ask if they have worked on similar projects in the past. If they haven't, explain that you prefer working with someone experienced in this type of work.

17. If they are experienced, invite them to bid on the project, in writing.

18. Request the names and contact information of home owners for whom they have done similar work. Contact these references, and if possible visit the homes to evaluate the work.

20. If you are able to review a project, evaluate the quality of workmanship and materials.

19. Ask reference(s) if they are satisfied with the work; if it was completed on schedule and within cost; if the professional was responsive to their concerns or questions before, during, and after the project; and if they would hire that professional again.

59

the basics

When you buy a house, you have a reasonable assurance of what you are getting. You know, for instance, that water and electricity are available, and you have some idea of what you can expect from your immediate surroundings. Buying vacant land offers no such assurances. In fact, anyone considering the purchase of vacant property faces as many concerns as a person who is buying a home, but they encompass an entirely different set of issues. Whether buying property as an investment or as the site of a future home, a buyer must both look back and look ahead before making the purchase. You want some sort of idea how the property has been used in the past, what rights of access the present or former owners may have signed away, and what you will and won't be able to do on the property. Then you want to try to anticipate how this site, and the surrounding environs, might change in the future. Will you be able to protect the view? Will the area one day be cluttered with the development and crowding you're trying to escape? Vacant property holds all possibilities.

There aren't many vacant lots in cities anymore, so if you're thinking of buying vacant land, it's likely you're investigating acreage in one of the spreading suburbs, as part of a planned development, or in the country. Many former estates and farms are now being carved up to make way for subdivisions and home sites. Some may consider such property a stable investment; others as a place for raising a family or retirement. No matter what your purpose, the first thing you must know when buying vacant land is how it is zoned. Check with the local planning or zoning commission to make sure you'll be able to build the type of home, rental units, or commercial building you want there, and operate a business, if that's a concern. Once you know you can pursue your plans on the site, you want to know exactly what you will be getting for your money. Preferably the landowner can provide you with a survey detailing the property's boundaries. If you're looking at country property, you may need to rely on the fence line and a deed description to know what you are getting. Always walk the boundaries of any property you are considering, deed or survey in hand, to make sure the actual property boundaries are established, understood, and respected by all neighbors. Next, learn what you can about the history of the property. How has it been used in the past? Has a former owner signed away any rights or a granted right-of-way that might interfere with your plans for the property? Conversely, are the rights of access by road or a water source you need secured and guaranteed? You also want to know if there are any other restrictions or designations that might interfere with your plans. Will utility connections be available, and at what cost? Has the site been approved for a septic system? Do water lines extend to the property, or is there a clean, reliable water source on-site? Has the property been declared a wetland? Is it in a designated floodplain? Then consider what could happen on surrounding properties. More than one city slicker has purchased a site for his rural retreat only to find others bringing similar dreams to the lots alongside his.

jargon

Encumbrance: A special condition attached to a deed that limits how you may use some portion of your property. For instance, an agreement may have been reached with neighbors by some former owner granting them permanent access to a water source or use of a road that passes through the property.

Mineral rights: A contract signed by a landowner, usually concerning rural property, that grants some company or individual the right to mine and remove a "mineral" from the property—gas, oil, coal, etc. If someone else holds the mineral rights to a piece of property and ever exercises them, the owner may have little power to stop them.

Right-of-way: Access through or across someone else's property. The buyer should look into this from all angles. You may need right-of-way through someone else's property to reach yours, or someone else may have a right-of-way that could limit what you can do in some section of your property. State roads and utility lines involve a certain amount of right-of-way that could impact your plans, as well.

fyi

Some of your best deals on rural property can be found at public auctions when an old farm or homestead is divided into lots. Drainage problems and susceptibility to flooding won't be obvious on a sunny day. If possible, try to visit the site in both wet and dry weather. The fact that there is a lot of vacant land for sale in an area could be a good sign; It may mean the area is in the midst of a period of growth and development. It may also mean that something else going on in the area is about to have a negative impact on land values. Talk to area residents to learn what's going on. You'll always do better to buy a large tract of vacant land in the winter months, when you can see the land as it actually is, without the obstruction of summer greenery.

warning

When you come from a city, where utility access is a given, you can easily overlook this crucial concern. Water and gas lines will never extend to some homesites. The electric company, on the other hand, may bring power to your remote lot—at a considerable cost to you. Check into the availability and expense of utility service. Without the protection of a survey, it's in your interest to speak with owners of surrounding properties and make sure all landmarks are understood and recognized. Otherwise you might one day have to meet them in court to resolve disputes. If your plans for the property include drilling a well, you want to know all you can about how the property has been used in the past. In fact, if you plan to rely on a natural water source, it's prudent to have it tested.

resources

Finding & Buying Your Place in the Country by Les Scher and Carol Scher (Dearborn Publishing, 2000): A thorough guide to all the considerations one should take into account when buying rural property, with advice on recognizing and avoiding the many potential pitfalls.

How to Buy Land Cheap by Edward Preston (Breakout Productions, 1998): As the title implies, a step-by-step guide for finding and buying land at tremendous savings, with advice on where to look and what to look for.

1. Check to make sure local zoning or any other restrictions will not interfere with your plans.

2. Ask the seller to provide you with a copy of the survey.

3. If none is available, get a copy of the deed.

12. Ask the present owner if the land has ever been used as a dump. If you suspect it may have, get confirmation in writing.

11. Have mineral rights been sold?

10. If not, contact neighbors to see if these are available.

13. If you are buying as a home site, does the site have or have access to a water source?

14. Test any natural water source.

15. Will utility service be available?

24. Is the price fair and in line with other properties for sale?

23. Check local real estate and newspaper listings for prices on comparable pieces of property.

22. If you're planning for commercial development or to run a business from the site, are there adequate transportation links?

4. Walk the property, deed or survey in hand, making sure fence lines and landmarks as described are established and accepted.

5. If anything seems questionable, contact neighbors on surrounding properties and make sure they accept and respect the boundaries.

6. Are fences in good shape? If not, use this as a bargaining point to lower the price of the property.

9. Are any necessary rights-of-way for access and/or water permanently secured?

8. Have rights-of-way been granted to surrounding landowners or utility companies?

7. Does the deed carry any encumbrances? If so, what kind?

16. Are you buying for the view? If so, will you be able to control its availability?

17. If possible, visit the property in the winter months, when there are few plants to conceal what might be concerns.

18. Also, visit the property after a rain to see there could be any problems from flooding.

21. What are the taxes on the property?

20. Could that impede your plans?

19. If surrounding properties were developed, how close would your neighbors be?

how to appeal the amount of your property taxes

the basics

Are you paying too much tax on your home or property? It's a question every American should ask annually. Each year thousands do and, as a result, succeed in getting their property taxes lowered. That's not to say your local tax assessor isn't doing his or her job or is abusing his or her power. But there are so many factors that impact the value of your property, the local tax assessor may not be aware of all them. Or there may be something unique about your property that demands it be considered individually, rather than grouped with other properties. Market value does increase, and local governments do make changes in how they assess property value or tax properties. But sometimes they make mistakes or something happens to reduce a property's value of which they're not aware. It's up to you to keep track of your taxes and what factors are considered in the assessment. Only then will you be in a position to appeal.

People in every community, every year, successfully appeal their property taxes and have them lowered—without using an attorney. The only requirement is proving you're being asked to pay too much tax. The process is relatively simple. You may file an appeal in writing or be required to make a presentation to an equalization or appeals board. Members are citizens like you, not agents of the government you may be tempted to blame for burdensome taxes. Your goal is to convince them that your home is worth less than its assessed value; that something has happened relative to your property that has decreased its value; or that you're entitled to some tax break that has not been applied to your property taxes. Before you can build your case, you must understand how property values are determined and the formula used for assessing taxes.

Assessed value: The dollar value of the property, as determined by the tax assessor, used to determine the amount of property taxes. This may reflect full market value or a percentage thereof.

Assessment ratio: The ratio of assessed value to full market value, used to determine the tax rate.

Comparables: Properties recently sold that were used as models in determining market value and tax assessment.

Equalization board: The board responsible for hearing property tax appeals, determining if the appeal is justified, and taking appropriate action.

Reassessment: The periodic process of reconsidering the tax rate on property in an area, based on recent sales trends. A reassessment may also be the direct result of a property tax appeal. Also called reevaluation.

Tax rate: The number of tax dollars imposed per thousand dollars of assessed value.

The most effective appeal is one in which you convince the equalization board that your property has been overvalued. Its members don't want to hear your complaints about a system you consider unjust. They want to help you get fair treatment, based on the evidence you present backing up your appeal. No more, no less. Be aware that in some cases an appeal backfires. That's because an appeal may result in an inspection of your property. The tax assessor may never have actually visited before, instead using formulas for real estate market trends in your area to set your property taxes. If you've made significant improvements that the assessor wasn't aware of, you could actually end up paying higher taxes.

fyi

Tax records are public documents. You have the right to review them to determine if taxes on your home or property are in line with what others in the area are paying.

resources

Appeal Your Property Taxes and Win by Ed Zalsman (Panoply Press, 1993): An insider's advice on the appeals process by the former head of the Board of Equalization for Clackamas County, Oregon.

Save a Fortune on Your Homeowners Property Tax by Harry Koenig and Bob Lafay (Dearborn, 1999): Step-by-step plans for researching property value, evaluating your assessment, and challenging your property taxes.

Challenge Your Taxes by James Lumley (John Wiley & Sons, 1998): A real estate counselor's insight into how to determine the real worth of your property and prepare and present a successful appeal.

Local tax assessor: Located in city or county government offices. Your best source for information about how property taxes are determined, tax records for comparison properties, and information on the appeals process.

1. When purchasing any piece of real estate, ask what the property taxes are and how they're assessed.

2. Keep track of your property taxes from year to year. Review your annual property tax statement.

3. If taxes climb significantly from one year to the next, contact the tax assessor's office for an explanation of the increase, how the rates are calculated, and what factors are considered.

5. Determine if you want to handle the appeal yourself or hire a tax attorney. Unless the grounds for your appeal are especially complicated, you can probably handle it yourself—as long as you have the time and initiative.

4. If you're not satisfied with the explanation or feel your property has been overvalued, consider appealing for a lower tax assessment.

6. Review your tax assessment records, looking for any obvious errors, such as the wrong address, inflated size of home or property, or "improvements" that do not exist.

7. If you find discrepancies, bring them to the immediate attention of the assessor and find out what you need to do to appeal.

8. If you find no errors but still feel you're overtaxed, ask about the appeal process: learn when hearings are held, what you need to do to have a hearing, and the cutoff date for setting up an appointment.

11. Contact area real estate agents and ask about the recent sales range of comparable properties in your area. Document and verify with tax records.

10. If appealing an overassessment, review public tax records for nearby, comparable homes and property.

9. Determine the grounds for your appeal and gather supporting evidence.

12. If appealing based on a devaluation of property, document the proof.

13. Photograph any recent damage to your home, former "improvements" that have been removed, and any developments in your neighborhood that would devalue area property.

14. If appealing based on some tax abatement or relief that has not been granted or recognized in the tax assessment, document your eligibility.

17. Estimate the amount you think the taxes should be.

16. If so, request that a hearing be scheduled.

15. After gathering the appropriate evidence, determine if you have reasonable grounds for an appeal.

18. Rehearse your presentation, making the case why your taxes should be lowered. Keep it short and to the point. If necessary, prepare and print supporting documents for distribution to board members.

19. Dress appropriately for your hearing. Present a case based solely on the facts you have gathered. Explain what you think your property taxes should be and why. Provide documents to support your claim.

20. Answer any questions posed by the review board members factually and concisely.

22. Whatever the outcome, thank the board members for their time. If you're disappointed with their ruling, don't launch personal attacks against board members, our system of taxation, or the government in general.

21. Be prepared for the board to offer a reduction slightly less than the amount you seek.

23. If their offer isn't acceptable or your request is rejected, consider a further appeal.

lifemaps for consumers

part four

how to choose a
long distance plan

61

You've seen the ads ad nauseum; an endless assault of commercials on TV and ads in print telling you why one long distance carrier offers a better deal than all others. They even cite competitors' rates, then try to entice you to switch to their service for the promise of free calling on certain days and hours and unbelievably low cost-per-minute charges. Should you miss the ads, there's always that call from a telemarketing representative, who can't even pronounce your name correctly, trying to win you over with a comparable pitch. And when you ask for the details, the conversation can turn so confusing you become lost and no longer care. But read on. There is a better deal for you in your long distance plan, but you won't find it in an advertisement or hear about it from a telemarketer. You must do the legwork to find it and review your bill each month to make sure you're still getting it.

Want a better deal on your long distance plan? It begins with knowing how you use this type of service. Your use profile—when you make the majority of your long distance calls, whom you call, and how much time you spend on the phone—outlines the essence of what you need in a long distance plan. Only when you understand that should you contact the long distance providers and ask what they can do for you. It's not that the carriers are trying to deceive you (although at times it may seem that way); it's just that what they don't tell you in their ads can add substantially to the cost of service. For instance, that attractive low cost per minute may be applied to all calls you initiate, whether someone answers at the other end or not, and there may be a minimum number of message units required for the rate to apply. Promotions for attractive overseas rates may not mention that there is a minimum service charge each month whether or not you actually use the service. The details are hidden in the fine print. To find the best deal, even after you think you know what you are getting, you need to read that fine print and make sure you're paying for the service you need and will actually use, no more and no less.

Basic rate: The standard cost per minute for long distance calling. Usually when companies draw comparisons between theirs and another carrier's rates, they are comparing some special offer of theirs with their competitor's "basic rate," which is also the highest.

Dial-arounds: Services that enable you to use a long distance service provider other than your primary carrier by dialing a special access code, such as 10–10.

Primary carrier: The company you select and designate to your local phone company as your supplier of long distance services.

Think you're confused about all the terms and conditions of a long distance plan? Sometimes the carriers get confused too, or at least that's how it can seem if you review your phone bill regularly. As calling offers are revised or dropped and new packages are added, there's plenty of opportunity to make a mistake on your bill. For this reason, even after you've found a better deal, take the time to review your bill every month. Make sure all the rates and service fees are what you agreed to and that the proper rates have been applied to all your calls. Should you find an error, pick up the telephone and contact Customer Service, bill in hand. Write down the name of the representative you speak with, when you placed the call, and how your call was resolved. Then, next month, check to make sure the adjustments to your bill have been made.

If you spend a lot of time dialing long distance, you may be surprised at how willingly some of the carriers will be to shape a plan to your particular needs. In fact, there's a lot more they can and do offer than what's touted in their national advertising campaigns. When comparing plans, be sure to pay attention to the interstate and intrastate rates applied to calls. Sometimes you can lose all the advantage of a low rate for calls outside your state due to the surprisingly high rates applied to the intrastate calls you may be more likely to make. The law requires that you must select a long distance carrier. If you don't select one, your local phone service provider will make the selection for you, and not necessarily with the company that offers the best plan for you.

Long distance carriers: You can't escape them because only they can put together the package and tell you what it will actually cost. Use the toll-free numbers or Web sites of long distance carriers serving your areas to see what type of service packages they offer, then compare the quotes to find the best package, based on how you already use your long distance.

1. Review your past bills to develop a profile of your long distance usage.

2. Note the days of the week, times of day, places called, and length of time you spend on each call.

3. Use this information to help you match a calling plan to your needs.

6. Explain what you need in a calling plan and ask if it can accommodate you.

5. When you have identified a long distance carrier that offers the features you seek, use a toll-free number to contact its customer service representative.

4. Review ads or log on to Web sites for a preliminary review of features offered in calling plans.

7. Check with other carriers, asking them to match or exceed the deal.

8. Before agreeing to any plan, ask for written documentation that describes all the features of and applicable fees for the plan.

9. Closely scrutinize any fees and/or minimum usage requirements to make sure this plan is what you thought you were getting.

12. Thoroughly review each monthly billing statement as soon as it arrives.

11. When you have selected a carrier, contact your local telephone company and tell it which carrier you have chosen for your long distance.

10. If you have any questions about the rates or fees, contact the company's customer service representative and have them explained to you.

13. Make sure you are being charged for the services and at the rates to which you originally agreed.

14. Before succumbing to the temptation to switch carriers again, thoroughly evaluate all details of the plan, as above, to make sure you really are getting a better deal.

how to choose an HMO

62

the basics

Right now, at your company's headquarters, the health benefits people are probably plotting to switch you and your colleagues out of your comfortable old "see-any-doctor-you-choose" health plan into managed care—if they haven't done so already. This is a money-saving move for your company. But is it going to be healthy for you? True, managed care plans generally offer more preventive care (such as vaccinations and mammograms) than nonmanaged care plans do. And patients generally pay only a very minimal fee (a copayment of $10 or $15) for a visit to the doctor. But managed care restricts access to specialists and medical tests and aggressively limits the time patients can spend in the hospital. Remember, these are the folks who brought you the twenty-four-hour stay for childbirth—and even (till protests forced them to back down) the outpatient mastectomy. If you're lucky, you'll be allowed to stick to your old "fee-for-service" ("indemnity") plan. But because fee-for-service plans are also expensive for your company, odds are you'll be asked to choose among competing managed care plans instead. If that's the case, it's crucial to select a plan that provides not only preventive care but high-quality treatment and hospitals if someone in your family has a grave illness.

inside information

When an illness is serious or rare, access to an eminent specialist can spell the difference between a patient's life or death. The smartest thing you can do is to make sure you choose a managed care plan that includes a point-of-service (POS) option. This means that the plan will at least partially reimburse you if you consult a specialist who is not a part of your health plan's network of doctors. Of course, going "out of network" will cost more than you'd pay if you stuck to your plan's own specialists. But some things are more important than money.

jargon

Capitation system: A system in which doctors are paid a flat monthly fee for every managed care patient on his or her roster whether a given patient comes in for a visit or not.

Utilization review: The requirement that doctors wishing to prescribe tests or hospitalize a patient must be preapproved by the nurses (or clerks) at the insurance company's headquarters.

Withhold system: A system in which insurers hold back a percentage of the fees they owe their doctors, then give the money to the doctors at the end of the year—but only if they have not referred "too many" patients to specialists or prescribed "too many" tests.

warning

Some managed care companies require the doctors they hire to sign a contract stating that they will not tell patients about treatment alternatives that the managed care plan will not pay for. Critics call this the gag clause.

resources

Managed Care and Your Mental Health: What You Need to Know About Your Managed Mental Illness Insurance Benefits: A free brochure from the American Psychiatric Association. Write to 1400 K Street N.W., Washington, DC 10005.

Consumers' Guide to Health Plans: A very helpful setting forth of patients' views on their managed care coverage. Some 72,000 federal employees were asked to rate their own plans according to standards that matter to patients: access to medical care, quality of care, competence of the plan's doctors, coverage, and customer service. Write to Center for the Study of Services, 733 15th Street N.W., Suite 820, Washington, DC 20005, or call (202) 347-7283.

National Committee for Quality Assurance: An independent, nonprofit organization based in Washington, D.C., that rates health plans. To find out if the plan you're considering has been rated, call the committee's customer service number, (800) 839-6487, and ask that its Status List be mailed to you. Or look up the status on the Internet at www.ncqa.org. Full accreditation (three years) is given to plans that "have excellent programs for continuous quality improvement and meet NCQA's rigorous standards." One-year accreditation is given to plans that "have well-established quality improvement programs and meet most NCQA standards." Provisional accreditation (one year) is given to plans that "have adequate quality improvement programs and meet some NCQA standards." Denial means the plan has been evaluated but does not qualify for any of the categories above. "Under review" means that a plan has requested a review of the accreditation it received.

1. Get copies of the full terms of coverage for each candidate plan.

2. Make sure they include information on premiums, copayments, deductibles, exclusions, etc.

3. Forget about plans that don't offer a point-of-service (POS) option.

12. Find out under what conditions the plan denies payment for emergency care.

11. Check whether emergency care must be approved in advance.

10. Check what local hospitals are under contract with each plan.

13. Find out the limits, if any, on psychotherapy visits.

14. Check into each plan's grievance procedures.

15. Check to see if review denials can be appealed to an independent agent.

23. Weigh your choices and select the plan that seems best for you and your family.

22. If the terms of coverage don't answer all these questions, call the plan directly.

4. Find someone who has used each plan and ask his or her opinion on quality of care and access.

5. See if the plans have been analyzed by the National Committee for Quality Assurance.

6. Consult a copy of *Consumers' Guide to Health Plans* and see how the plans stack up.

9. Check to see how many specialists of various kinds are included in each plan.

8. Ask the insurance department what percentage of each plan's premium is paid out in claims.

7. Call your state's insurance department to check for complaints against each plan.

16. Make sure that review appeals are binding on the HMO.

17. Find out about coverage for nonemergency travel illnesses.

18. Check into emergency travel illness coverage.

21. If not, ask them if they're planning to participate.

20. Check whether any of your current physicians participates in any of the plans.

19. Find out what percentage of the plan's primary care physicians are board certified.

how to appeal an HMO's refusal to pay

63

the basics

You've heard the horror stories; an HMO refuses to pay for a treatment someone desperately needs, placing profit before patient. Hopefully you'll never face such a dilemma. But if you do, be prepared for a fight. You have the right to appeal that decision—and can, with determination, documentation, and perhaps the presence of an attorney, convince the HMO that the care is necessary and in both their interest and yours.

inside information

Whether it's elective surgery or emergency treatment, time is always of the essence when you need to appeal an HMO's refusal of treatment. Therefore, it's important to anticipate that need when you sign up with an HMO. Make sure you thoroughly understand its policies and procedures before you ever need to file an appeal. Read up: know what's covered, what isn't, who decides when you must see a specialist, policies and procedures on seeking treatment, and the appeals process. It's also advisable to make yourself aware of state law as it pertains to HMOs and patients' rights of appeal. You also need to understand your medical condition that prompted the refusal to pay, and the costs and benefits of the treatment you seek. You should be documenting everything: dates of your appointments, all correspondence relating to your condition, and the HMO's denial of service. In the case of a medical emergency or a life-threatening illness, you can seek an expedited appeal. Whenever possible, try an expedited appeal first, since the standard appeal process can take months. In either event, representation by an attorney, even if only to carry on your correspondence with the HMO, can help your cause.

jargon

Cost containment: The term HMOs use to describe their controlling medical costs through a number of methods, sometimes including cash incentives to physicians for holding down costs.

Emergency care: Not necessarily what you think when it comes to HMOs. Each has its own definition of what comes under this term; therefore you need to understand how your HMO defines it.

Medical necessity: As with the term above, determined and defined by your HMO in its description of coverage. Your HMO's definition of what's necessary when it comes to treatment may not be as broad as you think—or need.

warning

When you contact your HMO, don't place blame on the person who takes your call. An HMO is a corporate bureaucracy. Your appeal can easily get lost in the maze. You need an ally, someone you can connect with on a personal level, whom you can turn to for answers or help. Try to turn the representative who works with you on that initial call into that person. Ask for his or her phone number and extension, and try to reach him or her first, whenever you call. Be your own best ally. Unless you persist, push, and follow up every bit of correspondence, your appeal may languish on someone's desk. No one has more at stake in your appeal than you; presume that no one else will pursue your appeal with as much urgency.

There are a number of reasons an HMO may refuse to pay for treatment, and it's not always because the type of care you seek isn't covered. It may be for reasons as simple as paperwork not being submitted properly or some step in the hierarchy of approving a treatment being skipped. You can also avoid denials by anticipating the possible need for health care. What will you do in the case of an emergency occurring outside the HMO's coverage area? Will using a doctor outside the plan automatically result in denial of service? When there is a denial of service, have it adequately explained in writing, and respond immediately. Waste no time, as the appeals process can move frustratingly slowly. Be prepared to pay for treatment out of pocket while your appeal continues, in order to get the treatment you need.

resources

Don't Let Your HMO Kill You: How to Wake Up Your Doctor, Take Control of Your Health, and Make Managed Care Work for You by Dr. Jason Theodosakis and David T. Feinberg (Routledge, 2000): A practical guide to the HMO system and how to work within it to ensure you get the care you deserve and need.

1. Thoroughly read and understand an HMO's coverage plan before signing on with it. Consider such factors as:

2. What are the HMO's policies on emergency care?

3. What constitutes an emergency, and who decides?

6. What happens if you require care when you are away from the coverage plan area?

5. What if you disagree with your physician about treatment? Can you see another one within the plan?

4. Who decides when care by a specialist is warranted?

7. What is the appeals process in the event of denial of treatment? How long does it usually take to resolve an appeal?

8. Be aware of all state regulations pertaining to HMOs and patients' rights to appeal any denial of treatment.

9. If, after signing up with the HMO, you are denied treatment, appeal immediately.

12. Respond immediately in writing if you cannot resolve the dispute by phone.

11. If satisfied with the answers, note the representative's name and number and make that person your primary contact.

10. Call a claims representative and have the refusal explained.

13. Consider the advantage of hiring an attorney during the appeal process, at least to write letters on your behalf.

14. Try to arrange for an expedited appeal.

15. Comply with the HMO's appeal process procedures to the letter.

18. Make sure every document has your case/appeals number on it.

17. Explain your appeal in a letter to the HMO representative, with information on the above.

16. Read up on your condition, its treatment, and how the treatment that has been denied would benefit you,

19. Always follow up written correspondence with a telephone call to make sure your letter has been received and learn about its status.

20. Keep notes on all contacts with HMO representatives regarding your claim.

21. Regularly check on the status of your appeal.

22. If an expedited appeal is refused, you may still pursue a standard appeal, following the same procedures outlined previously.

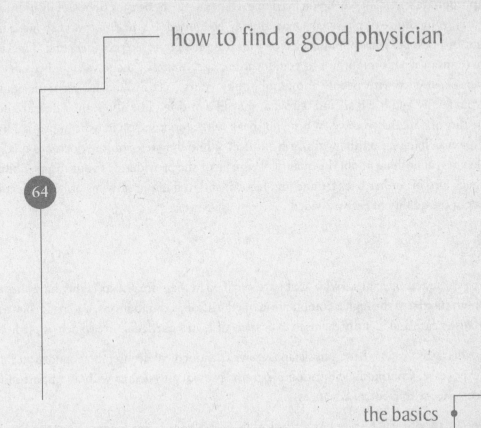

how to find a good physician

64

Think of all the trial and error you might expend to find the right haircutter. Isn't your health worth just as much? Surprisingly, many people go to greater lengths to find the "right" person to cut their hair than they do the professional to whom they entrust their health. Most wouldn't think twice about switching stylists, yet many stick with a doctor regardless of the quality of service provided. Just because you've always gone to a particular doctor or the office is conveniently located, it doesn't mean you're getting the best care. The right physician is one you can trust and confide in; one who listens to your concerns about your ailments; one who has the experience to make the right calls. That physician isn't hard to find, but you must be willing to undertake the search.

inside information

In the broadest sense, there are two types of physicians, general practitioners and specialists. A qualified general practitioner can handle most forms of illness and refer you to the appropriate specialist when you need one. Depending on the type of health insurance you carry, your choice of physicians may already be limited. If you don't want to incur much out-of-pocket expense, obtain a list of your insurer's preferred providers first. Then think in terms of what's important to you: location, age, or sex of the physician; bedside manner; experience with people and families like yours. Ask around for recommendations from family and friends. Find out what they like or don't like about their doctor and the quality of care they receive. When you speak with a doctor, you may be impressed by the diplomas hanging on the walls of his office. While they tell you the doctor is qualified, they reveal nothing about the quality of care he or she provides. It's your responsibility to check into his or her background and record, and to find out how his or her patients feel about the quality of care provided.

jargon

Board certified: Specialists who are board certified in their area of speciality have met minimum standards through a combination of education, examinations, and residency to administer care and identify themselves as specialists in a particular area, such as cardiology.

Continuing education: After physicians receive their medical license, their education should never cease. Continuing education programs provide physicians with an opportunity to keep pace with medical advances.

Licensing board: Each state has a medical licensing board that grants licenses to doctors, reviews their records, and even revokes licenses, if significant complaints are filed against a physician. It's prudent to check with your state's board to see if any disciplinary action is pending or has been taken against a physician before you become a patient.

warning

If you're not happy with a physician or the type of care you are receiving, don't hesitate to change. In your initial contact with a physician's office find out where he or she has admitting privileges, who fills in for him or her when she is away, which lab services he or she uses, and what the typical fees are for new and established patients. All these factors can impact the real cost of health care to you. Also, check the Internet. Many states now post information about physicians who have been disciplined, as do a number of consumer advocacy groups.

In your initial visit, perhaps even before your first exam, you need to learn as much about the physician as you can. Ask any questions pertinent to you and your health concerns. A doctor who is gruff, or who obviously doesn't take care of his or her own health, may not be the person you want to entrust with your well-being. The information in your medical records belongs to you. If you ever decide to switch physicians, be sure to request that your former physician forward the appropriate files to your new doctor.

resources

Guide to Top Doctors by the Center for the Study of Services (Center for the Study of Services, 2000): A consumer's guide to the country's best hospitals and physicians, based on criteria explained in the book.

Your Family Medical Record: An Interactive Guide to Getting the Best Care (John Wiley & Sons, 2000): Written for patients, this book explains how they can take charge of their health care and communicate with their doctors to make sure they always receive appropriate treatment for any illness.

HealthGrades.com (www.healthgrades.com): At this Web site, you can find this organization's ratings of hospitals, physicians, health plans, and nursing homes, based on extensive research and methods, for each region of the country.

1. Contact your health insurance provider or HMO. Request a list of preferred providers, or physicians who participate in the plan.

2. Decide what type of physician you would feel most comfortable with. Consider factors such as age, sex, and years of experience.

3. Also consider convenience factors, such as location and hospital admitting privileges.

12. Ask if the physician's office takes care of filing insurance claims.

11. Inquire about rates for new and established patients.

10. Ask who covers for the doctor when he or she is away or cannot be reached.

13. Verify that the doctor accepts your insurance plan.

14. How long in advance must you schedule an appointment?

15. Review all the information you have gathered, and decide which physician you would like to try first.

22. Decide if you are satisfied enough with the physician's qualifications, practice, manner, and experience to entrust your health care to him or her.

21. Try contacting the doctor after your appointment to have a question answered. Does the doctor or someone from the office call back with a response?

4. Do you need a primary care physician or some sort of specialist?

5. Ask family and friends for recommendations.

6. Ask what they liked and didn't like about each.

9. Ask about affiliations with local medical groups, labs, hospitals, etc.

8. Ask about the doctor's years of experience, board certification, and recent training through continuing education programs.

7. Contact the office of two or three candidates.

16. Before scheduling your appointment, do a background check. Verify that the physician is board certified.

17. Check with your state licensing board to see if any disciplinary action has been taken against this physician, or if any is pending.

18. If yes, move on to another candidate.

20. During your first meeting with the doctor, judge how well he or she takes care of his or her own health; how responsive he or she is to your questions; how well he or she listens to what you say; and how thorough he or she is in doing an examination.

19. If no, make an appointment.

should you buy or lease a car?

65

If you've been tracking the car ads looking for a new vehicle, your curiosity has probably been piqued by promises to put you behind the wheel for an incredibly low monthly lease payment. If you really want to know what kind of deal you're getting, you need to read the fine print. Don't be surprised if it leaves you feeling as if you're wandering through a verbal fog. But you need to cut your way through it because you don't really know what kind of deal you're getting in an auto lease until you know your financial responsibilities when the lease expires. Leasing a car does make sense for a lot of people, but it's definitely not for everyone, especially if you're looking for the best investment in an automobile. On the other hand, if you regularly trade up to a new model every three or four years, if it's important for your status that you always have a late-model car, or if you rely on a vehicle in your line of work and can claim the expense as a business deduction, leasing may make sense.

The typical lease involves three separate financial transactions. First, there are the costs involved in setting up the lease, including fees such as a down payment of some form, the destination charge, and a refundable security deposit. From day one through the end of the lease, you're responsible for monthly payments. Finally, a financial punch looms at the end of the lease, when you must pay all the fees, penalties, and possible surcharges you agreed to when you signed the original lease. If you're not careful when setting up the lease, you could find yourself presented with bills for things such as a cost per mile above the limit specified in your original lease; any needed repairs; and an additional surcharge for wear on the vehicle. In the worst case, you could end up owing money for a car you no longer drive. That said, there are people for whom leasing does make sense. If you consider a monthly car payment an unavoidable modern-day expense, are a cautious driver who doesn't do a lot of driving, and will carefully read and adhere to the terms of the lease, leasing may be an attractive way of driving a nice car—all the time.

Capitalized cost: The price you negotiate on the car, which determines all other financial aspects of the lease agreement. The capitalized cost reduction is the amount of money you put down, which is subtracted from the cost in order to determine the payment schedule and end-of-lease payment.

Closed-end lease: A car lease in which all the terms and fees, the assessed value of the car after depreciation, and your options for keeping or returning the car are clearly defined in the lease agreement.

Residual value: The value of the car at the termination of the lease, which should be stipulated in the original lease agreement. This residual value is the amount you could pay the dealer to own the car after the lease expires.

Think about how good you are about maintaining your car and its appearance before deciding to lease. Anything beyond normal wear and tear, as defined by the dealer, could significantly increase what you owe at the end of lease. Terminating a lease early can invite significant surcharges and should always be avoided. Before signing, make sure you can live with the terms of the lease, over the entire term. Dealers can lease a car for longer than the original warranty period offered by the manufacturer. If you do and the car requires out-of-warranty repairs, it's your bill to pay.

fyi

Since the cost of a lease is based on the selling price of the car, negotiate the best deal before you sit down and start discussing finance arrangements. Don't mention that you plan on leasing, or what you are looking for in a monthly payment, until after you've negotiated the best price on the car (see Lifemap 67). Compare the cost of leasing versus financing the car. Leasing's most significant drawback is that you don't build up any equity in the car as you make payments. If you can live without that or you need a better car than you can afford to buy, turn your car over every three or four years, or can claim the auto as a business expense, leasing makes sense.

resources

Have I Got a Deal for You! How to Buy or Lease Any Car Without Getting Run Over by Kurt Allen Weiss (Career Press, 1997): Straightforward advice on buying or leasing any car, based on the author's own experience as a car salesman.

1. Browse car ads to see what types of cars and what offers dealers are promoting for leasing an automobile.

2. Complete the steps outlined in Lifemap 67 to negotiate the best price on a new car.

3. Do not discuss leasing options with the dealer or salesperson until after you have negotiated your price and have it in writing.

6. Have the dealer work up a closed-end lease.

5. Decide what monthly payments you can afford and how much money you have available for a down payment or up-front costs.

4. Inquire about leasing the car.

7. Carefully consider all aspects of the lease, including such factors as:

8. Up-front costs to you.

9. Monthly payments.

12. Mileage limits and cost per mile for exceeding the limit.

11. Residual value of the car.

10. Any fees or penalties for early termination of the lease.

13. Applicable fees for wear and tear at the end of the lease.

14. Manufacturer's warranty period versus length of lease.

15. Compare the terms and cost of the lease against the cost of purchasing the car with an auto loan.

18. Keep the car properly maintained throughout the lease period.

17. Carefully review all terms of the lease agreement before signing.

16. Based on all of the above, decide if leasing is your best option.

how to buy a car from an auto dealership

66

the basics

Want a great deal on that new car you've been eyeing? It may be easier than you think but entail a little more work than you expect. Since car prices are negotiable, it means you must be prepared to do some haggling. Before you can claim the upper hand in the bargaining process, you need to know the dealer's real cost—the invoice price—and any current factors that may be encouraging the dealership to move some inventory. A slow market puts the pressure on, as do the final days of the month, when the dealership and salespeople strive to realize sales quotas. Car manufacturers may also offer dealer incentives, which can help you knock down the price.

inside information

Before you seriously start shopping for a new car, decide on the model you want. This may mean a couple of trips to the dealer to browse the selection or a couple of hours spent with a guide such as *Consumers Reports'* annual auto-buying issue, published each spring. In guides like that you'll find comparisons of models and features as well as vital information on invoice price, options and accessories, and cost. It's also helpful to know you have an auto loan arranged and what you can afford. Every penny above the invoice price should be considered negotiable. You want to negotiate up from what the car cost the dealer, rather than try to bargain down from the sticker price. There's more negotiating room than you might expect. Dealers can use your need for financing, or the fact that you want to trade in your old car for the new, to squeeze more profit from you in the negotiations. Don't discuss either until you've negotiated an acceptable price and have it in writing.

jargon

Extended warranty: Expensive and often unnecessary extended coverage for parts and repairs for a period of time beyond the manufacturer's original warranty. *If* you want this option, read the fine print to see what it adds and doesn't add before buying.

Invoice price: Also referred to as the dealer cost, this is what the car actually cost the dealer. The difference between dealer cost and sticker price should give you an idea of the least you could pay and the most you should pay.

Options: The invoice price is usually for a basic, stripped-down version of the car. Options are features you may want—everything from a different color and grade of upholstery to air-conditioning.

warning

Always shop around for the model you're after, and let dealers know you're speaking with competitors. It puts the pressure on them to come up with a better deal. Take someone with you when you shop for a new car. That person's presence can create a needed buffer between you and the dealer's high-pressure sales tactics. Your work isn't completed until you drive away with a great deal. After you've negotiated a price, don't succumb to a costly loan at a low monthly payment, unnecessary options, or overpriced extended service plans.

fyi

You don't need to put yourself through this hassle if you don't want to. Today you can entrust the process, and hassle, to a car-buying service. For a fee, it will negotiate a better deal. GM's Saturn broke new ground when it was offered with no-hassle pricing, a concept that has not really swept the industry by storm. In general, such offers are a good deal but not necessarily the best deal. For the best deal at the lowest price, you have to haggle.

resources

Consumer Reports New Car Buying Guide 2002 by the editors of Consumer Reports (Consumer Reports Books, 2002): Issued each year, this book combines useful information for the new-car buyer before shopping, with test reports, reliability records, and car reviews.

Have I Got a Deal for You! How to Buy or Lease Any Car Without Getting Run Over by Kurt Allen Weiss (Career Press, 1997): Straightforward advice on buying or leasing any car, based on the author's own experience as a car salesman.

Online: Depending on the make and model of car, you may be able to do a lot of the preliminary shopping online, even comparing how different option packages will affect the price. Start with the Web site of the manufacturer, then look at those maintained by dealers in your area.

1. Decide how much you can afford to pay for a car.

2. Investigate available auto financing and determine the amount you have available for a down payment.

3. Conduct a preliminary investigation of available models to determine which cars you are interested in.

6. Decide if you want to negotiate the price yourself or turn this over to a buying service.

5. Decide which options you must have and which you can live without.

4. Make a preliminary visit to dealers' lots to narrow your selection.

7. If doing it yourself, learn the invoice price and the cost of options from a new-car guide.

8. Learn whatever you can about any current incentives to dealers and special promotions through auto trade publications, as well as dealer advertising.

10. Make an appointment with a car dealer, specifying which model you're interested in. Take a friend with you to this meeting.

9. Decide which seasonal trends may help you negotiate a better price: end of model year; slow automobile sales; slow sales of particular model; end of month, when dealers need to reach sales quotas. Use this information as a guide to when to shop.

11. As the salesperson shows you the car, let him or her know how well informed you are about the invoice price, incentives, and trends that are currently shaping the market.

12. Test-drive the car.

13. Negotiate up from the invoice price, reaching at least a preliminary price before you cut the meeting short to visit another dealership.

16. Repeat the process with at least one other dealer.

15. Let the salesperson know you are shopping at other dealers and will get back to him or her. Leave your telephone number.

14. Resist the pressure to discuss financing or trade-in until you negotiate an actual sale price.

17. Compare preliminary offers and return to the dealerships.

18. Let each know the details of the other offers and ask them to match or improve.

19. After you have your best price, in writing, begin discussing the trade-in allowance and finance options.

22. Before you sign or commit to payment, insist on the opportunity to test-drive the car you are buying, not a comparable model.

21. During the final negotiations, resist the temptation/pressure to purchase frivolous options such as undercoating or extended warranty service.

20. Use what you know about other loan options to assess dealer financing.

23. Inspect the car and judge how it handles.

24. When you are completely satisfied with the car, pricing, and financial arrangements, close the sale.

how to buy a used car privately

67

the basics

If your goal in buying a used car is getting the most for your hard-earned bucks, you can't beat buying privately. The downside is that you have little recourse if you discover a problem with the car after you've handed over your greenbacks. That's why it's essential to do lots of preliminary research and conduct a thorough inspection.

inside information

The best way to find out what a particular used car is worth is to ask your friendly banker or insurance broker to look it up for you in his in-house valuation guide. If the only face you know at the bank is the teller at the drive-in window and you bought your insurance over the phone, pick up a copy of either *The NADA Official Used Car Guide* or *Edmund's Used Cars Prices and Ratings*. Both are available at bookstores and newsstands, but before you spend cash on them, see if you can find up-to-date copies at your public library. In addition to those listed in this map, you should try to ask all the following questions when looking at a used car. (Of course, take the answers with at least a grain of salt.)

- Is there anything wrong with the car?
- Do you sell a lot of cars?
- Are you the original owner?
- How long have you owned the car?
- How often has the oil been changed?
- Have you stuck to the suggested warranty schedule?
- When was the car last inspected?
- Where did you buy it?
- How did you drive it? Around town? Long trips? Both?
- Has the car ever been in an accident?
- Are there any liens on the car?

warning •

If the car you're looking at has surprisingly low mileage, watch for any of the following, all indications of possible odometer tampering: missing screws, scratches, or poorly aligned panels on the dashboard; signs that service stickers on doors have been removed; and overly worn or newly replaced front seats, pedals, floor mats, and windshield.

fyi •

Don't buy any used car until you've had a chance to examine the title. Here are some things to look for:

- Whose name is on the title? If it's not the person selling it, ask why and make sure to contact the person who's listed as legal owner before buying it.
- Does the vehicle identification number (VIN) on the car—located on a small plate secured with distinctive clover-shaped rivets on the left front of the dashboard—match the number on the title?
- Be wary of titles listing out-of-state owners or post office box addresses.
- Make sure there are no liens listed.
- If the title is marked "duplicate" and the car is only a couple of years old, there could be something shady going on.

- Make sure the title doesn't look phony. Pay particular attention to any changes made to the odometer reading.
- Any stamped codes on the title could mean the car was damaged, salvaged, classified as a lemon, or stolen and then recovered.

resources

Avoiding Shakes, Rattles and Rollbacks: How to Buy a Used Car: A good brochure, available from Consumer Protection Division, 200 St. Paul Place, Baltimore, MD 21202.

Buying a Safer Car and *Car Buying Checklist:* Two excellent booklets, free to AAA members; write to American Automobile Association, 811 Gatehouse Road, Falls Church, VA 22047.

Nutz & Boltz, Box 123, Butler, MD 21023: A very informative newsletter for used-car buyers (annual subscription: $19.96).

Federal Trade Commission, Public Reference Branch, Sixth and Pennsylvania Avenues N.W., Washington, DC 20058: Offers free information on auto service contracts.

1. List your goals, such as price, options, size, transmission, and mileage.

2. Study the classified ads for a week and take notes. Clip interesting ads, call for information, learn market price, pick out dealers.

3. Find a newsstand that sells Sunday's paper on Saturday night and buy it early; most ads start running on Sunday.

12. If you're interested, ask to see the car immediately.

11. Ask if there are service records; they provide documentation of the car's mileage and condition.

10. Ask why the car is being sold.

13. With the engine cold, remove the radiator cap and inspect the coolant. Avoid if it's rusty or milky, or has an oily film on top.

14. Check the dashboard warning lights. All should come on when the key is first turned. Missing lights might mean problems are being concealed.

15. Start the engine. Let the temperature gauge climb. Avoid if it doesn't stabilize or is already running when you arrive.

24. Watch the engine while the transmission is shifted. Rocking indicates worn or broken motor mounts.

23. Check the body. Look for signs of repairs. Use a magnet to find filler. Look for windshield cracks.

22. Check the tires. All four should look the same. Uneven tread or brand-new tires are a sign of alignment problems.

25. Check the shocks and struts by pressing down on each corner. The car shouldn't bounce, the steering wheel shouldn't move, and you shouldn't hear noises.

26. Look in the wheel wells and trunk and under the hood for signs of hidden damage, wear, or a recent paint job.

27. Go on a test drive. Get the car up to 65 mph and check for noises, hesitation, shimmy, or vibrations.

4. Compare the paper to your notes. Pick out the new ads and eliminate the dealer ads.

5. Make your calls between 7 A.M. and 10 A.M.

6. If you can't get through, start calling at 7 A.M. the next day.

9. Ask about the mileage: avoid four-cylinder cars with more than 100,000 miles, six-cylinder cars with more than 125,000 miles, and eight-cylinder cars with more than 150,000 miles.

8. If there's no telephone number but there is an address, go to see the car as soon as possible.

7. If the owner says the car has been sold, ask for how much and add the information to your notes.

16. Check the electrical system: turn on all accessories, check for battery corrosion, and check all the lights.

17. Rev the engine and listen for a deep-down rumble; that could mean there are bearing problems.

18. Look for leaks: dark and oily is oil; yellow or green is coolant; red is transmission fluid; red or clear is steering fluid.

21. Check the exhaust system: white smoke means blown head gasket; blue means burning oil; black means the mixture is too rich.

20. Check the door and window seals. A dollar bill closed in a door or window should be held tight.

19. Check the fluid levels: low oil means an oil burner or neglect; burnt-smelling transmission fluid means major repairs are needed.

28. Check the brakes. Take your hands off the wheel while braking; the car shouldn't veer, and the pedal shouldn't be mushy or sink too far.

29. Check the transmission. Noise or shifting problems may mean CV- or U-joint problems. Slipping means clutch problems.

30. Watch the car from behind while it's being driven. Make sure the front and rear wheels line up.

31. Be prepared to make an offer on the spot. Offer 10 percent less than your estimate of market value since the listed price is probably 10 percent above.

how to shop for an auto loan

68

the basics

For most people who want a new or good used car, an auto loan is a fact of life. Car prices are so high that it's far easier now to absorb the price of a car when you divide it up among monthly payments. Auto dealers love loans—maybe even more than their customers do. Depending on how eager you are to finance the car and how creatively they can accommodate you, they often stand to make more on the financing than on the actual sale price of the car. Shop around and compare features before you settle on the right make and model of car for you. You should be just as aggressive when shopping for a car loan. A poor choice in how you finance your car can turn your great deal sour and cost hundreds, if not thousands, of dollars.

inside information

The best time to shop for a loan is before you start shopping for a car. Contact your bank or credit union and find out what you qualify for in a car loan. This information will help you in several ways: it will steer you toward the cars you can reasonably afford; it will relieve you from the pressure of having to negotiate financing with a dealer after you've fallen in love with a car; and it will provide you with a base for comparing the terms of financing offered by a dealer. For the best deal on a loan from a dealer, you first want the best deal on the car. Negotiate a price, get it in writing, then talk about financing. It's also a mistake to walk into a dealership and announce that you have the financing taken care of or that you want to spend only a certain amount per month. Both undermine your ability to negotiate the best deal. That said, you may be able to negotiate your best financing package though the dealer, especially if there are many unsold cars sitting on the lot. Major car makers use low, even no, finance charges to spark a market to life. But don't assume anything about financing. Read the fine print as you would with any loan: know what you're paying, the real cost of the loan, and if there are any fees or penalties for early repayment.

jargon

Dealer financing: An often used enticement in automotive advertising in which the auto dealer puts the finance package together for you. You should shop around for financing, if only to determine how good a deal dealer financing really is.

warning

About the worst thing you can do to yourself when buying a car is to fall in love with it before you've worked out the financing. Don't think of the car as yours until you've signed a finance agreement. If you need more time to review the loan, take it. If the loan requires that you make a balloon payment after a set number of payments, make sure you can realistically expect to meet this obligation. And don't fall for enticements such as cash-back rebates. It's better to use such offers to negotiate a better deal on the car than accept what is, in reality, a loan to yourself, with interest.

fyi

The more of a down payment you can apply to the purchase of a new car, the better the financial package you'll be able to arrange. It's worth the extra wait if you can take time to save as much as 25 percent of the purchase price. If you own your home, you may want to investigate a home equity loan as an alternate source of financing your car. Your home can help you obtain the car of your dreams, as long as you are putting your home up as collateral on the loan. You may want to consider leasing your car, rather than purchasing it through financing, if you are using an auto loan as a way to keep monthly payments at a manageable level. Leasing is not for everyone, however, and the ultimate costs of leasing should be thoroughly evaluated against the cost of a financed purchase.

resources

Online: There are a number of online personal finance sites, such as **Quicken.com** (www.quicken.com), which provide information on shopping for all types of loans, loan calculators, and links to Web sites of lending agencies. Also, **FinanCenter** (www.financenter.com) offers guides to comparing auto loans, links to loan sites, and calculators for determining the real cost of any type of loan.

Local banks: Your local bank's loan officer can provide you with information on various ways to fiance your car purchase, including with a home equity loan.

1. Try to save as much as you can for a down payment on the purchase of a car. Ideally, you want to save between 10 and 25 percent.

2. Investigate your finance options before shopping for a car.

3. Contact your credit union or local banks for information on how much of a loan you qualify for and the terms.

6. Shop for a car.

5. Use this information as a guide to the price range of cars you can afford.

4. Also, investigate your options through a home equity loan.

7. Look for dealer ads on specials and special finance offers for an indication of models you want to consider.

8. When working with a salesperson, do not indicate how much financing is already available to you.

9. Do not indicate that you are looking to spend a certain amount per month on a car you want financed by the dealer.

12. Use your knowledge of other finance options as the basis for comparing dealer financing with other available loans.

11. After you have negotiated a price and a trade-in allowance for your older vehicle, inquire about what kind of financing is available from the dealer.

10. Negotiate the best price on the car and all features from the dealer (see Lifemap 67).

13. Consider leasing as opposed to buying or financing the new car.

14. Have all the terms of the loan adequately explained.

15. Inquire about the total cost of the loan, any additional fees, and any penalties that would apply if the loan is paid off early.

18. Don't finance the car for longer than you plan to own it.

17. Ignore recommendations that you buy credit life insurance for the loan.

16. Determine which loan offers you the best deal.

how to sell your used car

the basics

Want the most you can get for your old car? Then forget about taking it to a dealer; a dealer's business is selling cars. If they paid you what your car is actually worth, there wouldn't be any room for their profit. If you want to reap the full value of your car, you must sell it yourself. It's a pretty straightforward process: prepare the car inside and out; determine its actual value and your asking and/or target sales price; advertise; show it; and negotiate a deal.

inside information

Determining the current value of your car may be the most important step in realizing its current worth. There are a number of used-car price guides that can give you a good idea of the dollar range you can expect, based on the condition of the vehicle, engine wear, and age. Another good reference is the local classified ad section and penny-saver and "wheels-and-deals" magazines; browse them for an idea of the selling range of similar makes and models. Note that condition and appearance have much to do with the asking price and what a car will bring. If you want top dollar, your car must look its best inside, outside, and under the hood. Clean it up, top off or replace all fluids, even get a tune-up before you list it for sale. If it's going to require a major repair and you plan to sell it as is, get an estimate of what the repair will cost. That bit of information might help convince a wavering buyer. There are seasonal trends that impact sales. There's more call for four-wheel-drive and sport utility vehicles as winter approaches; it's also easier to sell a car without air-conditioning during the cooler weather. There are always more buyers in the months between January and April, as income tax refunds arrive. Unless you aren't willing to negotiate a price, leave yourself some room for negotiations in the asking price. Put a sign in the car window and start with an ad in the local classified. Be prepared to drop your price after a month if you haven't gotten any offers.

jargon

AC/AT/PS/PW/4WD: Popular acronyms used in car ads to economize the number of words used. Those used here refer to air-conditioning, automatic transmission, power steering, power windows, and four-wheel-drive.

Book value: What a car is worth, according to standard price guides such as *The NADA Official Used Car Guide* or *Kelley Blue Book*. For a dealer, book value means what he will give you in cash or trade for your car. "Book value" may also refer to the price or price range a car would bring on the open market.

warning

Remember the golden rule when you sell your car: if it's a lemon, don't try to unload it on someone else without telling that person. If a prospective buyer asks a direct question about something and you respond with a bald-faced lie, you'll have a lifelong enemy and could end up in small claims court. Present it for what it is—no more, no less—and answer any questions to the best of your ability. Before you allow strangers to test-drive your vehicle, check with your insurance agent to make sure they will be covered, whether you will need additional coverage, and what questions you should ask before you turn over your keys. Don't accept a personal check for your car from someone you don't know. If they insist on paying by personal check, meet them at their bank and make sure they have the funds to cover the amount before you hand over the title.

Once you've set an asking price, start with the cheapest form of advertising: put a sign in the window. Then try the local classified ads. After a week, place an ad in a more expensive wheels-and-deals publication if you have no success. There are a couple of simple ways to ensure that your car brings top dollar for its class. Clean it thoroughly, inside and out. Even a $200 paint job, well done, will add several hundred dollars to the price of an unsightly rusted car. If the turn signals, headlights, or wipers aren't working properly, a few bulbs or blades will more than pay for themselves in the final price. New tires—even newer used tires—can also make the car more salable.

resources

Kelley Blue Book: Standard reference for determining the trade-in and resale book value of a car. Its Web site, www.kbb.com, features forms you can complete to get an instant appraisal of a car's book value.

39 Ways to Sell Your Car Fast by Timothy Johnson (Spirit Drive, 1993): Tips on sales and promotion strategies to pique interest in and negotiate the sale of your used car.

2002 Edition Ultimate Collector Car Price Guide (Cars & Parts Magazine, 2001): Revised every few years, this guide gives price ranges for every major domestic and imported automobile built from 1900 through 1999, based on the condition of the car, engine wear, body condition, etc.

1. If you're not convinced you want to sell your car yourself, check with dealers or automotive price guides to see the trade-in price versus resale value.

2. Realistically assess the condition of the car inside and out, mechanically and cosmetically.

3. Make note of minor cosmetic repairs and parts replacements that could easily be done to make the car more appealing.

6. Decide if you can wait to sell your vehicle when seasonal demand will be at its peak.

5. Replace any tires that show excessive, uneven wear.

4. Decide if a new paint job will significantly improve the car's appearance and price, especially if older paint is peeling or has rusted through.

7. Browse classified listings for sales of makes and models similar to yours. Note the range of prices and factors affecting them.

8. Consult a price guide such as the *Kelley Blue Book* for a price range.

9. Use the information from the price guide, the current price range in your area, and the general condition of your car to set the asking price.

12. Vacuum the carpeting and clean the floor mats, seats, windows, and ashtrays.

11. Before you advertise the car, thoroughly clean it inside and out.

10. If you intend to negotiate the price, ask at least 20 percent above the minimum you are willing to accept.

13. Use a deodorizing spray, if necessary.

14. Top off all fluids, add to or change the oil, and replace filters as needed.

15. Clean out personal belongings from the trunk.

18. Put a sign in the window of the car noting the sales price and your telephone number.

17. Check with your insurance agent to see if your insurance will cover test drivers.

16. If the car requires any significant repairs you are not willing to make, get two estimates on the cost of both parts and labor.

19. Place an ad in the local newspaper classified section and the penny saver.

20. If these advertising efforts elicit no serious inquiries, consider placing an ad in used-car-type publications.

21. When dealing with prospective buyers, answer all questions to the best of your ability. If the car requires major repair, tell them about it and the estimated costs.

24. Do not sign or release the car's title until you have received full payment for the vehicle.

23. Request cash for the sale. If the buyer wants to pay by check, ask for a cashier's check or arrange to meet the buyer at his or her bank to complete the sale.

22. Negotiate a price.

how to deal with an auto repair problem

70

the basics

Your car won't start—now what? For many, dealing with a car repair problem is an experience regarded with as much enthusiasm as a trip to the dentist. Although most mechanics are honest, auto repair scams are common enough that a trip to the service station seems like "open season on your wallet." When you experience a problem with a car repair, it usually presents itself after the work is done: you'll be asked to pay for something you never discussed; the repair didn't fix anything; or there was nothing wrong with the car to begin with. That's why you should take these important steps before the repair is done: maintain your car properly; make yourself familiar with its basic features and operation; find a reputable mechanic; and never approve any repair until you have an estimate of the cost in writing.

The worst thing you can do is tell an unscrupulous mechanic you have no idea what's wrong, but your car is making a funny noise. The more knowledgeable you are, or appear to be, about your car's operation and the potential cause of the problem, the better the service. There are plenty of car repair books for every make and model with trouble-shooting guides. Even a novice can use these to narrow down the possible problem. Whether or not you have any idea what's wrong, always try to get at least two estimates before committing for a repair. You might be surprised at the difference in price quotes. Before you commit, get the estimate in writing, broken down into the costs of parts and labor. Always ask if the work and parts are guaranteed, and for how long. Make sure the mechanic has previous experience working on your type of car. When the repair is done, have the mechanic show you what was done. If you've paid for a new part, ask to see it or the old part that was removed. Test the car immediately, and return to the shop right away if there are any problems. If you can, pay for the repair by credit card, as, if further problems develop, it gives you the option of stopping payment until you are completely satisfied with the repair.

Core charge: A fee charged by the auto parts dealer if you do not turn in an old part when purchasing its replacement.

Original parts: Parts for a car that are made by the original manufacturer of your vehicle and are identical to the parts in your car. These are the most expensive parts you can buy.

Rebuilt parts: Parts that have been rebuilt and reconditioned from the core parts others have traded in.

Salvage parts: Used parts purchased at a junkyard at a greatly reduced price that have been removed from a car similar to yours.

Be wary of any mechanic who advises you that you need emergency repair after pulling off the highway from an uneventful drive; take your vehicle somewhere else for a second opinion. It's especially important to make sure the mechanic is experienced at working on cars like yours. Today's automobiles are not all alike, and the features and repair procedures are not always the same. Before you approve the work, find out what types of parts are to be used, their cost, and any warranty they carry. Ask around, and also check with your local Better Business Bureau about any repair shop's reputation and the number of complaints against, if any, before allowing it to touch your car.

fyi •

The best way to make sure a repair is done right is to take action immediately if it is done wrong. As soon as you discover a problem, head back to the mechanic immediately. You should not pay any additional fee for the work to be fixed. If the repair becomes a problem in itself, document every time you speak with the mechanic, and hold on to all copies, receipts, and estimates. If the repair shop will not work with you to fix their repair, take the car somewhere else. If possible, stop payment on the original repair. After it is repaired, consider taking action against the faulty service provider, through small claims court if possible.

resources •

Auto Repair for Dummies by Deanna Sclar (Hungry Minds, 1999): A useful guide for those who want to try his or her hand at auto repairs or at least wants to sound as if they know what he or she is talking about when taking it to a shop.

AllExperts.com (www.allexperts.com): This free Internet question-and-answer site has experts on all sorts of topics, including specialists on most types of cars, who will take your questions and offer advice on auto repairs or troubleshooting.

Auto repair guides: Publishers such as Chilton and Haynes, as well as all car manufacturers, sell detailed repair guides for most makes and models. Even if you don't plan to do the repairs yourself, the troubleshooting guides they contain can help determine the cause of your problem.

1. Keep your car in good working order by properly maintaining it as recommended by the manufacturer.

2. Ask friends and family for recommendations on mechanics before you need one.

3. Familiarize yourself with your car's basic features and operations so that if a problem develops you can isolate it at least partially.

12. Test-drive the vehicle.

11. When you pick up the car, ask the mechanic to show/explain what had to be done. If major parts were replaced, ask to see the old parts.

10. Ask that they call you for your approval of the repair after they have a look at your car and before proceeding with any work.

13. If not satisfied, explain the problem to the mechanic.

14. The mechanic should be willing to correct the problem immediately or by the next day, at no additional cost to you.

15. Pay only when completely satisfied

23. Get the car repaired at another shop and hold on to all receipts until your case with the first shop is resolved.

22. If it is still unresponsive consider legal action, file a complaint with the Better Business Bureau and possibly small claims court.

4. When there is a problem, diagnose it to the best of your ability, using a troubleshooting guide.

5. Then take it in to a mechanic for repair.

6. Get an estimate, in writing, broken down by parts and labor, on the cost of repair.

9. Find out if they will be using original, rebuilt, or salvaged parts, and make sure they are appropriately priced.

8. Ask if the mechanics who will be working on your car have experience working with this brand and model.

7. If this is a nonemergency repair, get at least two estimates before deciding which mechanic or shop to use.

16. Pay by credit card or check, which gives you the option of stopping payment if not satisfied with the repair.

17. If the car breaks down within the repair warranty period, contact the shop immediately for subsequent repairs.

18. Always try to resolve repair disputes amicably.

21. Have your attorney draft a letter and send it to the repair shop in an attempt to clear up the problem.

20. Inform the shop that you will report it to the Better Business Bureau and are considering legal action.

19. If the shop or mechanic refuses to work with you to correct the repair, stop payment if possible.

how to find the lowest possible airfare

71

the basics

The Internet has changed everything about getting the best deals when you travel. In the old days, if you wanted significant savings on an airfare, you had to call around, keeping copious notes, or engage the services of a travel agent. Today, you can let your fingers do the work: just log on to the Internet, type in "discount airfare" in your favorite search engine, and start exploring. Even the airlines have gotten into the act, selling tickets online and offering discounts to passengers who book electronically that are not available elsewhere. There are other ways to save, too: take a charter flight, or enjoy the group rates that go with joining a tour group. You can learn about these online as well.

inside information

To find a rock-bottom airfare, you need to understand how airlines price tickets. The same rules of supply and demand apply here as everywhere else: when there's the most demand for airline tickets, it will cost you. For a cheaper fare you will probably have to fly midweek and spend Saturday night at your destination. Seasonal trends apply, too. Don't expect significant savings around holidays or in any peak travel period. You can save, whenever you fly, by booking in advance. You may even be entitled to additional discounts if you book as long as a month ahead of your departure date. You would also do well to track newspaper ads and the latest promotions from major airlines in the weeks before you book your flight. The airlines run all sorts of promotions, but often you have to ask about a specific plan in order to reap its savings. If you're calling to book a flight, always ask what the lowest fare is and if there are any promotions currently running. Use the Internet to comparison shop and save. Great deals on airfares are everywhere; all you have to do is look for them.

jargon

Advance Purchase Excursion (APEX) fare: To get a low APEX fare, you have to buy a ticket in advance, usually at least a week before you fly. The longer in advance you purchase the ticket, the cheaper it will be.

Ticket consolidator: Consolidators purchase blocks of unsold tickets from the airlines at a deep discount and resell them to consumers. Some restrictions, such as ineligibility for frequent-flyer miles, may apply.

Travel agent: Travel agents were once the consumer's best ally for getting a better deal on airfares, and they still are if you don't want to book your flight yourself. They remain a good resource for coordinating travel plans and putting together packages of airfare, lodging, and car rental.

fyi

Airlines constantly go head-to-head in their competition for passengers. When one announces a major promotion but you prefer to fly on another, inquire if the other offers or plans to offer a comparable discount. You may be able to find a better fare simply by flying during off-peak hours. Indirect flights are often cheaper, too. You may even be able to get a much better deal than flying direct by transferring through a third city or flying partway and then driving to your final destination. The more flexible you can be about how and when you travel, the more opportunities you'll find to save on airfares.

Usually, the cheaper your ticket, the fewer options you have if you want to revise your plans. Certain cancellation fees may apply, so ask about these at the time you book your flight. Creative strategies can also cost you money if caught. One of the most popular involves purchasing two round-trip fares to your destination city at the discounted Saturday stopover rate, then using only half of each fare. The total still comes out cheaper than the usual midweek rate, but if you're caught, you'll have to pay full fare.

Fly Cheap! by Kelly Monaghan and Rudy Maxa (Intrepid Traveler, 2000): A handbook to finding and buying air travel for less, with contact information for all the major carriers.

Discount Airfares: The Insiders' Guide, How to Save up to 75% on Airline Tickets by George E. Hobart (Priceless Publishing, 2000): Various strategies for saving on airfare, with contact numbers, Web addresses, etc., of the major carriers.

Online: There is now an abundance of online resources available to help you book your flight at the lowest possible fare. Start with the Web sites of major airlines serving your destination, and proceed from there to resources such as **Priceline.com** (www.priceline.com) and **Travelocity.com** (www.travelocity.com). Use your favorite search engine.

1. Choose your destination.

2. Remember that flexibility in planning is the key to saving on airfare.

3. Plan your travel to take advantage of off-peak discounts in the time of day and week as well as time of year.

6. Contact an agent and explain your needs.

5. Decide if you want to do this yourself or entrust it to a travel agent.

4. Plan so you will be able to take advantage of midweek flights with a Saturday-night stopover at your destination.

7. If seeking lodging and/or car rental, see if there are any packages that can provide additional savings.

8. If booking the flight yourself, will you do it by telephone or online?

9. If by phone, contact an airline ticket agent and explain your plans. Ask for the lowest fares, what discounts or promotions you may be eligible for, and if any discount programs will soon be launched.

12. Search the fares for your destination. Note the fares and any restrictions that apply.

11. If going online, visit the Web sites of airlines serving the destination.

10. Call several airlines and compare their prices.

13. Compare the fares of several airlines found online, or use an online fare locator service to compare.

14. Note any restrictions that apply to these fares.

15. Investigate if an indirect flight with a stopover, or a flight to a nearby city and a second flight to your destination, would offer a better deal than a direct flight.

17. Before you book any flight, make yourself aware of any restrictions, fees, or penalties that would apply in the event that you change your travel plans.

16. If you need only a one-way ticket, compare the cost of the one-way ticket with the round-trip fare.

how to get the lowest rate at a hotel

72

the basics

Hotels charge two rates: the advertised rate and what you actually pay for your stay. During busy business travel periods or vacation time, the two may be one and the same. But whenever there are more available rooms than guests, you should be able to strike a better deal. To get it, though, you have to ask for it. When you step up and ask for a room for the night, you'll get the advertised rate. Ask if there are any discounts or special rates; you might be surprised to sleep in the same room at a savings of $10, $20, or more. Many specials and discounts are not advertised, but they are there and you'll find them—if you look and ask.

inside information

As with any consumer product or service, the laws of supply and demand govern the price of lodging. When the demand is there, the standard pricing holds. When the balance tips in favor of the buyer, the price is negotiable. Hotel chains, even locally owned independent motels, do a lot of advertising to entice guests. Part of this marketing effort may include some form of coupon or discount offer. You'll find it wherever they can reach potential guests: in the "green book" freely distributed at highway rest stops; in your monthly credit card statement; among the pages at the back of your road atlas or telephone directory. National chains also routinely offer discounts to members of groups such as the American Association of Retired Persons (AARP), military personnel, and even some large trade groups. Hotel discounts are also cross-promoted with other travel services such as airline tickets and rental cars. You may also be eligible for a discount by booking in advance or reserving your room yourself over the Internet. In fact, the Internet has revolutionized all aspects of the travel industry and can be your best source of savings, whether you're traveling in the United States or abroad. There are now a number of travel-oriented Web sites that let you compare local rates merely by entering your destination and the days you expect to stay there. Consolidators, who buy and resell lodging at a discount, are also using the Internet to pass savings along to consumers. Even when you walk up to a hotel desk in search of instant lodging, you may be able to negotiate a better deal. Go for the room that's up the extra flight of stairs, in the remotest reach from the pool, or not fully renovated, and you could enjoy extra savings. Such deals do exist for those who let a clerk know they are interested in cheaper lodging.

jargon

Consolidators: Companies that buy vacant hotel rooms in bulk from the major chains and then resell them to the public. They concentrate their business where the demand for lodging is greatest, such as major cities, and may have rooms available even when everyone else has hung out the "No Vacancy" sign.

Frequent-guest programs: Many hotel chains now offer programs that encourage frequent travelers to return to the company's hotels and motels wherever they roam. Such programs may entitle you to discounts, room upgrades, and other amenities, including free lodging, based on the number of nights you stay in a chain's facilities.

fyi

Many chains have a special corporate or business rate that may be available to anyone traveling on "business." The only proof required may be presentation of your business card. Time your travel during off-peak periods, and you will save substantially. Managers will welcome weekend guests with savings to the same rooms that are crammed with business travelers paying full price at midweek. Substantial discounts can be yours for traveling to and staying at a popular vacation destination just weeks before the tourist season begins. You may also realize savings by buying a package that includes airfare, lodging, and car rental, but don't take that for granted. Check the rates yourself to make sure you really are getting a bargain.

warning

You lose some of your bargaining leverage when you pull in off the road bleary-eyed, even if ample rooms are available. Book even hours in advance, and a clerk may pass along a savings for the knowledge that one less room will sit empty. Many discounts carry special stipulations: you may need to present proof that you are a member of an organization; present a coupon; and/or confirm a reservation a certain number of days in advance. Make sure you understand your responsibilities in order to qualify for the discounts. When traveling to third-world or developing countries, cheap lodging may not be worth the savings. If you're tempted by a deal that seems too good to be true, check the room before you check in.

resources

America's Cheap Sleeps by Tracy Whitcombe (Open Road Publishing, 1999): A guide to more than 7,500 locations where you can sleep for $45 or less a night throughout the United States, with information on what's available, where, and what the price includes.

Fly Free, Stay Cheap! "How-To" Strategies and Tips for Free Flights & Cheap Travel by Vicki Mills (Platypus Publications, 1998): A straightforward handbook detailing strategies you can use to travel and stay for less, whatever your destination.

Online: Start your search engine. There are literally hundreds of ways to find savings on lodging online. Some likely sources include the Web sites of national hotel and motel chains; city or regional sites; cross-promotions through airline or car rental sites; special travel sites; consolidators.

1. Plan and book your lodging in advance.

2. Travel during off-peak seasons or days of the week.

3. Always ask for a better deal when making a reservation.

6. Look for and use coupons and discount offers found in atlases, travel books, telephone directories, coupon mailings, and the chains' own advertising.

5. Inquire about corporate or business rates.

4. Be flexible about the type and location of your room.

7. Find out if any discounts are offered through clubs, organizations, or associations in which you or a family member participate.

8. Take advantage of discounts for seniors or military personnel if you or someone you are traveling with qualifies.

9. Enroll in a chain's frequent-guest program.

12. Choose a hotel/motel location that is removed from the main interstate, local airport, or downtown convention center or business district.

11. Contact travel agents to inquire if they can get you a discount on lodging.

10. Check to see if you can realize savings by buying a travel package combining airfare, lodging, and car rental.

13. Investigate renting a hotel room from a consolidator.

14. Use the Internet to shop and compare rates to find your best deal.

15. See if chains offer a discount for making a reservation online.

18. Know and abide by the rules or special stipulations governing any discount program.

17. Use travel sites to search for discounts on lodging at your destination.

16. Check city and regional Web sites for discount offers.

how to stop junk mail, telemarketing, and e-mail "spam"

73

At times the constant assault of people trying to convince you to buy their product, try their service, or support their charity is overwhelming. They pitch to you in the mail, over the telephone, and now in cyberspace. Is there no escape? Only if you take the initiative to stop them. Though you may consider your name, telephone number, and e-mail address to be your property, it's being sold by companies with your direct or indirect approval. The next time you fill out a warranty registration card or enter a "free contest," read the fine print: both are common ploys for building a database. You may, in completing a form, be giving permission for those collecting the information to use and distribute your name, address, and telephone number. It's the same on the Internet whenever you complete an electronic form for special offers or information, post to a newsgroup, or even visit certain Web sites. People are watching and tracking your activity so they can sell your name and personal information to someone eager to reach people just like you, whether or not you want to hear from them.

The first trick to stopping all forms of unwanted solicitations is to understand where and how personal information about you is being gathered, who is collecting it, and how it is being used. Unfortunately, your profile is being built and improved with many things you do routinely, without a thought. Ever use a supermarket club card? A credit card? A store discount card? Have a driver's license? Order a book on home repair? Apply for a loan? Subscribe to a magazine? Request free information? Spend a few minutes on an e-commerce site? In each instance you could be adding your name to a mailing or calling list and filling in details of your consumer profile. The gathering of personal information is just about impossible to stop unless you go by a pseudonym and use a false address and telephone number. What you can do is explicitly state that you don't want your name or number distributed without your permission and take action whenever you receive an unwanted call or solicitation. Request, in writing or by telephone, that you be removed from the list of groups, charities, and businesses that solicit you. Once you've notified them, they are breaking the law if they continue to contact you. Junk e-mail, or spam, as it's called, is a bit tougher to stop because the senders can hide who they are and where the spam is originating. Check with your Internet service provider and your software. Both should have filters for screening out some of the junk. Always read a Web site's privacy policy before filling out any electronic form.

Cookies: Pieces of data that are uploaded to your hard drive each time you visit a Web site. They are used to track your activity and build a profile of the places you go and the things you do online.

Junk mail: Anything that arrives in your mailbox unwanted and unsolicited. It takes many forms: catalogs, credit card offers, get-rich-quick schemes, requests for donations, etc. The bottom line on junk mail is that it's something you don't want and do want to stop receiving.

Mailing list: A database of names, including addresses, telephone numbers, and personal information, that companies sell and exchange for marketing purposes. Often these lists are organized related to some specific activity: you may have donated to a certain charity, purchased books on a certain topic, or completed a warranty registration for a recent purchase.

The only way to stop junk mail, telemarketing, and spamming is to take the initiative. Always specify that you do not want your name sold or distributed. Refuse first-class junk mail by writing "return to sender" and requesting to be removed from its mailing list on the envelope. Stop telemarketers by requesting that they stop calling you. Never give a stranger the kind of information—Social Security number, bank or credit card account numbers—that could be prone to abuse. Be especially wary of attachments in e-mail, from total strangers; they are the preferred means of spreading computer viruses.

Federal and state laws guarantee you protection against unwanted solicitation. Check with the Federal Trade Commission, your state's bureau of consumer affairs, and your local postmaster. Each can explain your rights and the steps you can take to ensure that the unwanted contact stops. If you want to find out who is selling your name and where, devise a code when you fill out a form or comply with a request for information. Use a variation on your name or address. When you find someone is selling your name, request that it stop. Immediately.

Stop Junk Mail Forever by Marc Eisenson, Nancy Cattleman, and Marcy Ross (Good Advice Press, 2001): A thorough guide to the steps you can take to stop the flow of unsolicited, unwanted mail to your mailbox.

Credit bureaus: People get more solicitations for credit cards than anything else. You can put a stop to this by asking credit bureaus not to distribute your credit history. One toll-free telephone call to (888) 567-8688 should take care of it for all credit bureaus.

Direct Marketing Association: Although this professional association has the interests of its member companies at heart, it does have programs that consumers can use to stop solicitations from member companies. Write to Mail and Telemarketing Preference Services, DMA, P.O. Box 9014, Farmingdale, NY 11735-9014.

Your local postmaster: He or she can explain the steps you can take to stop receiving junk mail, including what forms to fill out or who to contact.

1. Understand how and where telemarketers are getting your name, number, e-mail address, and purchase information.

2. When completing any form or request for information, state in writing that you are not authorizing the company gathering information to reuse or distribute it.

3. Be wary of all requests for personal information you do complete.

6. Contact the Direct Marketing Association and complete its forms for mail and telemarketing preferences, requesting to have your name removed from mailing and calling lists.

5. Contact credit bureaus and request that they not distribute any information they have compiled on you and your family.

4. Check with your local postmaster to see what you can do to stop unwanted mail and complete any necessary forms.

7. When you receive junk mail, return first-class mail to the sender with a request that your name be removed from its list.

8. Contact any companies sending unsolicited magazines, catalogs, or mailings and request you be removed from their mailing lists.

9. Do not respond to any junk mail solicitations or requests for donations.

12. If a representative of that organization calls again, report it to the National Fraud Information Center at (800) 876-7060.

11. When you receive an unwanted telephone solicitation, respond only by requesting you be taken off the calling list.

10. If you can identify a company or organization distributing your name and information, request in writing and by telephone that it stop.

13. Read the policy and disclosure statement of any Web site before you complete an online form.

14. When completing an online form, never check the box granting approval to receive information from other companies.

15. Frequently disable cookies from your preferences file in your Web browser and from commercial sites.

16. Do not respond to any spam received by automatically responding to that message, even to remove your name from the mailing list.

17. Draft and send a separate e-mail reply asking that you not be contacted again.

18. Contact your Internet service provider to learn what kind of filter you can activate to prevent spam.

19. Use the filters in your e-mail software to block as much spam as possible.

how to control how your charitable donations are used

If you've ever given even a dollar to a cause, you have quickly learned how many organizations need or want your financial support. Often one small gift opens a floodgate of solicitations from other charities. Many are from reputable organizations with well-meaning objectives and a track record of achieving them. But others are from organizations whose primary objective is to relieve you of a well-intentioned donation. If you want your charitable giving to make a difference, you must attempt to discern between the two. There's a considerable amount of documentation, including financial reports, that can help you understand which charities are worth supporting. Most charities are eager to share information and will willingly provide an annual report, newsletters, and program brochures describing their successes. Until you have an opportunity to review these, you should postpone giving.

It takes money to raise money, and as you check into the background of some charities you may be alarmed to learn how little of your charitable gift goes to actual projects and how much covers administrative costs. Any reputable charity will provide you this information. Be wary of any organization that does not spend at least 70 percent of collected donations on the actual projects and activities. Even before you look at the numbers, you should narrow down the field of potential beneficiaries of your generosity. There's a great sense of reward that comes from supporting activities and causes you believe in. Put your money where your heart is. When you've selected charities, look at the groups, what they propose to do, and what they are actually doing. Request a copy of their yearly report, newsletters, and brochures. How well stated are their goals? What are their short- and long-term goals? Who is on their boards of directors? What is their track record? Do they have the resources to continue with their work? Are they responsive to questions about operations and funding? These questions can help you find worthy charities. If the answers to your questions are vague or a charity is simply unresponsive, it's probably a good idea to take your altruism elsewhere. Charities are as varied as the people who run them. Restrict your generosity to those with leaders who are accountable, committed, and financially responsible.

501(c)(3): Designation given by the Internal Revenue Service to groups and organizations that meet its criteria for classification as nonprofit organizations, granted certain tax breaks.

IRS Form 990: A document completed and filed each year by many public charities to report information about their finances and operations to the federal government; these documents are available to the public.

Matching funds: One of the ways to enhance the impact of your gift is to make donations where matching funds are available. These match your gift dollar for dollar and may be offered by an employer or organization.

Charities that pursue you aggressively, through the mail or by phone, are often in the business of fund-raising. Your decision to support a charity should originate with you and not be a response to an aggressive pitch or sob story. It's good policy not to make any donation over the phone. And never give out your credit card number to an anonymous caller. If you have questions about a charity, visit its headquarters. Note how its key staffers are dressed and what types of cars they drive. These could provide insights into whether the charity is truly committed to its cause or merely a fund-raising mechanism for self-serving administrators. If you plan to claim a tax deduction for your donation, make sure you get a receipt.

Government cutbacks have put the squeeze on many charitable organizations, forcing them to be more aggressive in their pitch for donations. Of course, this situation also creates opportunities for unsavory solicitors, so be on your guard. Most charities require long-term support from donors to realize their goals. They should be eager to demonstrate how your money is being put to use. If a charity dodges your questions or can't produce satisfactory answers or documentation, look for another with a comparable mission. If you want your donation to be used exclusively for the charity's programs rather than administrative costs, use your donation to purchase sorely needed equipment or services. Whenever you make a donation, always request that the organization not distribute your name to others. Many charities routinely trade donor lists, resulting in the junk mail that clutters your mailbox, clamoring for your cash.

Robin Hood Was Right: A Guide to Giving Your Money for Social Change by Chuck Collins, Pam Rogers, Joan P. Garner, and Ellen Gurzinsky (Norton, 2000): A guide to charitable giving to promote social change, with profiles of foundations, a worksheet to determine how much you can give, and information on resources for responsible giving.

GuideStar (www.guidestar.org): A searchable database of information maintained by Philanthropic Research that includes recent financial disclosures for more than 640,000 nonprofit organizations in the United States. A good place to begin comparing charities and how much of the money they receive goes into actual program activity.

1. Try to ignore telephone and junk mail solicitations for donations. You should be the one to initiate contact with and donations to causes you believe in.

2. Decide how much you can afford to donate to charities weekly, monthly, or annually.

3. Does your company offer any type of matching fund program? If so, get a list of charities that qualify.

12. Who are the members of its board of directors?

11. What kind of support does it already enjoy?

10. What are its financial needs, and where is the greatest need?

13. Who plans and implements the charity's programs?

14. What kind of internal review and planning bodies are in place?

15. How will your support help this group?

24. Only when you have experience with the charity and are satisfied with its operation should you consider committing to any long-term giving plan.

23. Before making any donation, contact the Better Business Bureau to see if any complaints have been filed against the charity.

22. Are there any specific needs you could provide for by purchasing a product or service for the group rather than making a donation?

4. Do you prefer to spread your money among several groups or focus on one organization?

5. Identify the charities with a mission and commitment that match your concerns.

6. Contact them for information, annual report brochures, and financial disclosures on assets and spending. Review this information carefully.

9. What have its successes been?

8. Who does it serve, and how does it reach them?

7. Does a charity have well-defined goals and plans for reaching them, short and long term?

16. Is this charity a nonprofit organization?

17. How much money did the charity bring in last year? Over the last three years?

18. On an annual basis, what percentage of donations is spent on actual programs?

21. If you have questions about the charity's programs or finances, is a representative of the charity responsive to your questions with helpful information?

20. Is the charity strong enough financially to continue in its mission?

19. What percentage is used to cover administrative costs, including fund raising?

what to do if your purse or wallet is stolen

75

the basics

It happens in a flash. You're walking down the street or standing in a crowd. Someone briefly brushes against you, or you feel a tug at your arm. Instinctively you reach for your wallet or purse, and it's gone. Unfortunately, it's too common an experience, and it may mean months or even years of trouble for the victim. Pickpockets of the past might have been happy to get the cash and change in your wallet. For today's street criminal, it's the credit card and personal information you carry that are the real booty. They may use this information or resell it to make you a victim of identity theft long after your cash is spent. There's no way you can absolutely guarantee that your purse or wallet will never be stolen. But you can take steps now to protect and prepare yourself in the event it ever happens to you. Think ahead, and it will be much easier for you to minimize the impact of the crime on you, both emotionally and financially.

Pickpockets and muggers usually look for easy marks. A lot of what you can do to prevent these crimes is simply a matter of common sense. Don't leave your purse or wallet lying around in public places. When you carry either with you, keep it protected. Loop your arm and head through your purse straps; carry your wallet in a pocket that buttons shut or in a front pocket. Carry at least part of your cash somewhere else on your body, perhaps in a money belt. The best thing you can do to minimize the impact of such a crime is to know what you're carrying. Reduce the number of credit cards you carry, and keep a record of the account numbers somewhere else. Carry personal documents such as Social Security cards, birth certificates, and bankbooks only when you absolutely need them. When traveling abroad, leave copies of your passport and airline tickets at home and in your hotel room. When you are the victim of a street crime or discover your purse or wallet is missing, take immediate action. Contact the local police, and file a report. This is essential, as you may need it as proof for credit card companies and banks. Then, one by one, contact credit card companies, banks, and any other agencies to inform them of the theft. Cancel your old cards and change accounts or have the bank institute a password for all subsequent transactions. But the work isn't over with a few telephone calls. Once your wallet or purse is stolen, you have to monitor all bills and credit card statements to make sure you aren't also the victim of identity theft.

When you file a police report, keep a copy for future reference. It may be your only way of proving to credit card companies and banks that you really have been a victim of theft. There are liability limits for a person whose credit card, ATM card, or bankbook is stolen. Even the minimum $50 liability on an ATM or credit card may be waived for those who report the crime immediately. Besides, the quicker you respond, the less likely anyone will be able to use your name fraudulently and make you a victim of identity theft. Identity theft is a real long-term risk when your purse or wallet is stolen. Closely monitor your monthly statements and credit reports for a year after the theft. If you discover anything questionable, contact that company or agency immediately.

Some thugs aren't sophisticated enough to steal a purse or wallet cleverly. When a demand for either is backed with a knife or gun, give it up. There's nothing your wallet contains that is as valuable as your health or life. Before traveling abroad, make backup copies of your passport and airline tickets and leave them with a relative or friend. If your wallet is lost or stolen, it will make it much easier to secure replacements. If your purse or bag containing your keys is stolen, change the locks on your car and doors at home. The thief already knows where you live and what you drive from the information in your wallet.

1. Plan ahead: Anticipate that you may be the victim of such a crime and take appropriate measures.

2. Carry personal documents such as Social Security card, birth certificate, passport, and bankbook only when absolutely necessary.

3. Minimize the number of credit cards, debit cards, and ATM cards you do carry.

6. Conceal one copy somewhere in your luggage and leave another copy at home with a trusted friend or relative.

5. When traveling abroad, make backup copies of your passport and airline tickets.

4. Keep a record at home of the card numbers and customer service numbers to call in the event of theft of each.

7. Use common sense when out on streets or in crowds.

8. Know the contents of your purse and wallet.

9. Keep wallet in a buttoned or front pocket; loop your arms and head through the straps of a purse or bag.

12. Keep a copy of your report for future reference.

11. Contact the police and insist on filing a report.

10. When you discover your purse or wallet is stolen, take immediate action.

13. Contact credit card companies and credit information bureaus.

14. Inform them of the theft.

15. Cancel old credit cards and get new ones with new account numbers.

18. If this cannot be done, close the accounts and open new ones.

17. Request that your bank require passwords for any future transactions on your accounts.

16. Contact your bank and cancel ATM cards and get new ones.

19. Contact your long distance carrier and inform it of the theft. Change your account or calling card number.

20. Contact your state Department of Motor Vehicles and inform it that your license has been stolen. Request a new driver's license.

21. If your keys were stolen, change the locks on your car and the doors at home.

22. For the next year, closely monitor all billing statements, transaction records, and credit reports for any signs of identify theft.

23. If you discover fraudulent activity, take immediate action.

how to deal with identity theft

76

It can seem the ultimate affront: someone uses your good name and reputation to commit fraud, leaving you with the burden of proving your innocence. Identity theft is a crime that wreaks havoc with the lives of thousands of law-abiding, responsible citizens each year. It drags them through the emotional wringer of trying to explain away exhausted credit cards never applied for, loans in default never borrowed, and purchases never made. The thief, too rarely caught, can empty your bank accounts and enjoy a spending spree at your expense before you are even aware there is a problem. Often that awareness presents itself as a call from a collection agency or a refusal of a loan because of a bad credit history. You have two options: to react immediately when you discover a thief has compromised your good name and to realize that identity theft is a growing problem and take steps now to minimize the chances that you'll ever become a victim of these faceless criminals.

inside information

It takes any combination of surprisingly little information for someone to assume your identity: your name; address and phone number; credit history; employer's name; Social Security number; driver's license number; ATM PIN number; credit card numbers; a copy of a personal check; or the name of your bank. Think of how often you carelessly and routinely share such information. If thieves are watching—and they do—they could gather this information and make you their next victim. Unfortunately, with all the resources available online, they have easy access to all types of personal information you wouldn't want in their hands. And you can't assume that anyone else is as concerned as you about keeping this information away from spying eyes. Preventing identity theft requires a change of habits. Don't share information about yourself without knowing how it will be used and who will see it. Never give out credit card, Social Security, or driver's license numbers unless you initiate the contact, and then only when sharing this information is absolutely vital to the correspondence or transaction. If you discover you are a victim of identity theft, react immediately. Inform a law enforcement agency, your bank, the credit card companies and credit reporting bureaus, and the banks or credit card companies against which fraud in your name has been committed. It can take a thief minutes to steal your good name and months—even years—for you to repair the damage done.

jargon

Credit information bureaus: Companies that compile the credit and borrowing histories of consumers and store them in national databases. This information serves as the basis for deciding who gets loans and qualifies for credit. The companies include Equifax, Experian, and TransUnion.

fyi

Banks and credit card companies typically hold victims of identity fraud liable for the first $50 stolen in their name, but even that may be waived. However, there will be no compensation or relief for the time and money you'll have to spend to restore your good name. Too many victims have no idea their name has been compromised until they learn of a problem with their credit history. Request and review a copy of your credit history from the major credit information bureaus at least once a year and whenever you are denied a loan or credit card. Stealing a purse or wallet is still one of the easiest ways an identity thief can access all the information he needs. Carry as few credit cards as possible, and leave bank statements, Social Security card, birth certificate, etc., at home.

warning •

An identity thief will seize any opportunity to gather information about potential victims. Some merely lift credit card offers, bills, and financial statements from potential victims' mailboxes. A simple lock on your mailbox is enough to frustrate their efforts. Others "Dumpster dive" in search of credit card receipts and other paperwork. Eliminate the likelihood that they'll find any useful information about you. Destroy credit receipts, and rip up, shred, or burn canceled checks, credit card offers, and financial statements. You may find local law enforcement officials reluctant to file a report on identity theft. Insist they do, however, as a copy of your report will prove essential to your attempts to prove to credit card companies and financial institutions that you are a victim of identity theft.

resources •

Identity Theft: The Cybercrime of the Millennium by John Q. Newman (Loompanics Unlimited, 1999): A discussion of how identity thieves operate, where they get their information, what an individual can do to protect himself against identity theft, and how to protect yourself if you are a victim of this crime.

From Victim to Victor: A Step-by-Step Guide for Ending the Nightmare of Identity Theft by Mari Frank (Porpoise Press, 1998): An attorney, herself the victim of identity theft, details her experiences as she shows others how to prevent and deal with this criminal intrusion into their lives.

Privacy Rights Clearinghouse (www.privacyrights.org): This site offers detailed advice on what you can do to prevent identity theft and the actions you should take once it is discovered.

Credit information bureaus: You should review the credit history they have compiled about you at least once a year and anytime you are denied credit. If you suspect you are the victim of fraud, alert the credit information bureaus' fraud department immediately. Contact: **Equifax,** www.equifax.com, fraud hot line (800) 290-8749; **Experian,** www.experian.com, (888) 397-3742; **TransUnion,** www.transunion.com, (800) 680-7289.

1. Recognize where you may be exposing yourself to identity theft and take the appropriate precautionary measures.

2. Request and review copies of your credit history at least once a year or whenever you are denied credit.

3. Ask the credit reporting agencies to contact you for verbal confirmation of all future credit applications.

12. If your wallet or purse is stolen, take the steps outlined in Lifemap 78.

11. Review all financial statements and credit bills as received to check for accuracy and any fraudulent activity.

10. Install a lock on your mailbox.

13. If you discover you are a victim of identity theft, take action immediately.

14. Explain to collection agencies that you are the victim of fraud.

15. If they threaten criminal prosecution for debt, consult your attorney and have the attorney write them on your behalf.

24. Continually monitor your credit history, bills, and financial statements as needed until your credit history and good name have been restored.

23. If these efforts do not help clear up your problem, have your attorney write letters to each explaining the problem and your expectation that they will work to clear up this matter.

22. In addition to calls to banks, credit card companies, credit information bureaus, etc., contact each in writing, attaching a copy of the police report, to inform them of a problem.

4. Don't carry personal documents such as Social Security card, birth certificate, financial statements, etc., with you unless absolutely necessary.

5. Minimize the number of credit card accounts you carry.

6. When you make a purchase, destroy the credit receipt yourself.

9. On the Internet, don't fill out electronic forms requesting personal information unless you understand how the information is to be used and who will have access to it.

8. Don't give out your Social Security, driver's license, or credit card number to anyone unless you initiated the contact and understand how it is to be used.

7. Rip up, shred, or burn all credit card offers, canceled checks, and financial statements.

16. Contact bank or credit companies, inform them when fraud has been committed in your name, and explain the situation.

17. Contact your local law enforcement agency and insist that it take a report.

18. Contact your bank and inform it of the problem. Request verbal authorization or a password for future withdrawals from your account.

21. Contact the credit information bureaus' fraud hot lines and inform them of identity theft. Request and review a copy of your credit history. Inform them immediately of any fraudulent activity you discover.

20. If they cannot comply with your request for verbal authorization or a password for future purchases, ask that they cancel your old card and issue a new one with a new number.

19. Contact the issuers of all your credit cards and inform them of the problem.

how to resolve
consumer complaints

77

the basics

When you purchase any good or service, you rightfully expect that it will live up to your expectations. A new coffeepot should outlive its warranty, at the very least. When you drive away from a mechanic's shop, you expect the repair you just paid for to be a final fix. If a housepainter damages your carpet, you expect that he'll clean or replace it at his expense. When these things don't happen, you must assume the role of an assertive consumer and pursue your rights. Small claims court is your absolute last resort. You want and should expect to be able to resolve consumer complaints without having to turn to the legal system. The overwhelming majority of business owners consider their reputation a primary asset and will work with customers to resolve any reasonable complaint.

inside information

The most important step you can make toward resolving consumer complaints is to know and understand your rights before you buy. If a store doesn't have its return policy posted, ask the store owner. Read a product's warranty before buying the product. Have a service provider's guarantee written on your bill. Hold on to all receipts, owner's manuals, and warranty cards. You should know what's covered and what isn't before you agree to any service or purchase a product. It's now common for many products to carry one warranty for the repair or replacement of parts and a much shorter warranty to cover the labor required for the repair. A service provider may guarantee his or her work but not the materials you purchased for the job. A quick response is your best ally whenever a problem does occur. If you have a complaint, head first to a store clerk or the person who provided the service. If he or she will not address your complaint, speak with the business owner or manager. Present your complaint without getting emotional. Next contact the manufacturer, the central or regional manager of the business, or the main office and explain your complaint. Only when you've exhausted these reasonable efforts should you consider taking your case to small claims court and filing a complaint against the business with the Better Business Bureau.

jargon

Return policy: The terms and conditions under which a store will accept merchandise back. The return policy should state how long you have to make a return, whether or not you must present a receipt, and whether returns are eligible for a refund or store credit.

Warranty period: The length of time in which a warranty covers a product or service. Note that some of the longer product warranties are prorated; the longer you have and use a product, the higher the fee you will pay for a replacement, even within the warranty period.

warning

Losing your cool over a complaint only antagonizes the other party and makes it less likely that it can be resolved amicably. If you are required to call a vendor's service center for help or return authorization, be sure to write down the name of the person you speak with and your case number. If you don't, you might find yourself explaining your entire experience and complaint each time you call. Don't try to fix a product yourself if it's under manufacturer warranty, and then call for repairs or replacement. Most warranties are void unless the product is taken to an authorized service center for repair. Think ahead when buying, and make sure there is an authorized service center in your area. If not, you may need to ship the item off for repairs, at your own expense, and wait weeks for its return.

Credit cards offer an important form of consumer protection and give you some leverage when trying to resolve a dispute. Some credit card companies automatically double the warranty on purchases made with the card. If a problem occurs, you can request that the card company stop payment until your complaint is resolved. Extended warranties and service plans are usually not a good buy. Read the fine print before you agree to one of these programs. It's important to understand under what circumstances the coverage does not apply. Some unscrupulous companies, especially in the computer industry, have now started to charge for technical support for products right out of the box. If a product doesn't come with a minimum of ninety days of free customer service, purchase a different brand.

resources

Shocked, Appalled, and Dismayed! How to Write Letters of Complaint That Get Results by Ellen Phillips (Vintage Books, 1999): The secrets of writing letters of complaint that get results, with the do's and don'ts of letters of complaint, advice from legal experts, and information about dealing with some commonly experienced areas of consumer complaints.

The American Bar Association Guide to Consumer Law: Everything You Need to Know About Buying, Selling, Contracts, and Guarantees (Times Books, 1997): Much of this guide explains the contracts that are so often the root of consumer complaints. Separate chapters are devoted to consumer issues such as leases, warranties, consumer credit, and purchases made outside a store.

Local or state bureau of consumer affairs: Your state or city bureau of consumer affairs can prove a useful resource on your rights as a consumer and ways to resolve complaints with manufacturers and service providers.

1. Purchase big-ticket items with a credit card as a protective measure.

2. Know the store, vendor, or manufacturer's policies before buying.

3. What guarantees does the product or service carry? Get them in writing.

6. For products, what is the location of the nearest authorized service center?

5. What's covered—and not covered—under the warranty?

4. What is the policy on returns or refunds?

7. Hold on to all receipts, contracts, and warranties.

8. Record model and serial numbers for reference, if applicable.

9. When trying to resolve a consumer complaint, be polite but insistent about your rights.

12. Write down the name of the customer service representative, your case number, and the date and time of the call.

11. If you cannot return the item to the store but the product is still under the manufacturer's warranty, contact the company's customer service department.

10. For products, when a problem occurs during the store's return policy period, take the product to the store for refund, exchange, or store credit.

13. Explain your problem and follow the instructions.

14. If you cannot resolve your problem with the customer service rep, ask to speak to his or her superior.

15. Proceed up the bureaucratic chain until your complaint is resolved to your satisfaction.

18. For a service provider, if a problem occurs within the service provider's work guarantee, contact it immediately and alert it to the problem.

17. Take along or include a copy of the original receipt, case number, and repair authorization number.

16. Take or ship the product to an authorized service center for warranty repair.

19. Make arrangements for necessary repairs to be made at the service provider's expense.

20. If you cannot resolve a complaint, present your case to the next person in the business's or company's hierarchy: business manager, customer representative's superior, regional or central office manager, business owner.

23. If you are still unable to resolve your complaint, consider the merits of taking your case to small claims court (see Lifemap 81).

22. If you have to write to the company to try to resolve the dispute, contact your credit card company and try to stop the payment. You will be sent forms to complete and return.

21. If you are still unable to resolve the complaint, contact the individual or company in writing, outlining the nature of your complaint and how you would like it resolved. Include proof of purchase/payment and warranty.

how to file and win a case in small claims court

78

the basics

When you are unable to resolve a complaint or problem with a company, institution, organization, business owner, service provider, acquaintance, or neighbor, you can turn to small claims court. The only restriction is that disputes must fall within established financial limits. There are usually no lawyers involved and no jury. It's our judicial system at work on the most basic scale.

inside information

There are no national statutes when it comes to small claims court. The laws and procedures that guide them are set on the state or local level. If you're thinking about taking someone to small claims court, your first stop should be the local courthouse. The clerk should be able to provide you with brochures explaining the local small claims court system and how it operates; applicable financial limits on the size of disputes that can be brought to court; and procedures for filing and presenting your case. Once you learn how you can take someone to small claims court, you should carefully weigh whether you should. There are fees involved, for which you may be reimbursed if you win, but awards made in small claims court are not always easy to collect. So before you proceed to court, redouble your efforts to resolve your dispute. Your willingness to try to resolve a dispute outside of court, if well documented, will bolster your case if you must make a presentation to the judge. You'll be better prepared if you sit in on a few small claims cases before you prepare for court. Spend time rehearsing and preparing so you can clearly and concisely explain the nature of your dispute; present proof that the amount of damages you are seeking is reasonable; and demonstrate that you have tried unsuccessfully to resolve the dispute outside the court system. You'll have an opportunity to respond to the defendant's presentation, too, so try to anticipate how he or she may present the events that have brought the two of you to court. When you file a case, you agree to abide by the judge's decision. Usually the plaintiff has no right to appeal the decision, although the defendant may. Even if the judge rules in your favor, collecting the settlement is your responsibility.

jargon

Mediator: An impartial person who can help resolve the dispute and eliminate the need to go to court. Depending on the venue, the court clerk may be able to provide you with a list of court-sanctioned or private mediators who can help you and the defendant resolve your dispute without taking the case to court.

Statute of limitations: The amount of time you have from the date of occurrence of a dispute or injury to file a case in small claims court.

Venue: The municipality or county where the case will be heard. Your case must be filed in the proper venue, usually the court district where the dispute occurred or where the defendant lives or operates the business named as defendant in the suit.

warning

Although you may be driven to small claims court by a defendant's unwillingness to work with you, leave your anger outside the courtroom. Shouting angry accusations, calling names, and interrupting the other party's opportunity to speak will only make you look bad in the eyes of the judge. You must have evidence—supporting documents—to back up your claims. Hold on to all receipts, document any correspondence between you and the defendant, and log telephone calls. Build your case with proof that you have a right to the settlement you seek and have made reasonable efforts to get it. You only have a few minutes to make your case; keep it short, simple, and on topic. If the judge announces a decision in your favor, don't celebrate your victory. Conversely, the ruling upholds the defendant, accept the defeat gracefully.

fyi

You and the defendant have the right to reach a mutually accepted resolution of your dispute right up until the time you are summoned before the judge. It's in the best interests of all involved to resolve your differences amicably whenever you can. You usually can't be represented by an attorney in small claims court, but you can turn to one for advice in preparing your case. Witnesses can help or hurt your case and should be interviewed before you summon them to court. If an expert charges for his or her testimony, you may not be able to recoup the cost as part of your settlement.

resources

Winning in Small Claims Courts: A Step-by-Step Guide for Citizen Litigators by William E. Brewer (Career Press, 1995): An overview of how to win in small claims court, with information on the different systems in each state.

Local court: Your best source of information on small claims court, how it works, and how to file a case. Since every jurisdiction has different policies for small claims court, you must understand the local system before you decide to pursue a claim.

Local publications: Since the laws regulating smalls claims court vary from state to state, even city to city, check your library or a community bookstore for publications focusing on filing a case in small claims court in your area.

1. Hold on to receipts, warranties, and any correspondence for products or services, as well as any documents related to personal injuries or property damage.

2. Make every reasonable effort to resolve your dispute with the other party. Contact the other party and, in writing, outline an offer to resolve your dispute.

3. Contact or visit the local courthouse and request information on filing a case in small claims court. Read this information closely since it outlines the policies, procedures, and any limitations that apply to filing a case.

12. Take the necessary steps to ensure that the defendant is properly served with notification of the suit.

11. Fill out forms to file your case in the appropriate venue.

10. Determine the proper venue for your case.

13. Try to keep the channels of communication open in the hope of resolving your dispute with the defendant, even as you prepare your case.

14. Visit small claims court and sit in on cases to see how the system works.

15. Gather all your supporting evidence and documentation, including receipts, letters, warranty information, etc.

24. Rehearse your case, focusing on the brevity and clarity of your presentation.

23. If the defendant will not comply voluntarily, have it subpoenaed.

22. If there is any supporting evidence you need from the defendant, request it.

25. Be prepared to explain to the judge why the damages you seek represent a fair amount.

26. Before heading to court, make sure you have all your evidence and copies for the judge.

27. Contact friendly witnesses and make sure they are going to be there.

36. If you are unable to or experience difficulty in collecting the judgment from the defendant, contact the court to see what collectron options are available to you.

35. When the judge issues a ruling, in court or by mail, accept a win or loss graciously.

34. Respond without getting emotional.

4. As an alternative, consider using a mediator to resolve the dispute.

5. If you prefer mediation, contact the court for referrals to qualified mediators.

6. If you're not using a mediator, decide if you really want to take the case to court.

9. If a business or corporation, identify the appropriate representative.

8. Determine who you are going to file this case against: one or more individuals, or a business or corporation.

7. Will the defendant have the means to pay for damages and your court costs if the judge rules against him or her?

16. If photographic evidence is required, take photographs.

17. Make duplicate copies of all evidence for your files and to give to the judge.

18. Decide if any witnesses can help your case.

21. If they will not appear voluntarily, have them subpoenaed to appear in court.

20. If you plan to use them, ask if they will appear voluntarily.

19. Contact potential witnesses and determine their version of events.

28. Arrive early, dressed in proper attire.

29. When summoned to present your case, present your evidence to the judge.

30. Explain what you seek and what the request is based on, and review your supporting evidence.

33. Listen to the defendant's version of events.

32. Request that you also be reimbursed for court-related costs.

31. Demonstrate the efforts you have made to resolve the dispute, short of filing your claim in small claims court.

how to trace your family tree

79

the basics

Ever wonder what makes you the person you are? Certainly nurture has a lot to do with it, but there's a lot to be said for all that nature has endowed you with, as well. Each of us is heir to traits and characteristics passed along by generations of men and women who lived before us. We may never appreciate the sacrifices our ancestors made or recognize their achievements without delving into our family history. Tracing your family tree can be a rewarding experience that provides a real sense of who you are and where you came from. We cannot escape the past hidden in our family tree, nor should we want to. Rather, we should be eager to celebrate those who went before, the lives they lived, and the legacy they have given us in our name and traits.

inside information

Tracing your family history can be as simple as opening the pages of an old family Bible and reviewing the family tree recorded there in an old-fashioned hand. Or it can pose a lifelong challenge to unlock secrets hidden in the past, when even the spelling of a family name was sometimes arbitrary. In either event, the tools you need to start are close at hand: family records such as birth certificates and marriage licenses, and hopefully grandparents and older aunts and uncles who can give you some direction in your search. Any search for the history buried in the past should begin with the living. Get the names of as many relatives as older family members can remember, when and where they were born and died, where they lived, what they did for a living. Write down as much as they can recall. The toughest thing about researching your heritage is that the further back you push, the more difficult the search becomes. Your parents each had two parents, as did your parents and great-grandparents. You may find it best to search a single line at a time—for instance, your surname or your mother's maiden name—until you reach a dead end and then follow your search in another direction. Take copious notes of everything you discover, and prepare or purchase a family tree chart or genealogy software. Compile the details and complete the chart as you verify new information. Soon you'll find the branches of your family tree filled with the names of those who helped make you the person you are.

jargon

Genealogy software program: A program, such as Family Tree Maker, created to simplify the process of recording and organizing family data.

LDS Family History Library and Centers: The Mormon Church (Church of Jesus Christ of Latter-day Saints) has been acquiring and preserving genealogical data since its founding. Its Family History Library contains information on hundreds of millions of deceased individuals from all over the world in books and on microfilm. Much of this information can also be obtained through local LDS Family History Centers.

fyi

Tracing one's family tree once meant traveling to distant cities, poring over ancient records, and searching through forgotten graveyards. While a probe for family history may still involve some of that, the Internet has greatly simplified genealogical research in many ways. Many records that once had to be looked at or requested firsthand are now available online. These range from birth and marriage records to ancient military rosters and records of who arrived on these shores, when, and on what ship. With such a widespread interest in genealogy, a number of Web sites have been set up to assist both the amateur and professional genealogist. Not only do they provide links to vast stores of records, they also serve as a forum where you can connect with others who are on a similar search. Some may even be lost relatives. Valuable information may be hidden in places such as jewelry inscriptions, old diaries, diplomas, and news clippings. Exhaust all possible resources.

warning

The search for your family history can quickly overwhelm you with information or lead to frustrating dead ends. In either case it's advisable to step back and take an occasional break from the process so you can assess what you do and don't know and gather your bearings before you continue. You won't know what family secrets are hiding in the past until you uncover them. Expect and accept the unexpected, for better or worse. Services that contact you with offers to provide you with your family crest and history offer little more than generic information. The crest they provide may look nice on the wall, but it's not necessarily authentic, and the package won't help you fill in the blanks of your personal history.

resources

The Everything Family Tree Book: Finding, Charting, and Preserving Your Family History by William G. Hartley (Adams Media Corporation, 1997): A complete guide to discovering and documenting your history, with advice on conducting research and charts and forms for recording your family story.

How to Trace Your Family Tree: A Complete and Easy to Understand Guide for the Beginner by the American Genealogical Research Institute (Doubleday, 1975): A handbook outlining everything you need to know to trace your family tree: where to begin, where to turn for help, and how to organize your findings.

Online: One of the most extensive archives of genealogical information is maintained by the **Church of Jesus Christ of Latter-day Saints**. Start with its genealogy Web site, www.familysearch.org. Another good site, **Ancestry.com** (www.ancestry.com), offers a genealogy community with resources, links to databases, and surname bulletin boards.

1. Prepare a chart of your family tree, or download or purchase family history software or a family tree book.

2. Fill in all the details you can as far back as you can.

3. Add details as you uncover them; if possible, verify all before recording.

6. Sit down with your oldest relatives and ask them about your family history.

5. Also search less obvious places such as jewelry, news clippings, obituaries, and old telephone books and city directories.

4. Look in obvious places for information: family Bible, family graveyard or cemetery plot, old letters or records.

7. Take detailed notes on what they can tell you about names, dates, dates and places of birth and death, places lived, professions.

8. If possible, ask more than one relative for this information. Record all you learn.

9. Search a research library for relevant information.

12. Review records on Internet genealogy sites.

11. Concentrate on one line or one name (i.e., surname or mother's maiden name) at a time in order to simplify the process.

10. After filling in as much information as you can from these sources, prepare to take your search online.

13. See if there is a message board or forum for people with the surname you are looking for.

14. Post queries on genealogy bulletin boards, being as specific as possible about whom you are looking for information about.

15. Try to learn the places and dates of birth, marriage, and death, and the trade or profession of each ancestor.

18. Use your family tree and anecdotal information as the basis of a narrative about your family history.

17. Trace family lines back as far as you can to complete the family tree.

16. Also look for any anecdotal information: physical characteristics, special life events, etc.

how to craft a fair prenuptial agreement

80

With today's trend to marry later, once a career is established and personal assets are built up, and the prevalence of divorce and second marriages, prenuptial agreements have become increasingly common. Properly written, such a contract can protect the interests of both husband and wife should the marriage turn sour or when one partner outlives the other. A prenuptial agreement is especially important when either the bride or the groom has been previously married and has children from that marriage. The prenuptial agreement can establish the rights of these heirs and the rights of the spouse concerning any assets or property brought into the marriage. Anyone considering signing a prenuptial agreement should consult an attorney. That way there can be no claims of deception or coercion later on.

A prenuptial agreement is essentially a contract between bride and groom, and, as with any contract, its contents should be carefully considered. Even though you trust your prospective spouse enough to plan your future together, it's in your best interest to have separate attorneys review the terms of the agreement. What's critical is that you and your spouse be completely honest in disclosing your finances in this agreement. Lack of complete honesty in preparing this agreement will undermine its legality if the two of you, or you and your spouse's heirs, ever wind up in court. Most people equate a prenuptial agreement with the disposal of property in the event of a divorce, but the document can encompass many other areas, even if the two of you remain married the rest of your lives. A good prenuptial agreement will also determine the rights of your children from a previous marriage when you pass away, who gets your retirement benefits, and which of your personal assets are to be considered jointly owned. The latter will affect your new spouse if he or she ever needs to qualify for government-subsidized medical benefits. This agreement should also define your responsibility, if any, for debts your new spouse incurred before your marriage.

Full disclosure: As it pertains to a prenuptial agreement, an honest and complete reckoning of your financial situation, including property and assets, income sources, retirement plans, investments, and pensions, as well as all outstanding debt each brings to the marriage.

Postnuptial agreement: A contract between husband and wife, similar in scope and content to a premarital agreement. Also called a postmarital agreement. It can be more suspect than a prenuptial agreement, especially if either spouse files for divorce soon after signing it.

A prenuptial agreement is rarely called into question until the marriage has ended in divorce or there's disagreement on the use or disposal of assets either spouse brought into the marriage. Common grounds for challenging a prenuptial agreement include claims of coercion, asset hiding, misrepresentation, or having the husband's or wife's attorney represent both parties when drawing up the agreement. It should be easy for the two of you to draw up an agreement without argument. If not, it is better and potentially much cheaper to discover the type of person you're marrying before you formalize the relationship.

fyi

There is no law that states that you must have an attorney draw up your prenuptial agreement. But a prenuptial agreement is a binding legal contract that has many long-term legal implications. Even mere phrasing can betray your intent if you are not careful and precise in your wording. What's not spelled out in the agreement can be as important as what is.

resources

How to Write Your Own Premarital Agreement by Edward A. Haman (Sourcebooks, 1998): An overview of the prenuptial agreement, what it is, how it can protect you, and how you and your prospective partner can prepare your own.

1. Speak with your future spouse about the need for a prenuptial agreement.

2. Reason 1: Either or both of you have built up significant financial assets and investments prior to the marriage.

3. Reason 2: Either or both of you have financial obligations or benefits resulting from a previous marriage.

6. Reason 5: Either or both of you are burdened with a significant amount of debt.

5. Reason 4: Either or both of you own a share in a family business.

4. Reason 3: Either or both of you have had children prior to this marriage whom you want to share in your estate.

7. If circumstances warrant a prenuptial agreement, decide if you want to draft the contract yourselves or consult an attorney.

8. If consulting an attorney, each spouse should have an attorney.

9. The document must define any prior marriage history and the names of children resulting from that marriage.

12. The document must define who is entitled to those earnings after the marriage.

11. The document must define any income-generating business and investments you presently own.

10. The document must define property you own that you are bringing into the marriage.

13. The document must define any debts you carry and who will be responsible for them after your marriage.

14. The document must define how you want your estate divided and the rights of your children prior to the marriage.

15. The document must define any special circumstances related to your or your spouse's finances, such as health care needs, retirement plans, etc.

18. Have anything you do not understand explained to you by your attorney.

17. If your attorney did not draft the agreement, have him or her review it before you sign it.

16. Carefully review all the terms of the document.

19. Make the revisions your attorney recommends before signing.

20. After you have signed it, make copies for yourself, your spouse, and anyone else affected by the terms of the agreement.

21. Ask that your attorney keep a copy of the agreement in your file.

how to plan a wedding

81

the basics

Your wedding is one of the milestone events in your life and could be the largest project you and your prospective spouse ever pull off together. You both deserve a perfect wedding, however you define it. That takes planning, whether it will be a catered event for hundreds or an informal gathering of close family and friends following a trip to city hall. The months or year leading up to this big event can prove a stressful period for both bride and groom. Make it easier for yourselves by working together, with help from those closest to you, so that no detail is overlooked, from flowers to food.

inside information

Weddings are big business, and you'll have no trouble discovering ways to pour money into yours. So after you've chosen a date and agreed on the setting your concern should be the budget, as it's going to dictate everything else you do. The cost can prove staggering, and if you or your parents haven't been able to plan ahead and save, you may have to share the cost, pay for the event with your spouse, or plan a more modest affair. Someone has to take responsibility for all the details that contribute to a wedding. If you're planning an ambitious event, you may want to consider using the services of a wedding planner or coordinator, who can work with you so your dreams are realized. At the very least, consult a wedding-planning book or software or one of the many Web sites that offer planning guides and checklists to guide you through the process. Many of these details can be taken care of in the months or weeks leading up to the actual day. Other aspects of the event—church, hall, musicians—should be booked well in advance, or you may be forced to revise your plans. Depending on you or your spouse's faith, there may also be religious requirements that must be met before you can marry. There's much more to a perfect wedding than you realize until you've planned and enjoyed your own.

jargon

Bridal registry: A registration or selection of gifts the couple would like to receive as wedding gifts. The registry can include anything from a particular pattern of china or stemware to a range of items needed for their new home. Registering gifts relieves guests of the burden of deciding what to give the bride and groom and provides the couple with items they actually want and will use.

Wedding planner or consultant: A professional who specializes in coordinating all the details that go into a wedding. The more ambitious your wedding plans, the more valuable his or her assistance can be.

fyi

Your wedding day belongs to you and your spouse, and should be the event you want. Don't let others shape your plans or force you to compromise on the type of wedding they think you should have. If your budget is limited, consider having a quiet private ceremony and an informal party sometime afterward as a celebration. Forget the old rules that the bride's family pays for this, the groom's family for that. All should work together, as circumstances allow, to create an event all will be proud of and enjoy.

Don't go into debt for an extravagant affair on the assumption that gifts will cover the costs. (They may, but then again they may not.) Find out about any religious requirements well before your wedding day. If you leave them until the last few months, you may find you cannot get married within your faith when you want to. Success in marriage means mastering the art of compromise. Remember that as you work with your spouse to plan your big day.

Bridal Guide: A Complete Guide on How to Plan Your Wedding by Pamela Thomas (Bridal Guide Ltd., 1999): A revised and updated guide to planning for the perfect wedding, with lists to help make sure nothing is missed.

The Knot Ultimate Wedding Planner: Worksheets, Checklists, Etiquette, Calendars, & Answers to Frequently Asked Questions by Carley Roney (Broadway Books, 1999): A stand-alone guide to the nuts and bolts of planning a wedding, this planner walks the bridal couple through each major step from initial planning through the wedding day.

Emily Post's Guide to Weddings (Multimedia 2000, Inc.): Software version of a wedding planner, with advice on wedding etiquette, for both PC and Macintosh platforms. Contains a number of worksheets users can print and use.

Online: A number of sites are devoted to the needs of the aspiring couple, including software planners you can use to plan your event. Enter "bride" or "wedding" in your search engine, or start with sites such as **Wedding Web** (www.weddingweb.com) or **WeddingChannel.com** (www.weddingchannel.com).

1. If possible, plan and save ahead—years ahead if possible—anticipating the type of wedding you would like to have.

2. Decide with your prospective spouse on the type of wedding you'd like to have.

3. Choose a date.

12. Determine your budget for major expenses.

11. If handling the details by yourselves with close family and friends, obtain a printed wedding planner and begin filling in details.

10. If using a planner, meet with her, explain budget, plans, and proceed.

13. What will the costs of the wedding banquet hall and meal, photography and videography, musicians, and all related expenses be?

14. What will the costs of the wedding event—invitations, limousines flowers, organist, clergy's fee or donation to church, lodging for guests—be?

15. What will the costs of the wedding attire for bride and groom, attendants, etc., be?

22. Periodically review the list with all assisting in planning to make sure plans proceed on schedule and everyone is completing assignments.

4. Contact your church, temple or synagogue, or desired hall to make arrangements to be married on that date.

5. Make arrangements with the clergy or officiating person whom you want to perform the ceremony to be there on that day.

6. Inquire about any special religious requirements you must meet in order to be married in your faith.

9. Decide if you want to handle all the details yourself or hire a wedding consultant or planner.

8. Determine a budget.

7. Determine who will pay for the wedding.

16. What will the costs of miscellaneous expenses, such as favors for guests, engagement picture, newspaper announcement, etc., be?

17. Determine who will pay for these expenses.

18. Using a printed wedding planner as your guide, make a detailed list of all activities that must be completed and deadlines that must be met.

21. Note any responsibilities assumed by or assigned to others.

20. Make sure this chronology is as detailed as you can make it.

19. Categorize these activities on a schedule, such as one year before wedding date, nine months before, six months before, etc.

how to find quality child care at home and away

82

If you have children, there's nothing in the world more precious. Therefore, deciding how they are to be cared for when you are at work or away should be one of the most carefully weighed decisions you make. Unfortunately, it is often a choice dictated by economic concerns. Too many people, even those with considerable means, entrust the care of their children to the "best buy." You cannot escape your responsibility for finding the child care that offers the greatest value for your child. That value cannot be measured in the facilities and equipment, nor in the price, but in the human interaction that takes place in a safe, supportive environment. Only by actively investigating your options and meeting with and interviewing caregivers can you determine what's best for your child—and you.

There's no substitute for the care of a loving family member or friend when you cannot care for your child yourself. When that's not an option, you must consider several solutions and decide what's best for you and your child. These include licensed child care centers; in-home care providers; or an at-home nanny or au pair. Before you begin comparing the facilities, you should make yourself aware of your state's licensing requirements for child care facilities. In every child care scenario, the most important evaluation you must make concerns the person or persons who will be involved with your child. Does she seem truly interested in children? Why has she selected this type of work? What does she consider the most important aspect of the care she provides? Answers to questions such as these can give you real insight into the kind of person your child will be dealing with. There are pros and cons to each type of child care solution. A licensed child care center is a regulated facility with set requirements for safety, meals, student-teacher ratio, activities, and facilities. In-home care providers are usually run by women or couples who care for several children in their home. The structure is usually less formal than in a center, and they tend to be more willing to adapt to parents' scheduling needs. An at-home provider is technically your employee, and you can work out any scheduling arrangements that are acceptable to both. Some will even travel with you and care for your child when you are away. This can be the most expensive form of child care, but it offers the advantage of one-on-one attention in familiar surroundings. Always check the background and references of anyone you are considering entrusting with your child. With nannies or au pairs, check on the referring agency as well as the candidate. The search should always include an unannounced visit to any facility to see how things are run and how children are treated throughout the day.

fyi

Be sure to ask the caregiver what the policy on sick children is. Some simply will not care for a child who is ill, thereby forcing the parents to arrange for alternative care. On the other hand, if a center doesn't accept sick children it will lessen the chances that your child—and you—will be exposed to every bug making the rounds. When you will be entrusting your child to a child care center or in-home provider, it's important to know who will interact with your child and what criteria are used when hiring. Meet and interview these people as well. If you want to keep track of your child throughout the day but can't break away from the office, some child care centers now have Web sites where parents can view live images of the activity at the child care center. If this interests you, make sure the center has a secure Web site.

If a facility refuses to allow unannounced visits from parents, strike it from your list; it's likely it has something to hide. Your responsibility toward your child does not end with selecting a child care facility or individual. You must continually monitor the care and speak with both caregiver and child to make sure the relationship continues to serve the needs of your child. If you have any suspicion or concern about anything related to your child's care, take immediate action. No matter who is caring for your child, the ultimate responsibility for his or her welfare and well-being is entirely yours.

The Anxious Parents' Guide to Quality Child Care: An Informative, Step-by-Step Manual on Finding and Keeping the Finest Care for Your Child by Michelle Ehrich (Perigee Press, 1999): Steps parents through the considerations they must make when determining who will take care of their children.

The Safe Nanny Handbook: Everything You Need to Know to Have Peace of Mind While Your Child Is in Someone Else's Care by Peggy Robin (Quill Books, 1998): An informative book on hiring the right caregiver, based on the author's own experiences, surveys, and interviews.

The Unofficial Guide to Child Care by Ann Douglas (Hungry Minds, 1998): A mother of four's time- and money-saving tips on choosing child care, drawn from her considerable practical experience.

Child Care Action Campaign: This organization offers a selection of guides to child care for parents and providers and also publishes a newsletter on child care topics. Call (212) 239-0138.

Online: National Network for Child Care (www.nncc.org): This Web site includes many resources for child care professionals and parents, including a list of questions to use when considering in-home child care.

1. Decide what type of child care you want for your child: child care center, at-home care provider, or in-home provider.

2. Decide what you can afford to spend.

3. Ask friends, family, and coworkers for recommendations.

6. Make an initial visit to the facility unannounced. Note the cleanliness and overall maintenance of the facility.

5. Check with your local Better Business Bureau and state licensing board to see if there are any complaints against facilities you are considering.

4. Check with a state or local child care licensing agency for information on licensing requirements.

7. Are there any safety hazards?

8. Are the children being well cared for or neglected?

9. How are the groups organized?

12. Do the care providers seem angry or worn out?

11. What kinds of meals are provided?

10. How many students are there per teacher?

13. Are any of the children neglected or unattended?

14. Is there a medical professional on staff or affiliated with the facility?

15. Ask the center operator, in-home care provider, or candidate for nanny/au pair why he or she has chosen this type of work.

18. What does the care provider hope to accomplish with your child?

17. What will your child's typical day be like?

16. What licenses or relevant training and experience does the care provider have?

19. How flexible is the care provider in terms of scheduling or providing care on short notice?

20. What is the care provider's policy in the event a child becomes sick?

21. Does the care provider carry any liability insurance directly related to child care?

24. Ask for and check at least three references of parents who have children enrolled in this program, or former employers of a nanny/au pair.

23. What are the fees, and how are they structured?

22. Are drop-in visits from parents allowed and encouraged?

how to get help for a child with special needs

83

the basics

Most children's needs are met by the routine policies and procedures of social and educational organizations. For a child with special needs, however, some modifications and adjustments may be required to ensure that they have the same opportunities as their peers. Such planning must cater to the needs of each individual child. Some children with special needs are physically or mentally challenged in ways that require individualized attention and therapy. Others may be gifted with an intellectual capacity demanding the development of a more challenging school curriculum. Whatever the child's special needs, there are a variety of local, state, and federal laws designed to guarantee that the rights and needs of each individual child are met. As well intentioned as they are, they are often ineffectual without persistent lobbying by parents and others concerned with a child's welfare and well-being.

In order to ensure adequate help and attention for a child with special needs, it's important to understand the nature of his or her handicap or special abilities and the challenges this poses to the child and those who care for him or her. This may require consultation with and special counseling by physicians, therapists, psychologists, and educators—anyone involved with caring for the child. Once the special need is identified, it's important to know your child's legal right to support and services. Several federal laws apply, including the Individuals with Disabilities Education Act, Section 504 of the Rehabilitation Act of 1973, and the Americans with Disabilities Act. There may also be state and local statutes that apply specifically to children with special needs. Often the people who will be dealing directly with your child—teachers, coaches, youth leaders—are ignorant of these laws and the rights they guarantee your child. As the parent, you cannot escape your responsibility for knowing what these laws state, what guarantees they grant, and how they can be enforced. That knowledge will prove invaluable in working with educators, social service agencies, and community organizations. Ideally, you want to secure the kind of help that will not isolate your child from other children but will give him as normal an existence as possible. It may seem an uphill battle at times, but the law is on the side of you and your child. Once others become aware of the laws, they have no choice but to comply.

Early intervention: Support or services that may be required to foster the growth and development of an infant or toddler with special needs. Usually determination for such support can be made through a combination of the child's physician, public health or social service agency representative, or specialists employed by the local school district.

Individual Education Plan (IEP): An annually reviewed plan required under IDEA to meet the special education needs of a child. It is developed through the cooperative efforts of parents working with school district personnel and educators.

Individuals with Disabilities Act (IDEA): Federal legislation that stipulates that any state receiving federal monies must provide a free, appropriate education for all eligible children with disabilities. Eligibility is usually determined through a series of tests and evaluations conducted by the local school district.

The trend in legislation and practice over recent years has emphasized trying to integrate children with special needs into the mainstream in everything from classroom learning to outside activities such as scouting and organized sports. Since there may be resistance to taking steps to include special needs children into such programs, parents often need to become directly involved in the child's day-to-day activities to ensure that their needs are met. It is imperative that parents know the letter and intent of applicable laws and, if necessary, be prepared to solicit the help of an attorney to ensure that such laws are complied with for the good of their children.

warning

The earlier a child with special needs is identified, the better for his or her short- and long-term growth and development. If you have any doubts or questions about your child, discuss them with your pediatrician as soon as possible. Planning, lobbying for, and ensuring that your child's special needs are adequately served can seem emotionally overwhelming. Parents should not lose sight of their own needs. Support groups composed of parents facing the same challenges can prove a source of inspiration and advice for meeting these challenges. A child with special needs affects the lives of all around him or her, especially siblings. Keep their needs in mind, too, and help them deal with the special challenges they face.

resources

The Child with Special Needs: Encouraging Intellectual and Emotional Growth by Stanley I. Greenspan, M.D., Robin Simon, and Serena Wieder (Perseus Press, 1998): This comprehensive book for parents and educators outlines ways to help special needs children realize their emotional and intellectual potential.

The Survival Guide for Parents of Gifted Kids: How to Understand, Live with, and Stick Up for Your Gifted Child by Sally Yahnke Walker and Susan K. Perry (Free Spirit Publishing, 1991): An easy-to-understand, commonsense approach to addressing the unique challenges and problems faced by the parents of gifted children.

National Information Center for Children and Youth with Disabilities (www.nichcy.org): This Web site provides information and links to resources on disabilities and related issues for parents and educators.

1. Accept that it is your responsibility to see that the special needs of your child are adequately met.

2. If you have any concerns about an infant's or toddler's growth and development, discuss them with your physician immediately.

3. If the child is of school age, express your concerns to the child's teacher or school psychologist.

12. First focus on educational programs: contact the school system and request that your child be evaluated.

11. Outline what you want for your child, identifying the steps that must be taken to enable your child to live as normal a life as possible.

10. Investigate support groups for parents of children with special needs.

13. Based on this evaluation, arrange a meeting with education officials to develop an IEP responsive to your child's needs.

14. Understand your rights before you attend this meeting.

15. Express your concerns and goals and try to work with educators to develop an appropriate plan.

23. Continually monitor all your child's educational plans and participation in activities to ensure that his or her needs are adequately met.

22. Involve yourself in your child's school and other activities as much as possible.

4. Request that an assessment of your child be made to identify special needs.

5. Inform yourself as best you can about the need, how it affects the child, the challenges it imposes, and recommended therapies and treatment.

6. Involve other family members and friends by explaining the child's condition and the needs it creates.

9. Read up on federal, state, and local legislation concerning children with special needs.

8. Contact local public health and social service agencies to see what resources and facilities are available to help your child.

7. Solicit their help and support to include the child in normal, everyday activities.

16. Don't approve any elements of the plan that you feel are inadequate.

17. If necessary, exercise your right to an appeal or special hearing.

18. Identify school or social organizations you believe would be beneficial to your child.

21. Also be prepared to have an attorney draft a letter on your behalf if there is resistance.

20. Be prepared to cite any applicable laws if they express resistance.

19. Contact officials of these organizations and explain your child's special needs and your plans for participation.

how to make college tuition bills more manageable

84

For most families, college tuition is a major concern. In fact, funding a child's college education may be one of the family's major financial undertakings and investments. Ideally, this is an event you have been planning for since the birth of your child, and you have the resources to cover tuition and related expenses without sacrifice. For many people, though, the expenses of raising a family preclude adequately planning for college. They dread the college years for fear that they may not be able to give their child or children the kind of education they want or deserve. Many of those fears are unfounded. There are a variety of financial resources available to the college-age student and family that ensure that any child who wants a college education should be able to finance it. Pooling the resources to pay for education is the easy part; the challenge lurks in managing their use in such a way that the family or student isn't burdened with long-term debt.

Today's students pay for their education using whatever combination of resources is available to them: family savings, trust funds, educational IRAs, academic or athletic grants, school or private scholarships, federal or state grants, government-backed loans, home equity loans. Like everything else, the costs of college keep climbing, so the earlier parents begin planning to finance an education, the better. Even a small amount invested or saved on a regular basis while the child is growing will help defer the impact of costs later. With an educational IRA, a parent can set aside as much as $2,000 per year in anticipation of costs and enjoy the same tax advantage as with other IRA investments. After long-term savings and investments, the next steps in making education costs most manageable come when it's time to select a school (see Lifemap 88). Costs vary widely between private and public institutions. Colleges can be very responsive to the needs of the students they want most when it comes to putting together a financial aid package. A student who has demonstrated special academic or athletic ability has the most to gain. Unless a student receives a full academic scholarship, he should apply for financial aid and scholarships. A school may have its own criteria for awarding each of its scholarships. Determining financial need, and what the family or student is expected to contribute toward costs, is based on accepted formulas established by state or federal legislation. Qualification determination is based on information supplied in such applications as the Free Application for Federal Student Aid (FAFSA) and the College Board's Financial Aid Profile. Based on family and student income and expected contributions toward tuition costs, the school will put together a financial aid package, which may include grants, scholarships, and loans. Consider loans a last option; exhaust all other potential sources of financial assistance before assuming future debt. If other sources won't cover all the expenses, ask the school about a payment plan that will allow you to make monthly payments to cover costs.

jargon

Estimated family contribution (EFC): The cash amount the parents and/or student are expected to contribute to cover tuition and related expenses each year. This is determined using set formulas, based on an analysis of information provided in the student's application for financial aid.

Financial aid package: The combination of grants, loans, and work-study programs the school's financial aid administrator creates to enable a student to cover tuition and related education expenses.

Work-study: A form of financial aid in which part of the cost of tuition is paid for in exchange for work done by the student, usually on campus.

Careful choice of a career or plans for after college can help reduce costs. Enrollment in the ROTC, for example, can be a source of assistance in exchange for a commitment to enter military service after graduation. Some communities also offer special grants or assistance to students who pledge to return there as teachers or medical practitioners. Community colleges typically cost less than four-year colleges, yet four-year institutions may accept many credits earned at two-year schools. You can dramatically reduce the total costs of a college education by enrolling in a community college, then transferring to a four-year school. It's important to understand how the government determines student need and expected family/student contributions before applying for aid. For example, you may be able to increase the amount of available aid by having more than one family member enrolled in school or by reducing the amount of reportable assets in savings accounts. In order to qualify for any state financial aid, students must usually attend a school in their state.

Submit applications for financial aid as early as possible, and always meet deadlines. Financial aid decisions are often made on a first come, first serve basis. Tuition is only one of the costs of a college education. Unless the student will continue to live at home, there may be considerable expenses involved in room and board. And a semester's worth of books for four or five courses quickly adds up to several hundred dollars. As a student nears college age, expect to hear from companies offering scholarship search services. Be wary: many provide little more information than you could gather on your own.

How to Go to College Almost for Free by Benjamin R. Kaplan (Waggle Dancer Books, 2000): Drawn from the author's own success in winning scholarships and grants, an insider's guide to scholarships with tips on how to find, apply for, and win them.

College Financial Aid for Dummies by Herm Davis and Joyce Lain Kennedy (Hungry Minds, 1999): A thorough yet easily understood guide to finding and applying for all the financial aid a student qualifies for.

Online: 2001 Colleges, College Scholarships, and Financial Aid Page (www.college-scholarships.com) provides college-bound students with information on hundreds of college scholarships and a free college scholarship search engine. **FastWeb** (www.studentservices.com) offers a directory of more than four thousand schools with information on admissions, financial aid, and scholarships.

1. Plan ahead: set up a college fund, special savings account, or educational IRA in anticipation of higher education expenses.

2. Begin investigating schools and scholarships as soon as a student enters high school.

3. Apply for all applicable scholarships before the deadlines.

11. Compile a list of all resources available to cover college costs.

10. Investigate such sources of financial aid as enrollment in the ROTC or community grants for teachers.

9. Consider enrolling in a two-year college initially for cost savings, then transferring to a four-year college that will accept its credits.

12. Familiarize yourself with how the estimated family contribution is computed.

13. Take any steps you can to reduce this amount.

14. Complete the Free Application for Federal Student Aid and any other applications required by individual schools as early as possible in the calendar year.

4. If your child's performance on the ACT or SAT falls just short of qualifying for academic scholarships, consider enrolling him or her in a program to improve scores.

5. If your child has special academic or athletic ability, discuss with your school's guidance counselor what special scholarships he or she may qualify for, or what schools might be most interested in attracting such students.

8. Make a realistic assessment of the total cost of education, including living expenses, transportation, and books.

7. Compare the cost of private and public education, in state and out of state.

6. Contact any appropriate schools and their financial aid departments to see what assistance may be available for your child and how to apply.

15. Carefully review all elements of any financial aid package that comes back.

16. Consider student loans to be a last resort.

17. Investigate payment plans as a way to make tuition costs manageable.

20. If the student plans to work while attending school, be aware of the student's expected contribution to cover costs above set income limits and how a higher personal income can affect available financial aid.

19. If you must borrow to cover the cost of education, consider the advantages of a government-backed loan with deferred payment.

18. Consider taking fewer courses at a time to reduce expenses.

how to choose and gain admission to the right college or university

85

There are hundreds of schools eager to accept application fees from aspiring students, whether or not they qualify. Selecting and gaining admission to the right college or university is a decision that demands careful consideration and planning. A college education provides part of the foundation for the future, and it should be a foundation that takes into account your child's strengths and abilities, his personal preferences, and the type of environment that will inspire him to excel. It's not an endeavor that should be entrusted to a last-minute decision. Rather, a college-bound students should start thinking in terms of higher learning as soon as they enter high school. Challenging themselves in high school will allow them to hone the skills that will serve them in their subsequent academic careers. That work will also help identify the special talents and abilities they will want to develop further in college. Their final choice should take into account the talents, interests, and abilities they identify while in high school, the school that offers the best program in support of these, and what they can reasonably afford.

Applying to the right college requires first that your child identify what he or she wants from the college experience. Then, he can match his skills and expectations with schools where he has a reasonable chance of getting accepted. Colleges are as varied as the students who enter them: some are sprawling cities-within-cities; others quaint retreats in the countryside. Some are known for their athletic programs, others for academics. Your child may want the personalized attention of a school where there's a high faculty-to-student ratio or thrive in an environment where the latest technology opens up new options in the learning experience. The point is that selecting a college should be a personal choice. You may want your child to attend your alma mater, but what was right for you isn't necessarily right for your child. Parents should certainly help with the selection process, but if they dictate a choice, they may be doing the student a disservice. So the selection process begins by honestly assessing one's abilities and interests and then identifying the colleges with the best programs and schools to complement them. In the application package you'll find descriptions of these programs as well as a profile of the student body. The percentage of students who actually graduate from the school, and how long it takes them to earn their diplomas, may indicate overall satisfaction with the school. The information accompanying the application also details costs, what financial aid is available, and who receives it. Financial considerations must enter into the selection process, as the cost of a college education can overwhelm a student or family with limited resources. Ideally, you don't want your child to finish his or her education saddled with debt. Unfortunately, sometimes there's no choice.

Academic ranking: Where your child ranks in his or her high school class; academic ranking is one of the important criteria colleges consider during the selection process.

Application essay: As part of the application process, most schools require students to submit an application essay. It should be well written and grammatically correct: a description of who your child is, what matters to him, what he wants from the college experience, and what he, as a person, can offer the school.

In evaluating applicants, colleges use a variety of criteria, including rank in class, grade point average, standardized test scores, involvement in outside activities and the community, personal essays and interviews, and letters of recommendation. A letter from a distinguished alumnus or alumna can help, especially if that person is a strong financial supporter of the school. Students should limit their applications to schools they'd really like to attend, with a clear first preference and then backup choices. If your child can't get into the college of choice the first time around, he or she can always transfer there later after proving him- or herself in another institution. College fairs are a good source for gathering information about different schools and their financial aid packages and having preliminary questions answered by school officials.

warning ●

Any place can be made to look good in an expensive brochure. Don't base decisions on which colleges to apply to on such materials. If your child is really serious about a school, encourage him or her to visit the campus. Ask the admissions office to arrange a tour and an opportunity to speak with students and faculty. If your child waits until his or her senior year to start worrying about college, he or she may be unprepared and unable to demonstrate the academic qualifications his or her first choice wants in its students. Students who have decided they're college bound need to think ahead and take the "tough" courses that will develop their skills as they prove themselves. Take application deadlines seriously, and make sure your child provides everything in his or her application the school wants. If the application isn't in on time, his or her name will be at the very bottom of the acceptance list—if it even makes it.

resources ●

College Admissions: A Crash Course for Panicked Parents, 2nd edition, by Sally Rubenstone and Sidonia Dalby (IDG Books Worldwide, 1997): Admissions experts' insight into the admissions process, with practical, straightforward advice for parents nervous about getting their child into the right school.

College Match: A Blueprint for Choosing the Best School for You by Steven Antonoff and Marie A. Friedmann (Octameron Associates, 1999): A step-by-step guide that helps students determine what they should look for in the college experience and find the right school.

Online: There are a number of Internet sites dedicated to helping students select, apply for, and receive financial aid from the schools right for them.

1. Think ahead: if you're college bound, concentrate on the tougher academic and college prep courses.

2. Colleges want a well-rounded individual: get involved with school and community activities.

3. Start thinking in terms of what especially interests you and careers you might want to pursue.

6. Before you begin writing away for application packages, conduct a self-assessment of what you want from the college experience.

5. Sit down with your parents and discuss your options in college and what you can afford.

4. In your sophomore year, sit down with a guidance counselor to begin exploring schools you might like to attend.

7. What are your special skills and academic abilities?

8. Do you have any special athletic, musical, artistic, or other talents?

9. What majors are you considering?

12. Urban, suburban, or rural setting?

11. Public or private institution?

10. Would you prefer a large or small school?

13. A large campus or a smaller school?

14. Will you board or live at home or off-campus?

15. What school activities would you like to be involved in?

18. Visit their Web sites and request application packages.

17. Use a Web search engine or college guide to narrow your selection to a handful of schools.

16. What can you afford? How much financial aid will you require?

19. Review these with parents and advisers to narrow your selection to a few schools.

20. Compare your academic profile with that of the typical student.

21. If possible, visit each campus to get a feel for the school.

24. Inquire about and apply for any scholarship programs for which you may qualify.

23. The summer before your senior year, narrow your selection to the schools you would actually like to attend.

22. Talk to students or alumni of these schools about their experiences there.

25. Get letters of reference from teachers, employers, school alumni, and others who know you.

26. If a personal essay is required, take time to make it your best expression of why you want to attend this school, what you can offer, and what you hope to gain from the experience.

27. Submit applications, fees, and support materials before deadlines close.

30. If disappointed that you are not accepted by your first choice, consider starting college somewhere else and transferring to that school later.

29. Compare financial aid packages before deciding which school to attend.

28. Wait until you hear from all the schools you applied to before deciding which one to attend.

31. If you attend a school and decide you are not happy there, explore transferring to another school that originally interested you.

how to craft a fair divorce settlement

86

The decision to marry is an emotional one that creates a financial and legal institution. Dismantling that union can prove emotionally and financially wrenching, especially when either husband or wife looks to the divorce procedure as a way to get even with or punish the former partner. It's in the best interest of neither to go this route. If you truly want to craft a divorce settlement that is fair to your spouse and yourself, you need to set your differences aside. Work together one final time to negotiate a mutually acceptable division of property and assets, as well as custody arrangements if you have children from the marriage. For some couples, that doesn't seem an option. But even those who are at odds may see the wisdom of working things out together when the emotional and financial strain that can be part of a prolonged court battle to undo what's already broken is considered.

The laws governing grounds for divorce, division of property, and child custody arrangements vary from state to state. The first step for any couple considering dissolution of their union should be an investigation of the state laws where they plan to seek the divorce. There is no law that says you must involve an attorney in your divorce proceedings. Still, it's in the best interests of both parties to have their own attorney review any agreement they do work out before filing it with the court. A divorce agreement has long-term legal implications that neither of you may understand or foresee. The two areas where a divorcing couple are most likely to be at odds are the division of property and child custody. If the couple cannot agree on how to divide all they've accrued while married, the courts will decide based on state law. Most states divide property based on a concept called equitable distribution, while a few treat everything as community property. Knowing how the court will divide your property can provide encouragement to work things out on your own and save the expense of going to court. A fair settlement is one that is acceptable to both sides. It takes both parties' needs into account and recognizes the contribution each has made to the marriage. If the couple cannot work together to draft a mutually acceptable settlement, both are likely to feel that the decision imposed by the legal system is unfair.

Community property: In states that use the community property principle, property owned by the couple together, or its value, is divided equally between the couple at the time of the divorce.

Contested divorce: A divorce is contested when the spouse who has been sued for divorce does not accept or challenges the grounds on which the other partner is seeking the dissolution of their marriage. A contested divorce often results in a bitter court battle.

Equitable distribution: The "fair" distribution of a couple's property following a divorce. Often, "fair" means that the principal wage earner will receive a larger share of the assets, as much as two thirds, with the remainder going to the other partner.

No-fault divorce: A simplified divorce proceeding in which a couple seeks to dissolve their union based on reasons that do not have to be proven in court, such as irreconcilable differences or incompatibility.

When couples bring significant assets or possessions into a marriage, it's in their best interest to draw up a detailed prenuptial agreement. It should stipulate who owns what prior to marriage and even how property and assets acquired during the marriage are to be divided in the event of a divorce. Couples who can agree to work together, even when there are considerable differences, often turn to divorce mediators as an alternative to the ordeal of divorce court. Impartial mediators are trained to counsel couples in resolving their differences and crafting a divorce agreement that has the best interests of both parties at heart. Mediators typically charge by the hour and can help reach an acceptable agreement at a fraction of what it would take to achieve a comparable result in court.

When a marriage sours, some spouses who are looking toward divorce try to run up exorbitant bills as a way of "getting even." In the end they often harm only themselves. The divorce agreement will address the division of liabilities as well as assets. A protracted courtroom battle over the divorce settlement can cost more in expenses than what you are fighting for. Be realistic about what you can expect to gain from pursuing this course. And carefully consider whether it's worth your while to contest a divorce, unless to demonstrate that the grounds for divorce are without merit. If you can prove that, the deciding judge will take it into account when determining the settlement. It's highly unlikely, though, that a judge will order a couple to stay married against the wishes of either husband or wife.

Divorce Yourself: The National No-Fault Divorce Kit (Legal Self-Help Series) by Dan Sitarz (Nova Publishing, 1998): A divorce guide with instructions, questionnaires, checklists, and sample documents, designed to help consumers prepare for divorce without the need for an attorney. Includes a sample marital settlement agreement and an appendix on divorce laws in all states.

Divorce & Money: How to Make the Best Financial Decisions During Divorce by Violet Woodhouse and Dale Fetherling (Nolo Press, 2000): A guide to divorce and the many financial considerations that should be taken into account for the long-term good of both parties.

1. Recognize a substantial share of marriages ultimately end in divorce. If you each have sizable individual assets, think ahead and work with your spouse to develop a fair prenuptial agreement before you tie the knot.

2. Consider divorce a last resort. Try to work out your differences with the help of a marriage counselor before you take that step.

3. If there seems no alternative, read up on your state laws pertaining to divorce and dissolution of property.

12. When the agreement is acceptable, have it reviewed by your attorney before signing.

11. Develop a mutually acceptable plan for child custody and alimony.

10. Under a mediator's guidance, work with your spouse to hammer out an acceptable agreement on the division of property and assets.

13. Make revisions as recommended by your attorney.

14. Sign the final agreement and file it with the court.

15. If you and your spouse cannot work together on the divorce, retain an attorney to represent you in the divorce proceedings.

4. Inform your partner of your decision.

5. If this is a mutually acceptable no-fault divorce, begin working together to craft a mutually acceptable, fair divorce settlement.

6. Consider crafting your settlement yourselves or using a divorce mediator.

9. Prepare a list of children's names, Social Security numbers, schools, etc.

8. Gather information on all jointly owned property, bank accounts, investments, pension funds, and other resources.

7. Consult with an attorney, even before you visit a mediator, about what you need to take into account when you draft an agreement.

16. Inform your attorney of all property, investments, children, etc., involved.

17. Determine the grounds for divorce.

18. Have your attorney prepare a divorce proceeding, detailing your grounds for divorce, property assets, children, and what you seek from the divorce settlement.

20. Be prepared to justify any claims or accusations in court proceedings.

19. Entrust the courts to apply the laws of the state to your request.

how to win custody of your child

the basics

Going through a divorce can be an emotionally draining experience for all those involved. There is no one more likely to carry the scars of this breakup of a family longer or more deeply than the children of a broken marriage. Powerless to stop the changes redefining their lives, they often find themselves caught up in a tug-of-war over affections and allegiances they cannot win, no matter which side they take. And most children don't want to take sides; they don't want to see their family dissolve at all. Unfortunately, the battle over child custody can be the most contentious part of the divorce proceedings. But it shouldn't be if the best interests of the children are considered. Unless either parent is abusive, suffers psychological or emotional problems, or is an alcoholic or drug addict, each should remain a vital influence on the child's life after the formal breakup of the marriage. The only real winners or losers in a child custody case are the children, and concern about their best interests should guide their parents through these difficult negotiations.

There was a time when the "natural" assumption about divorce was that the mother would get custody of the children. Today, though, the courts tend to favor some form of joint custody that keeps both parents involved for the good of the children. How the law determines what's in the best interests of the children varies from state to state. As with divorce law, it's prudent to look into what the laws in your state favor when it comes to deciding custody issues and who should assume primary responsibility for raising the children. Ideally, the parents should be able to set aside their other differences and put the needs of their children first when trying to work out a custody arrangement. If they can't, the decision will be left to the judge presiding over the case. Unless a parent has been abusive or can be shown to pose a real threat to the child, the court ruling will likely favor some form of joint custody. Any parent seeking sole custody will have to present a strong case that the other parent poses a real threat to the child. Supportive evidence may include police, hospital, and social services reports detailing incidents of abuse. The stability of the household where the child will live and the relationship between parent and child can be the determining factors in deciding custody. Attempts to resolve child custody inevitably entail discussions about alimony and child support. Ultimately, these decisions will determine the quality of life for both children and parents after the dissolution of the marriage. Even if the parents are able to resolve all other issues related to the divorce settlement, those contentious issues often drive them to court, where a judge will make a decision based on all other factors in the case and the ultimate needs and welfare of the child or children.

jargon

Joint custody: Arrangement whereby parents who do not live together share responsibilities for the raising of their child or children.

Legal custody: The right and responsibility to make legal decisions for a minor child whether or not a parent has physical custody of that child. This is often a right equally shared by both parents, no matter what other custody arrangements have been made.

Physical custody: The parent with whom a child resides is said to have physical custody. This may be a shared right, worked out by the parents as part of their divorce settlement, or decreed by the judge presiding over the case.

Visitation rights: When one parent does not have physical custodial rights to the children, the divorce settlement may include the granting of visitation rights. These may include a set visitation schedule if either parent is unwilling to cooperate and allow the other to visit the child.

Unless there are mitigating circumstances, the courts tend to favor some custodial arrangement that keeps both parents directly involved in the child's upbringing. This may mean some structure that promotes joint physical custody as well as joint legal custody. Although the courts consistently uphold the rights of parents to see their children, one recent ruling by the U.S. Supreme Court established that no such right exists for grandparents. Among the factors the courts take into consideration when deciding which arrangements are in the best interest of the children and who is to be awarded custody are the children's present lifestyle and well-being, the willingness of either parent to work with the other to put the children's interests first, and sometimes, if a child is older, the preference that child expresses.

Children rarely have the experience or insight to understand what is going on in a divorce or why their home life has taken this turn. Some may even blame themselves. Parents should be sensitive to how their divorce is affecting their children and keep their welfare at the forefront of their concerns. Anyone who approaches winning custody of the children as a way to "punish" a former spouse should seriously consider whether he or she has the emotional stability to be a good parent. Divorce can be traumatic for children. Don't make it worse by putting the burden on children to demonstrate whom they love most or pushing for an arrangement that divides close siblings between different households.

Child Custody Made Simple: Understanding the Law of Child Custody and Child Support by Webster Watnik (Single Parent Press, 2000): A handbook on how child custody issues can be resolved, with real-life examples drawn from family court cases and insight into how the legal system tends to look at child custody issues.

The Best Parent Is Both Parents: A Guide to Shared Parenting in the 21st Century by David L. Levy (Hampton Roads Publishing Company, 1993): A work promoting the idea that joint child custody is the best thing for children of divorce. The book also includes an index of the custody laws and mediation statutes for all fifty states.

1. Read up on your state's laws pertaining to divorce and child custody.

2. In the light of what you learn, try to set aside your differences and hostilities in order to work out arrangements that put the best interest of the child or children first.

3. Counsel your children about what is happening in the marriage.

4. Try to get them to discuss their feelings and preferences without asking them to choose one parent over the other.

5. If necessary, seek the help of a divorce mediator to resolve these issues.

6. Among things to consider when trying to reach custody agreement are the children's present home and overall environment.

7. Consider their involvement in school and other activities.

8. Consider the ability of either parent to continue providing such an environment.

9. Consider the stability of both parents and the stability of their households.

10. Consider the potential resentment of children in a home with a new spouse or partner.

11. Consider the ability of either or both parents to provide adequate financial support for the children.

12. Strive first to reach some custodial arrangement that keeps both parents directly involved in the children's life.

13. Work toward some form of joint physical and legal custody arrangement.

14. Develop a plan that describes what these arrangements are, who will get the children when, and what types of decisions each parent will handle separately or jointly.

15. If you decide it's in the children's best interest that one parent have sole custody, work out the details of a visitation schedule.

16. Work out a mutually acceptable plan for child support payments, when they are to be made, by whom, and the amount.

17. If you cannot work out custody or child support arrangements on your own, be prepared to let the courts impose a custodial agreement.

18. Work with your divorce attorney to determine what type of arrangement you want.

19. If you want sole custody, gather documentation that establishes why the other parent should not have or share custody.

20. Include any police or hospital reports or orders of protection that demonstrate that the other parent poses a real threat to the welfare of the children.

21. Include in your request that any visitation rights granted by the court stipulate that visits be supervised and monitored.

how to plan a funeral

88

Everyone recognizes the importance of carefully weighing major decisions such as buying a home or car or paying for a college education. But there's another major expense most individuals and families neglect until the last minute: a funeral. Unfortunately, when the need for a funeral arrives, those who must make the decisions are so overwhelmed by emotion and grief that they often can't make rational decisions. Expenses can quickly get out of hand in a last effort to demonstrate love for the deceased, without really abiding by what they may have wanted for themselves. A funeral is an event we can all anticipate and something we can easily plan for. Advance planning saves family and friends the burden of trying to do the right thing by us. It can also protect them from making purchases under duress and assuming debt it may take years to pay off. Planning a funeral in advance also gives each of us the opportunity to be remembered with favorite readings, music, and speakers that testify to who we were as people and what mattered in our lives.

Funerals are big business, and the cost of the typical wake, funeral, casket, vault, and burial can quickly run into thousands of dollars and leave survivors with debt. Loved ones may equate what they spend with an expression of what the deceased meant to them, but their best intentions may not reflect the real wishes of the deceased. No one will know unless you take the time in advance to outline how you would like to be remembered. If it seems like a morbid undertaking, think of it as a service you are doing for your loved ones. Planning ahead will spare them emotional decisions and unnecessary financial burdens. Your funeral should be an expression of who you are. Your plans can be as detailed as you want them to be, right down to the type of casket, what type of flowers you'd like, and where you want donations sent in your name. Make your plans as specific as possible; outline the type of memorial service you want, who you want to preside, where you want it held, who you'd like to deliver eulogies, what you want done with your remains, what type of marker you want. Be specific, but leave some room for flexibility. A funeral may celebrate the dead, but it is a ceremony for the living. Leave them the opportunity to use it to exorcise their own grief in whatever way will help them as well.

Preneed insurance: A specialized type of life insurance policy that pays out benefits for the projected costs of a funeral.

Preplanning: Planning and arranging your funeral in advance as a way to spare loved ones emotional decisions and save costs. Preplanning often includes prepaying the funeral costs, either in a lump payment or on a payment schedule.

Many funeral homes now offer individuals the opportunity to prepay their funeral costs in scheduled payments set at the time the individual makes his plans. This course offers protection against inflation, relieves family members of an emotional burden, and ensures that your wishes are carried out. If you opt for cremation, for instance, an ornate casket may be an unnecessary expense. Those who prefer cremation should also provide specific plans on what they want done with their remains, as family members often have trouble deciding what's proper.

Avoid any type of funeral package. A funeral director should be willing to provide an itemized list of all expenses related to the cost of a funeral. Without such a list, you have no way to compare costs or identify areas where you may be able to save. The casket is often the major funeral expense, with many people paying an exorbitant amount for a coffin they believe will protect their remains indefinitely. A coffin, however, may postpone but will not prevent the inevitable. If you opt for a prepaid funeral plan, make sure you have a written, itemized list of exactly what you are paying for. Find out how the money will be used until the time of the funeral and what will happen to any amount left over after the funeral expenses are met. What happens to the fund if your death takes place away from home? Also, make sure you have the option to cancel the plan and get your money back.

resources

At Journey's End: The Complete Guide to Funerals and Funeral Planning by Abdullah Fatteh, Naaz Fatteh, and David R. Pearson (Health Information Press, 1999): A complete guide, reference, and resource for an event most would rather not discuss: planning one's own funeral and/or the funeral of a loved one.

Before It's Too Late—Don't Leave Your Loved Ones Unprepared by Sue L. Thompson and Emily J. Oishi (Sue Thompson Press, 2000): A workbook guide with simple step-by-step instructions for everything related to advance planning, from recording personal information through final arrangements for the funeral service, obituary, and disposition of remains.

1. Contact area funeral homes and see if they can supply checklists, forms, or brochures to help you plan your funeral in advance.

2. Also inquire about preneed insurance and prepaid funeral plans.

3. Use forms from funeral homes, books, or the Internet to plan the details of the funeral.

12. What type of casket do you want?

11. Or do you want the family to make that decision?

10. Do you want an open or closed casket?

13. What type of flowers do you want?

14. Are you a veteran who wants a flag on his casket?

15. Are there any favorite photographs you want displayed at the wake?

24. What do you want done with your remains after the service?

23. Whom would you like to deliver eulogies at the funeral service?

22. Make sure to include a copy of the texts of any special readings.

25. If opting for cremation, what should be done with your ashes?

26. If opting for burial, where do you want to be buried?

27. What type of graveside service do you want?

4. Where do you want your obituary to appear?

5. Do you want a public viewing?

6. How long should this public viewing last?

9. If so, who do you want leading them?

8. Do you want prayers during your viewing?

7. Where do you want the viewing held?

16. In lieu of flowers, identify any charities to which you would like donations in your name to be made.

17. Where would you like your memorial or funeral service held?

18. Whom do you want to officiate?

21. What readings from scripture or literature would you like?

20. If you want live music, whom do you want to perform or sing?

19. What music selections do you want played?

28. Are there any special readings or prayers you want read there?

29. What would you like written on your headstone?

30. Once your plans are finalized, tell family members what you've done and let them know where they will be able to find these plans when needed.

31. Provide them with an itemized list of any prepaid funeral arrangements and/or a copy of a preneed insurance policy.

how to become a naturalized U.S. citizen

89

Every year, tens of thousands of immigrants, of all races and from all corners of the world, take the proud step of becoming naturalized citizens of the United States. They recognize that American citizenship is a privilege that allows them to participate in and enjoy the benefits of our unique freedoms and system of government. As citizens they can vote freely in local and national elections, carry an American passport, and participate in the many government programs designed to improve life for all Americans. And as U.S. citizens they can help other members of their family take the same steps by sponsoring their applications for immigration, residency, and citizenship. The process through which these immigrants become citizens is called naturalization. It is not a complicated process, but there are certain requirements that all applicants must meet before they are granted citizenship.

Every applicant for naturalization must be at least eighteen years old, have entered the United States legally, and have lived within its borders for at least five years, including the full two and a half years prior to applying. For the spouse of an American citizen, the residency requirement is just three years total and the one and a half years immediately preceding the application. In either case, the applicant must be able to demonstrate that he or she has been of good moral character for the five years preceding the application. Those who meet these basic requirements must formally apply for citizenship at an area office of the Immigration and Naturalization Service. Some application requirements include a set of fingerprints, proof you entered the United States legally, photographs, and brief information on personal background. After the application is processed, the applicant will be subject to an interview conducted by an INS representative. At this interview he is expected to demonstrate basic proficiency in reading, writing, and speaking English. Special circumstances, such as the age of the applicant and the length of time he or she has lived within U.S. borders, may be considered to waive the English-language requirement. All applicants for naturalization must also demonstrate a basic knowledge of U.S. history, government, and citizenship as part of the application-interview process. Once these hurdles are cleared and the application is approved, the applicant must take an oath of allegiance to the United States and its Constitution before he or she is officially granted citizenship. As part of this oath, he or she must renounce allegiance to any foreign government and agree to take up arms for the United States or work for the national interest if called upon to do so.

Alien: A person who resides in the United States or its territories but is not a citizen.

Green card: The registration card given to legal permanent residents by the Immigration and Naturalization Service.

Legal permanent resident: A person who has legally entered the United States and is registered as a resident with the Immigration and Naturalization Service. The length of time a person has carried LPR status may be one of the factors considered in the application for citizenship.

Naturalization petition: The application form completed and submitted by a legal permanent resident to apply for U.S. citizenship. This petition is filed with a naturalization court through the Immigration and Naturalization Service.

Naturalization is not the only way a person born outside the United States can gain citizenship. Children born in U.S. territories, such as Puerto Rico and Guam, are automatically granted citizenship at birth. Also, children born outside the United States to parents who are American citizens are also eligible for citizenship at birth. Children under eighteen who have legal permanent resident status may also become citizens at the same time their parents—or parent, if only one is surviving—meets the qualifications to become a naturalized citizen. The process, from completing the initial application for naturalization through taking the oath granting citizenship, takes, on average, from three to six months.

Certain circumstances automatically disqualify an application for citizenship. Habitual drunkards, polygamists, prostitutes, drug addicts, and career gamblers are all considered to lack the good moral character required of citizens. Additionally, conviction for murder or any other aggravated felony crime automatically and permanently disqualifies an applicant for consideration for citizenship. Members of the Communist and Nazi parties, or any subversive group bent on the overthrow of the U.S. government, need not bother to apply, either.

Local office of the Immigration and Naturalization Service: Everything an applicant for naturalized citizenship needs to study, apply, and qualify for citizenship is available through the local or regional office of the INS. To find the office nearest you, call (800) 375-5283 or visit the INS Web site at www.ins.usdoj.gov.

1. Enter the United States legally.

2. Register with the Immigration and Naturalization Service as a legal permanent alien.

3. Reach the minimum age requirement of eighteen.

4. Meet the residency requirements for an individual or for an individual married to an American citizen. Don't meet any of the criteria that automatically disqualify an applicant for naturalization.

5. Visit the local INS office and complete Form N-400, "Application for Residency."

6. Have photos taken to submit with the completed application.

7. Provide details to demonstrate that you have been of "good moral character" for the five years preceding the application.

8. In the weeks or months while the application is being processed, study the information supplied by the INS on U.S. history and government and citizenship in anticipation of the interview/exam.

9. Submit to an INS interview/application review. At this interview, demonstrate the ability to read, write, and speak basic English unless special circumstances apply.

10. Also be able to demonstrate a basic understanding of U.S. government, history, and the responsibilities of citizenship.

11. Be prepared to demonstrate that you are of good moral character and have not been in trouble with the law.

12. Upon approval, participate in a ceremony in which you take the oath of allegiance to the United States, renounce any foreign allegiance, and vow to uphold the U.S. Constitution and serve in the armed forces or national interest in some other way if called upon.

how to research a
health problem

90

Modern medicine is one of the marvels of our time. Diseases and injury that once required prolonged care in bed, if not worse, are now treated routinely. Thanks to the advances in health care, more people can look forward to living longer, more productive lives than in any previous generation. Today's medical consumer often finds, however, that physicians and other health care providers rarely take or have the time to adequately explain the nature of a health problem, the rationale for its treatment, or the benefits and possible side effects of the drugs they prescribe. For many consumers, that's fine. But those who want a deeper understanding of what's going on in their bodies must undertake their own research. This need to know may be especially critical when someone is diagnosed with a serious or uncommon disease. Many patients aren't sufficiently prepared for how their illness may progress, or they may dwell on groundless fears. Thoroughly researching a health problem can also alert a patient to alternative therapies and potentially harmful drug interaction or put him or her into contact with groups of people who have grappled with the same condition.

There's no substitute for a physician's care and experience; anyone interested in research-ing his or her health problems should not take his or her layman's knowledge as a substi-tute for a doctor's. That said, there are a number of standard reference books that should be on the bookshelf of anyone interested in learning more about his or her medical condi-tion. These include a thorough medical guide for men, women, or families; a medical dic-tionary; and an updated guide to prescription drugs. A guide to symptoms can also help identify the preliminary signs of an illness and what warrants a visit to the doctor, but it should never be relied on for diagnosing a disease. It's a good idea to have more than one of each of these books on hand, as no single volume has all the answers. Today, access to the Internet is as critical as the volumes in your library to learning about your health problems. There are many Web sites devoted to medical topics and issues, with up-to-the-minute reports on the latest research and breakthroughs in medical technology. News-groups can also prove an invaluable source of information on particular illnesses and to share experiences or concerns with other patients. Your physician and his staff should also be willing to advise you on what you need to know and where you can look to learn more.

jargon •

Alternative medicine: An all-encompassing term that describes a broad range of treatments and medical traditions that take a different approach from modern medical science: acupuncture, herbal medicine, Chinese medicine, homeopathy, etc. Modern scientific re-search is only now being applied to these therapies, proving some claims and disproving many others.

fyi •

Nearly all medical conditions have both a common and a scientific name (German measles and rubella, for example). Knowing both will make your research easier and alert you to information resources you might otherwise miss. Anyone who is under the treat-ment of more than one doctor and taking a combination of prescription drugs should learn about the possible interactions of those drugs and make sure each doctor knows what other drugs you are taking. Research into your health problems can alert you to lifestyle changes that you can make to reduce their health risks. Such knowledge is power only when put into practice.

Your own research is a poor substitute for the insight and experience of a trained physician or health care professional. If your research leads you to question your doctor's treatment or diagnosis, switch doctors rather than rely on your newfound "expertise." When you research any health topic today, you are likely to find information about alternative therapies such as homeopathy and herbal or Ayurvedic medicine. Discuss these with your physician before embarking on any self-prescribed therapy. Some of these therapies are little more than modern versions of snake oil, while others have proven to be powerful treatments that can mimic or interfere with the effects of prescription drugs. As you visit Web sites on health-related topics, you'll find that many ask you to fill out a medical history survey so you can become an official "member." Check to see how the site plans to use this information, or you could be compromising your medical privacy.

The Merck Manual of Medical Information, Home Edition, by Robert Berkow, Mark H. Beers, and Andrew J. Fletcher (Merck, 1997): A comprehensive medical guide, written for the layman, with information on and illustrations of all aspects of family health issues, symptoms, treatments, and prescription drugs.

American College of Physicians Complete Home Medical Guide by David R. Goldmann (Dorling Kindersley, 1999): Medical guide to more than seven hundred different diseases and disorders with a companion CD-ROM. Each article discusses the causes, symptoms, diagnosis, treatment options, and prognosis of the condition. Two thousand illustrations and seventy symptom charts.

The Complete Guide to Symptoms, Illness, and Surgery by H. Winter Griffith (Perigee, 2000): Guide to diagnosis and treatment of most illnesses, with information on new medical therapies, drugs, and surgeries.

Online: There's a wealth of online information about every aspect of health care, as well as news forums and online support groups. Use your search engine if you're looking for information on a particular condition. For general information on health care issues, try sites such as that of the **Centers for Disease Control and Prevention** (www.cdc.gov), **HealthAtoZ.com** (www.healthatoz.com), or the directory of health resources on a search engine such as **WebCrawler** (www.webcrawler.com).

1. Stock your library with a good selection of basic medical reference books: one or more family medical guides; a medical dictionary; a current guide to prescription drugs; and a guide to symptoms.

2. If you suspect an illness or injury, use the symptoms guide to decide if a condition may exist and when to visit your physician.

5. Write down both the common name and the medical name of the illness or disease.

4. Be sure to alert your physician to any other drugs you're currently taking, as well as asking what side effects you should expect and what to look for.

3. When diagnosed with an illness or injury, have your physician explain the condition, its treatment, and why certain drugs are being prescribed.

6. Look both up in your medical references; also check the references for information on the underlying causes of these ailments and related symptoms and effects.

7. Read any brochure that came with your prescription drug and look it up in your drug reference guide.

8. Pay close attention to any warnings about this drug, its side effects, or possible interactions with other prescription drugs.

11. Conduct a search for the prescription drug you have been prescribed.

10. Conduct a keyword search on Internet search engines for both the common name and the medical or scientific name of your condition.

9. Alert your physicians to any potentially dangerous interactions with other drugs you are taking.

12. Read relevant articles and save, bookmark, or print any content that seems especially informative and useful.

13. Conduct a search through your news forum server for groups that are devoted to your particular medical condition.

14. Monitor newsgroup postings and subscribe if relevant.

17. If your research introduces you to alternative therapies you want to consider, gather information and discuss them with your doctor.

16. Visit more than one site; no site has all the information you need.

15. For general health information, conduct a keyword search or use Web directories to find relevant material.

18. If your research leads you to question some aspect of your treatment, discuss this with your physician.

19. If you're not satisfied with the response of your physician, take your concerns to another doctor.

20. Recognize and accept that the information you uncover through your research is no substitute for the care provided by a trained health care practitioner should you even suspect a serious illness.

what to do if you are diagnosed with a serious illness

91

the basics

Nothing can prepare you for the shock of learning you have a serious, life-threatening illness. The news is met with a flurry of emotions: anger, worry, frustration, disbelief. And pain for oneself and those we care about. It's all right to feel any or all of these things. But it's critical to your well-being and ability to conquer the challenge that you summon the strength to deal with it openly and honestly. There are no rules, no secrets for coming to terms with a prognosis that threatens your future. The right way to deal with it is to do what feels right for you. But you'll do better in the long run when you can accept the situation, make an objective assessment of your options, and decide on the course that's best for you. Keeping your feelings to yourself and attempting to hide or deny the turn of events will do more harm than good. When everything you've believed about your life and future comes under sudden threat, you'll fare best and improve your chances for recovery and cure by accepting the emotional support of those who care about you and your situation and will be there to help you deal with whatever comes your way.

Your first reaction may be disbelief or denial. Get a second opinion. If the original diagnosis proves correct, sit down and discuss your situation with your physician. What does this diagnosis mean, long and short term? What's the long-term prognosis? What are the preferred modes of treatment? What can you do to prepare your mind and body for the battle ahead? Don't rely only on your physician for information. Learn all you can about your illness, including the preferred modes of treatment and any new experimental therapies. Find out if there are support groups for people in a similar situation. If so, try to speak with people who have survived the illness. Get them to share all they can. Talk about your situation with someone who can offer you objective advice on dealing with your emotions: a minister, psychologist, or friend. Involve your family, drawing close to those who matter. Their support will prove a crucial source of strength in the months ahead. Express your needs, and be willing to understand theirs as well. They want to help and will try in their own way. Appreciate that effort, whether or not you fully understand what they are trying to do. Do everything you can to equip yourself for recovery, but don't neglect your personal affairs. If you don't have a will, prepare one. If you want specific people to have some of your possessions, think about giving them to them so you can see them enjoy the gifts. Turn to your own religious beliefs. Accept that once you've done all you can, whatever happens is beyond your control. Trust, pray, and seek peace as your source of strength, and try never to surrender to your darker emotions.

Alternative therapies: Unconventional and often unproven modes of treatment. Most proponents are well intentioned, but some prey on the seriously ill and their families by offering false hope at an exorbitant price. Thoroughly investigate any unproven alternative therapy before embarking on it.

Support group: A community of individuals brought together by a similar experience to help one another deal with a special challenge or issue in their lives. Support groups for those diagnosed with a serious illness can prove a valuable source of information, insight, updates on the latest scientific breakthroughs, and inspiration.

Attitude really does play a role in overcoming serious illness. People who are optimistic and prepared to fight fare better and improve their chances of regaining good health. Nevertheless, it's appropriate and realistic to feel a certain amount of anger, frustration, or despair upon learning of your condition. Venting these feelings and moving beyond them can be important first steps in the healing process. Many people who survive a serious illness find that the experience has helped them grow and develop as a person. Suddenly everything takes on a new perspective, and much of what worried them before seems trivial. This perspective can serve you the rest of your life. One of the most important things you can do for yourself is to speak openly about your feelings, your hopes, and fears. No one else can fully understand your needs unless you voice them.

It can be far more dangerous, emotionally and physically, to live with fears of a possible illness than to have it properly diagnosed. You know your own body, and if something concerns you, bring it to your doctor's attention immediately. It's better to be proven wrong than wait and be proven right after the condition has progressed. Often people suffering from a chronic condition are so desperate they turn to the false hope offered by medical quacks. Before you rely on any unorthodox treatment or therapy, thoroughly investigate it. Speak with others who have completed the program. See what kind of scientific research has been done to test or back up any aspects of the treatment. Be skeptical about any claims. If you do not have faith in your physician or the treatment you are receiving, turn to another doctor. Lingering doubts can only sap the energy and positive attitude needed to overcome your illness. You alone have the final say on how to deal with the illness. If you are uncomfortable with or don't believe in any aspect of the treatment, you have the right to stop or refuse it.

The Chronic Illness Experience: Embracing the Imperfect Life by Cheri Register (Hazelden Information Education, 1999): An exploration of the psychological and emotional aspects of chronic illness to help those diagnosed with one come to terms with their condition so they can continue to enjoy meaningful lives.

A Delicate Balance: Living Successfully with Chronic Illness by Susan Milstrey Wells (Perseus Books, 2000): A compelling mix of useful information and inspiration, based on the author's hard-won experiences, to help others cope and enjoy full lives and learn from their experience. Discusses such issues as the diagnosis, health care providers, traditional and alternative treatments, and strengthening personal relationships.

SupportPath.com (www.support-group.com): An alphabetical roster of bulletin boards, chat rooms, news forums, national and local support organizations, and support-related information on the Internet.

1. Have your physician explain your diagnosis, how it was determined, and its short- and long-term implications.

2. Have him or her explain the different treatment or therapy options available to you and the pros and cons of each, including side effects.

3. Ask what you can do to prepare yourself for the battle ahead.

6. Discuss your situation with your family or any others you may lean on for emotional support.

5. Vent your emotions in whatever way seems best. It's appropriate and normal to experience anger, despair, uncertainly, and depression.

4. Get a second opinion on all of the above.

7. Learn all you can about your illness, long-term prognosis, and routine and experimental modes of treatment.

8. Contact your health insurance company to learn what treatment options are covered and to what levels.

9. Decide with your physician how you will deal with the illness.

12. Sit in on or monitor these groups to see if you would feel comfortable participating.

11. Find out if there are any support groups in your area or online for people with this illness.

10. Follow this plan as prescribed, taking all medications or treatment as scheduled.

13. Try to speak with people who have survived this illness long term or been cured. Ask them to share their experiences and insights.

14. Confide in friends or family members about your feelings.

15. Seek counsel from a religious leader, therapist, or psychiatrist to help you deal with the mixed emotions you are experiencing.

18. Speak with them about your feelings and theirs.

17. Give them the opportunity to help you in whatever way they can.

16. Recognize how your condition will affect those around you.

19. Take care of any personal business that might be impacted by your situation.

20. Do all you can to overcome your situation, but recognize that ultimately things are beyond your control.

21. If you are religious, draw strength from your faith and regular prayer.

23. Before embarking on any unconventional therapy, investigate it thoroughly. Find out if any research has been done to verify that it offers any real benefits.

22. If you lose confidence in your physician or treatment, discuss this with him before you entrust your care to another physician.

what to do when a relative shows signs of depression

the basics

Everyone suffers from an occasional bout of the blues. But when the blues won't quit, they could be a sign of a serious, underlying illness: depression. Real depression—prolonged sadness, loss of interest in things that once mattered and/or suicidal thoughts—is a chronic illness. And like any illness, it can be effectively treated with a combination of prescription medications and other therapies. Too often, though, it's not the person who is suffering depression who reaches out and seeks medical help. Rather, it's intervention by friends and family that sets a patient on the road to recovery. Effective intervention can mean as little as staying involved in the life of your loved one, learning to recognize the symptoms of depression, and convincing him or her to see a doctor for this treatable illness. That involvement and caring concern can be one of the most important ingredients for overcoming what can be a debilitating, even fatal, illness.

We tend to think of depression as an emotional state. Modern science, however, has found a direct correlation between depression and a lack of the chemical serotonin in the brain. The resulting imbalance results in many of the symptoms associated with depression: irregular sleeping patterns; too much or not enough rest; changes in appetite; changes in the ability to concentrate or memory; and sexual dysfunction. When attempting to diagnose a case of depression, physicians look for a combination of any of these with other symptoms: an overwhelming sense of sadness or melancholy; feelings of guilt or inadequacy; lack of energy; a tendency to jump from one thing to another; or lack of interest in anything. Any talk of suicide underscores the real threat of depression to an individual; as many as 15 percent of people who suffer from depression attempt suicide. Recognizing these signs or changes is perhaps the most important contribution you can make for a friend or loved one. Depression may strike anyone from any social group at any time in their lives. We often hear of cases of depression among teens, but the disease tends to become more prevalent as we age. The elderly, who have often experienced severe illness and the loss of loved ones and who have a sense of diminishing control over their own lives, are especially susceptible. When you suspect that a loved one is suffering from depression, get him or her to a doctor. The majority of cases of depression are treatable, but it may take some time before a physician can arrive at the right combination of therapies. And since depression tends to be a recurring illness, the importance of developing and following a long-term treatment plan cannot be overstated.

Depression often accompanies diagnosis of a serious disease, or it can be a symptom of some diseases, such as Alzheimer's disease or dementia associated with aging. Certain drugs may also make a person more susceptible to depression. Often, depression is masked by other personal problems, such as alcoholism and drug addiction, which may actually be signs that the individual is suffering from depression. More than two thirds of the people who are prescribed antidepressants for depression recover within three to six weeks. Since these patients are prone to recurring bouts of depression, however, it may be necessary for them to continue to take these drugs so they can live and enjoy a normal life.

Depression is not just a state of mind but a real chronic illness that can get progressively worse over time. Untreated, it can prove fatal when it results in suicide. If you suspect that someone may be depressed, get him or her to a doctor as soon as possible. Individuals with a family history of depression are more prone to depression themselves. Some, on initial observation, may not show any of the outward signs of depression but still seem somewhat withdrawn or uninterested in things that used to matter to them. If you notice significant changes in a friend's or loved one's day-to-day habits, try to get him or her to talk about how he or she feels and what may be bothering him or her. If you suspect that a loved one may be suffering from depression, speak with a doctor.

When Someone You Love Is Depressed: How to Help Your Loved One Without Losing Yourself by Laura Epstein Rosen and Xavier Francisco Amador (Fireside, 1997): A guide by psychologists to dealing with depression without letting it take a toll on your own outlook and well-being.

What to Do When Someone You Love Is Depressed by Mitch Golant and Susan K. Golant (Henry Holt, 1998): A book written for caregivers or concerned friends and family of those suffering from depression to help them deal with this condition more effectively.

1. Learn to recognize the symptoms commonly used to diagnose depression. Check to see which and how many are present.

2. Does the person exhibit a general sense of sadness or melancholy?

3. Do you notice a change in the person's sleeping patterns?

12. If the symptoms continue, suggest that he or she see a physician. Explain that depression is a treatable disease that can be cured, in most cases, under a physician's care.

11. When you observe a combination of these symptoms, talk with your loved one about how he or she is feeling. Find out what's bothering him or her.

10. Does the person talk about, or seem preoccupied with, suicide?

13. Contact your physician and explain your concerns. Arrange an appointment. Be adamant that the patient must see a physician, but be supportive. Explain your concerns for his or her well-being and how seeing a doctor may improve his or her health.

14. Accompany your loved one to the physician's office. Explain your concerns again if necessary, but leave the patient alone with the physician to make the diagnosis.

23. Remain supportive and involved in the patient's life, and continually monitor his or her behavior and use of medication.

22. Recognize that the risk of recurrence is always there even after the patient is "cured."

21. Continually monitor the patient's condition if alternative therapies are tried.

24. Contact the physician if you think there may be a recurrence of the disease.

4. Is the person's sleeping pattern irregular?

5. Do you notice changes in the person's eating habits?

6. Do you notice a loss of interest in normal activities?

9. Does the person speak of a sense of guilt and futility?

8. Does the person seem to be unable to concentrate?

7. Does the person complain of fatigue and lack of energy?

15. If the patient is diagnosed with depression, ask the doctor to explain the mode of treatment, the drug(s) prescribed, and any potential side effects.

16. Ask about depression support groups for patients and families. If there is one in your area, enroll in it. Attend meetings with the patient when appropriate.

17. Continually monitor that the patient is taking drugs as prescribed. Ask how he or she feels and watch for any improvements or side effects.

20. Report to the physician on the patient's progress or lack of progress.

19. If the patient does not live with you, visit or call on a daily basis. Encourage others to do the same.

18. Involve the patient in the lives of others in the household. Explain to the other household members the nature of the disease and how they can help the patient.

93

the basics

Your medical records may not be as confidential as you think. In fact, you may unwittingly be making them available to businesses, organizations, and individuals you probably don't want peering into your private life. Every time you apply for health insurance, visit your doctor, participate in a health fair, or fill out a form on a health-related Web site, you could be adding details to your health profile and opening a door to any who want to view them. Short of any strictly enforced federal or state laws to protect your medical privacy, you have to assume responsibility for keeping those records private. It begins with recognizing where the information about you is being collected, who is gathering it, and how it may be used. When you are aware of this, you can make your concerns known and do all you can to limit access to those records.

With the prospect of genetic mapping on the horizon, the need for guaranteed medical privacy is becoming increasingly critical. And it will in all likelihood require sweeping federal mandates to protect the rights to medical privacy of all citizens and how this information is used. Many states already have laws concerning medical privacy on the books. Contact your state health department and find out if yours is one of them; if so, familiarize yourself with the law. Realize that there are some situations where you simply cannot avoid agreeing to disclosure of your medical records. Few life and health insurance underwriters will grant you a policy without requiring a physical examination and access to your medical records. Whenever you visit your physician or stay in a hospital, you probably sign a waiver granting both permission to access your records, without a second thought. In these situations, you have no choice but to comply, but you can request that both doctor and insurer not divulge information about you to third parties. When you do, put it in writing. The need for confidentiality is especially important when you are suffering from a serious or embarrassing illness or when disclosure of a medical condition could impact your ability to get or retain a job. Become aware of places where information about your medical history may be collected for other uses. Web sites on health-related topics routinely gather information on visitors through the health forms they are invited to fill out. Free health screenings are used to collect vital data about participants that may be sold or shared with third parties.

Talk with your physician and the medical staff at your hospital about your concerns about confidentiality. When asked to sign a blanket waiver granting access to your records, modify it with stipulations as to what information you are granting disclosure for and for what purpose. If your medical records are subpoenaed for a court case, they will become part of the public record. Ask the judge to restrict the portion of the records to be seen to what's relevant to the case, or to seal your records once the case has been decided. Although your medical records technically belong to the physician or health care institution that gathered the data they contain, many states have laws guaranteeing citizens a right to view their records. Even if your state is not one of them, you should try to review your records. Most physicians and health care facilities will comply with such a request.

Health insurance policies stipulate that the company must have access to your case records before they can settle a claim. If there's something you don't want to become part of your record, expect to have to explain the situation to your doctor and pay out of pocket for the treatment. The Internet, with its health-related Web sites, user groups, and chat rooms, is an increasingly important resource for gathering and disseminating all sorts of personal information. Assume that nothing you do online is confidential or private, and act accordingly to protect your medical privacy.

Medical Information Bureau: This centralized database contains medical information on individuals used by insurance companies to determine eligibility for health and life insurance coverage. Contact it and ask to review your records at www.mib.com, or call (617) 426-3660.

Electronic Privacy Information Center: An online clearinghouse with information on all aspects of privacy. Its medical privacy section, www.epic.org/privacy/medical/, includes updates on the latest legislation related to medical privacy as well as advice to consumers.

University of Buffalo: This university's Web site includes a page with links to the latest information and developments concerning medical privacy: http://wings.buffalo.edu/faculty/research/bioethics/privacy.html.

1. Accept that it is your responsibility to protect the confidentiality of your medical records.

2. Familiarize yourself with any state statutes protecting the rights of citizens to medical privacy and the confidentiality of their records.

3. Keep track of efforts at the federal level to create some national guarantee of medical privacy.

6. Contact the Medical Information Bureau and request a copy of your medical records.

5. If you find any mistakes, alert the appropriate person to them and see that they are changed.

4. Request and review a copy of your medical records from your physician and any hospital where you have been a patient.

7. Purchase a copy of your records, review them, and alert the MIB to any mistakes.

8. If you find mistakes, ask to see the record with the corrections in place.

9. Discuss with your physician and health care providers your concerns about the confidentiality of the records.

12. When asked to complete any waiver granting access to or disclosure of your medical records, find out how the information will be used.

11. Ask how the information in your records will be used or distributed, and impose restrictions in writing if you have concerns.

10. If receiving treatment for a condition you don't want to become part of your record, explain your concerns to your doctor and pay for your treatment out of pocket.

13. Amend these forms before signing, and restrict authorization for access or distribution as needed.

14. If your medical records are subpoenaed in court, ask the judge to limit access to what's pertinent to the case or seal the records after the case is decided.

15. When participating in health care or free medical screenings, ask how information about you will be used before completing forms.

18. Read health-related Web sites' policies and procedures on how information gathered will be used.

17. Be aware of how and where health information about you may be gathered online.

16. If concerned about their use, don't complete the forms.

19. Don't fill out forms; alternately, use a fictitious name and address.

20. Don't use your real name and address when participating in online user groups or chat rooms devoted to a specific medical condition or concerns you have if you are worried about others learning about your condition.

how to manage medical care from many miles away

94

the basics

In our increasingly mobile society, it's common for family members to be scattered in all regions of the country. This rarely presents any problems until a parent or loved one becomes ill or is injured and requires care and round-the-clock attention that family members cannot provide. The alternative is to arrange, manage, and monitor that care from far away. It's not easy, but it can be done. You must be willing to assume the responsibility and direct involvement it takes to ensure that a loved one receives adequate care. And you must work with someone "on the scene" who can regularly update you on the patient's treatment and condition. More and more of us will face this challenge in the years ahead as our parents, relatives, and friends live longer.

inside information

When it comes to managing another person's medical care, there simply is no substitute for being there to see and know firsthand all that is being done for the patient. That said, more and more of us have no choice but to manage the care as best we can from far away. Sometimes this is easier to do because it doesn't impose the same demands on our time. At other times, it can be especially frustrating to make decisions through intermediaries, without the benefit of firsthand observation. Anyone who must face this responsibility should begin by making sure the patient has a living will. Ideally, you, as care manager, will also have power of attorney to make decisions for the patient if he or she is incapable of doing this. This situation is increasingly common, and you will find most health care practitioners responsive to the special needs of a family member who must mange care from a distance. Contact the patient's doctor and explain the situation. Let him or her know under what circumstances you are to be notified. Since doctors are always pressed for time, find out who on the staff you should contact for regular updates on the patient's condition and needs. If the patient is hospitalized, use the telephone to introduce yourself to each shift nurse, and again explain your situation. Find out when it's best to call, and ask that they inform you immediately of any changes in condition or decisions that must be made. If the patient is homebound, you will also want to arrange for him or her to receive any and all home care services he or she is entitled to. Contact the local social services office and inquire about programs for the aged or homebound such as Meals on Wheels. Arrange for a caseworker to coordinate all care, and contact her or anyone else who is directly involved with care and treatment. Contact a neighbor or religious leader and ask that he or she look in on the patient occasionally and report to you. Finally, speak with the patient regularly, if possible. Arrange to speak together when no one else is around, and take to heart anything he or she tells you. Managing care from far away is possible, but only when you work as a team with all other caregivers and the patient to ensure that all needs are addressed.

jargon

Geriatric case manager: A health care specialist directly responsible for managing all aspects of care for an elderly patient. He or she may work on the staff of an institution such as a nursing home, for a home care provider, or for a social services program. Usually he or she will have training in social work, psychology, nursing, or another specialty.

Home health care services: Health care administered to a patient in his or her home. This may be administered by a nurse, psychologist, therapist, social worker, or someone trained in one or more of these disciplines. Home health care may be provided through a local social services agency or a private company specializing in home health care.

Power of attorney: The right to make legal decisions for another person in the event he or she cannot make decisions for him- or herself. Anyone who will be responsible for the care of an elderly or injured person should make sure he or she has the right to make any necessary decisions as quickly as possible.

fyi

Trained case managers may prove your best allies if you are forced to manage care for a loved one from a distance. Working for public or private agencies, they can serve as your primary contact and coordinate all aspects of the patient's care. If you consider using one, thoroughly interview the candidate about his or her credentials, experience, and skills. Ask for a written plan describing what services he or she will provide, when, and how you can monitor progress. Investigate the company and its history, as well as the individual caseworker. Any homebound patient should be equipped with some means to contact emergency services, as well as his or her physician, police, or family members. Some cellular telephone companies now offer one-button 911 service for a modest fee, and many home security firms have programs and devices that will automatically dial emergency numbers.

warning

There is no substitute for being there. Anyone who must manage care for another person from a distance should make a point of visiting the patient as often as possible, preferably unannounced. This is the only way to get the full picture of the treatment your loved one is receiving and who is providing that care. When you interview potential case managers or other potential care providers, ask about their education, skills, and experience in caring for this type of patient. Get the names and contact information of their superiors and other families they have worked for. Check the references. Also, ask for an explanation of all fees, how they are assessed, and what you should expect in weekly or monthly expenses for their services.

resources

A Family Caregiver's Guide to Planning and Decision Making for the Elderly by James A. Wilkinson (Fairview Press, 1999): Written for the family member who must oversee care of an elderly patient, this guide provides worksheets and checklists to organize responsibilities to help ensure that the patient receives proper care.

Elder Care: What to Look For, What to Look Out For! by Thomas M. Cassidy (New Horizon Press, 1997): Straightforward advice for the aging and their families who must make decisions on elder care, written by a former investigator of medical fraud.

1. If possible, discuss other options with the patient, such as relocating to a facility in your area, moving into your home, or relocating nearby.

2. Make sure the patient has a living will.

3. Ask that he or she give you power of attorney to make decisions.

6. Get the name and telephone number of the primary contact on the physician's staff.

5. Let the doctors know that you are the primary contact and under what circumstances you want to be notified.

4. Explain the situation to the patient's physician(s), and ask for their assessments of the patient's situation.

7. Get the names of shift supervisors on the floor of the hospital or nursing home where the patient is staying.

8. Call, introduce yourself to each, and explain the situation and the need to keep you updated on the patient's condition.

9. Find out when the best time to call is, and call regularly for updates.

12. Enroll the patient in the appropriate programs, if he or she agrees to participate.

11. Contact local social services or senior services agencies to see what types of programs are available.

10. If the patient is to receive care at home or in a nursing home, contact the health insurer and see what types of benefits are available and if there are any preferred providers.

13. Consider using a case manager to simplify and coordinate all aspects of care management.

14. Find out about the candidate's education, background, experience, and fees.

15. Check with the candidate's supervisor and references before agreeing to have him or her handle the case.

18. Talk to the patient as often as possible about the care he or she is receiving.

17. At least once a week, regularly contact everyone providing any aspect of care for an update.

16. Contact neighbors or minister and ask that they look in on the patient from time to time and report to you.

19. Make sure that all insurance claims are filed promptly.

20. Equip the patient with some means of making emergency telephone calls.

21. Arrange to visit the patient as often as possible or in the event that you receive any reports that concern you.

22. Stay involved with the care, thank caregivers for their concern, and act immediately on any problems you may discover.

how to get a parent onto Medicaid

95

the basics

If you're providing care for an elderly parent or loved one who may require long-term hospital or nursing home care, expect to be applying for Medicaid on that person's behalf at some point in the future. Unless a person has sufficient long-term insurance to cover the costs of health care or the financial resources to pay these expenses out of pocket, it's likely that he or she will eventually require government assistance to meet the considerable costs. It's not Medicare but Medicaid that provides most of that coverage. A joint program of federal, state, and local governments, Medicaid was originally set up to provide financial assistance in meeting medical expenses to individuals with low income and limited financial assets. Many baby boomers who have been counting on a hefty inheritance nest egg may be alarmed to learn that their parents must deplete their financial resources in order to qualify for this assistance. Such expenses—$30,000 a year might be a good starting point—can quickly consume a life's worth of assets.

The laws governing the Medicaid program, its administration, and its qualification requirements are continually reviewed and revised by lawmakers at the local and national levels. If you foresee the need for Medicaid coverage, it's in your best interest to keep abreast of these changes. It's also advisable to confer with an attorney or financial planner with experience in Medicaid-related issues before taking any steps to transfer or protect assets. Some of this activity may be in direct violation of existing law and subject to criminal prosecution, as well as disqualifying an applicant for Medicaid assistance. The rules on qualifying for Medicaid are pretty straightforward but may vary slightly from state to state. Eligibility requirements include limits on the maximum monthly income from all sources, as well as limits on the amount of financial assets a person may have before he or she is eligible for Medicaid. The laws also stipulate which assets can or cannot be counted when determining qualifying amounts and how income may used to meet Medicaid costs. For instance, the value of a home, one motor vehicle, and business property may not be counted if the applicant plans to return home or eventually resume operating the business. Among the assets that are counted are checking and savings account balances, bonds, annuities, property other than the primary residence, boats, and income from pensions and other sources. These same laws also stipulate how some assets can be transferred without disqualifying the applicant for Medicaid. It is these areas that are often of most concern to caregivers who want to protect their own long-term financial interests while ensuring and financing the best care they can for their elderly parent.

Allowable transfers: The transfer of certain assets from the applicant to another party, usually a child or sibling, that will not disqualify the applicant for Medicaid eligibility.

Asset shifting: The transfer of assets from the applicant to other individuals so they cannot be tapped by Medicaid or included when determining eligibility.

Spend-down: Depleting resources in order to meet the eligibility requirements for Medicaid. This may include outright spending of resources, legally transferring title to some properties, and establishing trusts to reduce the amount of assets to qualifying levels.

Laws governing qualifying income and assets, as well as what assets will and won't be counted when determining qualification, are slightly different for individuals and married persons applying for Medicaid. Once a person qualifies for Medicaid, the responsibility for financial disclosure does not end. Rather, applicants or their legal representatives must report any changes in the financial circumstances of the person receiving Medicaid.

Improper transfer of assets in order to qualify for Medicaid can automatically disqualify an applicant's eligibility for a long period of time. Weigh the real costs and savings before making such a move. Since the laws governing Medicaid and eligibility are so complex and constantly changing, it's advisable to consult with an attorney specializing in these issues before you take any steps. Concealing assets to ensure eligibility can be a crime, subject to criminal prosecution and sentencing. If you have any doubts about a particular course of action, confer with an attorney. Take your parents' realistic financial needs into account before completely spending down or transferring assets to someone else. They may need some of these resources for expenses not covered by Medicaid or if their health returns and they no longer require Medicaid assistance.

The Medicaid Planning Handbook: A Guide to Protecting Your Family's Assets from Catastrophic Nursing Home Costs by Alexander A. Bove, Jr. (Little, Brown & Company, 1996): This guide to the Medicaid maze for seniors, disabled individuals, and their families discusses different ways of preserving and protecting personal assets while ensuring adequate long-term care.

How to Protect Your Life Savings from Catastrophic Illness and Nursing Homes: A Handbook for Financial Survival by Harley Gordon (Senior Planning Group Publications, 1995): The essentials of what family members should know about the ongoing changes in Medicaid law and strategies and options for protecting family financial resources.

Note: Medicaid rules and regulations not only vary from state to state but change often. Do not rely on printed material for anything other than a general introduction to the topic and the concepts.

Centers for Medicare & Medicaid Services (www.hcfa.gov/Medicaid/mcaicnsm.htm): this site has information on the Medicaid program, application and eligibility, and the type of assistance that is available for long-term care.

1. If the need for long-term care in a nursing home or hospital seems possible, plan ahead.

2. If possible, purchase long-term care insurance.

3. Familiarize yourself with the state requirements for Medicaid eligibility for both individuals and married couples.

6. Compare the above figures with the eligibility requirements.

5. Calculate the monthly income from all sources.

4. Compile a list of all "countable" assets.

7. Before embarking on a "spend down" plan or transferring any assets to others or a trust, fully familiarize yourself with the law.

8. Recognize the complexity of the law and confer with an attorney or financial planner familiar with Medicaid issues for advice in developing a plan.

9. Include your parent in these discussions, or, if this is not possible, advise him or her about every step you are considering.

12. Discuss each approach and its potential repercussions with your parent to make sure he or she understands the implications.

11. Have the pros and cons of each option thoroughly explained to your parent by yourself or an adviser.

10. Investigate the merits of different modes of allowable transfer of assets or establishment of a Medicaid trust or some other trust as a way to protect assets.

13. Make sure any steps taken to protect assets will leave your parent with sufficient income and resources, should he or she return to living on her own.

14. Before taking any steps on your own to shift assets or establish a trust, confer with an attorney about the legality of what you are trying to do.

15. If the establishment of a trust or transfer of assets will make the parent ineligible for Medicaid for a set period, weigh the savings of the action against the costs of long-term care for that period.

17. Recognize that your parent has the right to decide how his or her assets are to be used or protected, and respect and abide by his or her decision.

16. Recognize the long-term implications of taking any irrevocable action, such as creation of an irrevocable trust.

how to get a loved one into a good nursing home

96

the basics

If you care for a person, placing him or her in a nursing home is a decision rarely welcomed. The fact is, though, that it's a responsibility more of us will have to face in the coming years. Medical technology is allowing people to live longer lives, but it can't guarantee the fulfillment of their desire to live independently. Too often, discussions about nursing home care are postponed until all other options have been exhausted. Then the choice comes down to whatever nursing home has the space to accept your loved one. If you want to ensure the best possible care, the selection process should begin much earlier, in anticipation of the need. Think about all of the issues you weigh when selecting a house or apartment. Very often the nursing home will be the final home of your loved one. It should be selected with as much sensitivity and scrutiny as any other home.

Several considerations will guide you to the right choice in a nursing home. But before you even begin the selection process, learn about the economic realities. A prolonged stay in any facility is expensive, and Medicare is not going to pick up the tab. Without long-term care insurance, you will need to exhaust your loved one's financial assets and resources before Medicaid begins to cover the costs. Think of a nursing home as a community of caring. Many issues and services contribute to the overall quality of the facility. Of course, medical services should be at the forefront. You want to make sure that any facility you consider is adequately staffed by qualified personnel. It's also important that it be situated near a hospital or major medical facility in case there is ever a need for emergency care. If the stay is to be enjoyable and rewarding, the patient also has to have something to do. Therefore, you should review the types of activities available to patients and speak with the activities director about what types of recreational and therapeutic programs are available, how often, and who conducts them. Your best resource for determining the quality of care at a nursing home is present patients and their families. Talk to them about what they like and don't like about the facility, and their overall satisfaction with the care.

jargon

Assisted living facility: An alternative to nursing home care for seniors who require assistance with routine household activities but don't need the daily health monitoring provided in a nursing home.

Long-term care insurance: A special type of insurance policy that can be purchased to offset the costs if nursing home or other long-term care is needed.

Medicaid: A program, administered jointly by state and federal governments, that covers the costs of medical expenses for people with limited income and resources. Because of the significant expense of nursing home care, many families ultimately rely on Medicaid to cover the costs of a nursing home stay.

fyi

Nursing homes are state licensed and regulated, so make sure all licenses are current. Also, check with the licensing agency to see if a facility's license has ever been pulled or denied, and if so, for what reasons. A good facility will have staff available to help the family as well as the patient make the transition from independent living to nursing home care. No two nursing homes bill the same way, so you should determine the fees and how they are incurred before making your decision. Nursing homes may have a set daily or monthly rate. Ask what the basic fee covers, what services are billed separately, and how the rates are determined. Not everyone is a willing candidate for a nursing home. As best you can, involve your loved one in the selection process and explain to him or her why this is a necessary transition.

warning

Given fair warning, anything can be made to look good. When you are comparing nursing home facilities, make your first visit unannounced. Is the facility secure, or are you free to wander the facility and grounds unchallenged? If the latter, who's watching the patients? Note the overall cleanliness and atmosphere of the facility. Are patients involved or left stranded in beds or hallways, calling for attention? Does the staff seem friendly, annoyed, or overwhelmed? No matter what nursing home facility you choose, it's the family and friends of the patient who contribute most to determining the quality of care. Frequent visits and occasional forays outside the facility give a patient a sense of worth and involvement. And only with regular visits can you continue to monitor the quality of the care and ensure that your loved one receives all the attention and care he or she deserves and that you are paying for.

resources

Beat the Nursing Home Trap: A Consumer's Guide to Assisted Living & Long-Term Care by Joseph L. Matthews (Nolo Press, 1999): Information on arranging long-term care, including how to evaluate nursing home insurance and understand Medicare, Medicaid, and other benefit programs.

The Inside Guide to America's Nursing Homes: Rankings & Ratings for Every Nursing Home in the U.S., 1998–1999 by Robert N. Bua: This informative guide rates and ranks every certified nursing home in the country, helping readers make the right decisions for their loved ones.

The Nursing Home Choice: How to Choose the Ideal Nursing Home by Marian R. Kranz and Adolph Caso (Branden Books, 1998): Written as a guide to nursing homes and long-term care facilities, this book includes interview questions to ask the staff and administration when trying to select a nursing home for your loved one.

1. If possible, years in advance investigate the feasibility and value of long-term care insurance.

2. Anticipate the potential need for nursing home care in advance and begin investigating your options.

3. Involve the patient in discussions as much as possible, explaining, in the kindest terms, why the move will be necessary.

12. What types of activities are going on?

11. Are the patients well attended?

10. Is it clean and well maintained?

13. What is the attitude of the staff?

14. Talk to patients and family members about the pros and cons of this facility. How satisfied are they with the quality of care?

15. For a nursing home that passes this preliminary test, is it conveniently located for family visits and close to a hospital?

24. Is there a nutritionist on staff, and what does the typical week's menu look like?

23. What will the typical day be like if your loved one becomes a resident there?

22. What kind of assistance will they provide the individual patient, and how often?

25. What type of counseling is available to patients and families?

26. Speak with the activities director about the types and and frequency of activities and their entertainment and therapeutic value.

27. What type of recreational activities and resources are available to patients?

4. Determine how the cost of care will be covered and who will pay for it.

5. Contact a local social services agency or Medicaid office to determine qualifications for Medicaid and if the patient qualifies.

6. Based on the above, determine what the patient and/or you can afford for nursing home care.

9. Is it secure?

8. Visit facilities unannounced, with the following checklist of concerns:

7. Ask friends, neighbors, and area social services agencies for recommendations of nursing homes.

16. Make sure licenses are current and up to date.

17. Contact state and local licensing agencies to see if the license has ever been denied or pulled.

18. Contact the health department and inquire if this facility has ever failed inspection.

21. What is the ratio of nursing and support staff to patients?

20. Who is the medical chief of staff?

19. Are there any problems or unresolved complaints against the facility?

28. What are the policies on family visits and outings?

29. What are the visiting hours?

30. Discuss fees and billing with the director of finance. What do the basic fees cover, and how are other services determined and billed?

32. If possible, take the patient to visit acceptable facilities, based on the above, and allow him or her to decide where he or she would like to be.

31. What type of liability insurance does the facility carry, and what does it cover?

how to arrange home care for a loved one

97

the basics

The decision to provide home care for a loved one who can no longer care for him or herself, or who is suffering from a terminal illness, is an especially generous one. By making it possible for the patient to remain in familiar surroundings among friendly faces, you are assuming a tremendous responsibility and reordering the priorities in your life. For both patient and caregiver, this can be a rewarding experience that strengthens the bonds of love that define family and friendship. The home care patient has the comfort and reinforcement of knowing how much she matters to those she cares about. That support can make it easier to deal with the disappointments and frustrations brought on by failing health. If you are thinking of providing home health care for a loved one, you must also realize how this decision will impact your family life. Providing—even simply monitoring—care for a patient at home can be a full-time job plus. It involves a responsibility that you can neither leave nor ignore and that must claim precedence over whatever else is going on in your life.

Home health care requires an unquestioned commitment on the part of the person who will be the primary caregiver. Before you discuss this option with the patient, you must ask yourself if you have the time and energy to fill this role, as well as the support of your family. Your decision will impact their lives as much as your own. Then make a realistic assessment of the patient's present and foreseeable needs. Can he or she remain in his or her own home? Must she move in with you? Do you have the space and facilities for someone in his or her condition? Is he or she capable of taking at least some care of herself, or will he or she require constant bedside attention? How will his or her medical needs change? What about daily routines such as eating, bathing, etc.? Can he or she take care of these herself, or will he or she need assistance? What kinds of outside services and support agencies can assist you in providing home care? Is there insurance or sufficient resources to cover these expenses? Does the patient qualify for Medicaid? If so, what expenses will it cover? Only when you have thoroughly examined all these issues should you broach the possibility of home health care with the patient. When you do, be careful not to make promises you cannot keep. The patient's medical condition might one day reach a point where you are left with no alternative but a long-term nursing home or hospital stay.

Hospice care: A program that provides medical care and emotional support care for a terminally ill patient, often administered in a home care environment.

Primary caregiver: The person primarily responsible for overseeing the care of the patient. With home health care, it may be a friend, a family member, or a professional who visits on a regular basis or lives there.

Although the costs related to home care are expensive, they can be less costly than a stay in a nursing home or hospital. But you must know beforehand what insurance or Medicaid will and will not cover so you can develop an appropriate treatment and payment plan. Although no two patients are alike, you can gain valuable insight into what home health care entails by speaking with someone who is already fulfilling this role. That person can also be a source of much-needed emotional support and advice once you are providing that care. If you can't find someone on your own, inquire at a home health care agency.

warning

Be sure to discuss home care with the patient's doctor before embarking on this course. Make sure the patient has no special conditions that would preclude him or her from being treated adequately at home. Over the last decade a number of home health care agencies have sprung up. Most are legitimate, but a few are more interested in billing the insurance company, Medicare, or Medicaid than they are in the service they provide. Exercise the same cautions when shopping for home health care as you would any other health care professional service: get recommendations, inquire into care providers' background and experience, and observe how they interact with the patient. Don't make a martyr of yourself when providing care to someone at home. If you wear yourself down, who will be there to provide the care? Ask friends and family for help, and hire outside professional help when needed.

resource

Home Care Organizer: A Resource for Your Family by Laura Nieboer (State of the Art Publishing, 1997): An organizer for dealing with all the responsibilities involved in home care, such as medications, physicians, and appointments. Includes a glossary and resource guide.

1. Make a realistic assessment of the patient and how he or she will function and benefit from home care.

2. What does the patient think of home care?

3. What does the patient's doctor think?

6. What type of medical assistance is required?

5. What type of assistance does he or she need for daily living?

4. What can the patient do for him or herself?

7. Are there outside resources you can use to address special needs?

8. Can all the patient's needs be met at home?

9. Assess your abilities as the primary caregiver.

12. What outside assistance will you require to maintain adequate care?

11. Are you trained in CPR or for other medical emergencies?

10. Do you have the time, skill, and patience to provide and/or monitor home care?

13. Is it available, and at what cost?

14. Who is prepared to help you with caregiving, transportation, sitting with the patient, preparing meals?

15. Will they be available as a backup should you ever need it?

18. Where will home care be administered, in the patient's home or yours?

17. Are they supportive and willing to help?

16. How does your family feel about you becoming the primary care provider/monitor?

19. Is either properly equipped to meet the patient's special needs?

20. Will remodeling be required, and how soon can it be finished?

21. Is there an alert/alarm system so the patient can quickly reach you?

24. Does the patient have sufficient resources or insurance?

23. What outside fees will there be for medical care, therapy, prescriptions?

22. How will you pay for home care?

25. Does the patient qualify for Medicare or Medicaid?

26. What other financial resources are available?

27. Considering all of the above, is home care possible for you?

30. Thoroughly check the background and experience of any home health caregiver or agency before agreeing to use its services.

29. Decide what other assistance you will need that you or family members cannot provide.

28. Before you commit, speak with someone who is already providing home care about his or her experiences.

how to deal with domestic violence

98

Domestic violence is commonplace: a 1995 Department of Justice study estimated that "husbands, ex-husbands, and current and former boyfriends commit over one million violent crimes against women every year, including assault, rape, and murder." But at least there is a safety net, fragile though it is. Laws have been toughened, police forces retrained, and victim services organizations established. But an abused woman (the overwhelming majority of abusers are men) can still fall through a hole in the net unless she knows how to make the justice system work for her. To do so, a victim must know what to expect as her case moves through the court system; she must find the courage to file charges against the abuser; and she must speak up whenever she suspects the police or prosecutors are being careless about her safety.

inside information

When you file a complaint against an abusive spouse (or live-in lover), your case will be handled under state law, in a state court. Until 1994, abusers could escape arrest by leaving the state after they had violated an order of protection. But in 1994, Congress passed the Violence Against Women Act, which allows a woman to bring a case if an abuser has crossed a state line to cause her physical injury.

jargon

Battery: Physical contact with another person that causes bodily harm.

Domestic abuse: The National Organization for Women's Legal Defense and Education Fund defines this as "extreme coercion and control by the batterer accompanied by the victim's loss of self-will. . . . Batterers establish control through systemic, repetitive infliction of physical and emotional trauma, social and physical isolation of the victim, and other coercive acts."

Mandatory arrest: In some states police are legally required to arrest an alleged abuser if they respond to an incident.

Order of protection: A court document requiring the abuser to stay away from the abused. This document creates a record of complaint that a district attorney, judge, and jury will later take into consideration. And it is the mechanism that allows the police to make an arrest.

warning

Advocates for battered women stress that victims should usually press charges. Studies show that arrest, or threat of arrest, does cut down the rate of domestic violence. But they acknowledge that some abusers are so dangerous that the victim's refusal to press charges is sensible—indeed, lifesaving. When an offender is obsessed and deranged, the woman's judgment must be respected. She should not press charges until she is in a place of long-term safety.

Few victims of domestic violence are ever assigned security guards by the police. And so, in November 1996, Carolyn Miller, who has been a victim of domestic violence herself, established the World Security Bureau, a not-for-profit organization that supplies security guards to women in imminent danger of being killed. Call (800) 865-6645.

National Domestic Violence Hot Line: For answers to any question about domestic violence. Counseling is confidential. Trained hot line staffers can offer information on local shelters; where to call for legal advice; protection and restraining orders; options if you're not ready to leave home; and support groups. Counseling is available in English, Spanish, and more than 130 other languages. Call (800) 799-SAFE.

State domestic violence hot line: Every state has its own hot line, staffed by counselors who will advise callers about local shelters, legal services, and other available resources. If your local operator doesn't have a listing, call your state capital and ask for the state coalition against domestic violence (another commonly used name). Your own city may also have established a hot line.

Crime victims board or victim services agency: Call to learn what help your state will give you if you've been victimized. If there is no local branch in your city, call the board in your state's capital. Services may include installing a new lock for free; crisis intervention counseling; help in finding emergency shelter, transportation, food, and clothing; help in obtaining an order of protection; advocacy for court appearances; and assistance in obtaining housing.

Domestic Violence and the Law: An excellent, free resource kit offering an explanation of battered women's legal problems, a realistic look at how police departments respond to reports of abuse; and a state-by-state list of organizations set up to help battered women. Write to NOW Legal Defense and Education Fund, 99 Hudson Street, New York, NY 10013, or call (212) 925-6635.

1. Call the police.

2. In mandatory arrest communities, your abuser will automatically be arrested.

3. If you're not in a mandatory arrest community, ask the officer to arrest the abuser.

12. Apply for an order of protection at the local police department.

11. Put important documents together in one place for quick and easy access.

10. Have a friend take photos of your injuries, then have her sign, date, and store them.

13. Speak with the local district attorney.

14. Ask the police about an order of protection; sometimes they can do the paperwork.

15. Ask for a full order of protection if you've left the abuser.

24. Resist efforts at referring your case to mediation; this rarely works in abuse cases.

23. Call the police if the abuser violates the order. It will lead to an arrest.

22. Show the order of protection and a photo of the abuser to the police department near your workplace.

25. Tell the district attorney that you want to be continually notified of the status of the case.

26. Stand firm, and the district attorney will push for a severe penalty.

27. Submit a victim impact statement to the court if the abuser is convicted.

4. Note police officers' names and badge numbers if they refuse.

5. Ask the police to get you medical treatment if you need it.

6. Ask the police to help you gather your belongings and take you to a friend's home or shelter.

9. Keep medical records of battering, along with emergency money, at a friend's home.

8. Begin planning ahead, whether the abuser is arrested or not.

7. Take your children with you. They'll be protected, and it will be easier for you to win custody.

16. Ask for a limited order of protection if you're still living with the abuser.

17. Ask for your child to be included in the order of protection if he or she was present during the abuse.

18. Show the order to the domestic violence unit at your local police department.

21. If the employer won't cooperate, say that he or she may be liable under sex discrimination laws.

20. Show the order of protection and a photo of the abuser to your employer.

19. Show the order to officials at your child's school if he or she is included in it.

28. Ask for the statement to be filed with the parole board.

29. Fill out a victim notice so you'll be notified when the abuser is released.

30. If the parole board considers early release, seek publicity for your case.

31. Consider suing for damages under the Violence Against Women Act.

how to stop a stalker

the basics

Stalking—watchful, obsessive intrusion into another's life—is more common than you may be aware. Although you regularly read and hear of a crazed fan who wants only to get close to his or her idol, stalkers pose a daily agony for far too many average Americans who never step into the limelight. One recent survey estimates that as many as one in twelve American women will be stalked at some time in their life, and one in forty-five men. Stalkers disrupt the lives of all racial and social groups and pose a threat to people of every age and physical description. Unfortunately, there is no single profile that describes typical stalkers, other than the fact that they have an obsession about another person that is symptomatic of a deeper mental instability. The real danger is that stalkers may be overlooked or ignored until they pose a real physical threat to their victims. Although many stalkers never move beyond a stage of unreasonable infatuation with another, others progress from wanting to know to wanting to possess, then needing to control. Anyone who suspects he or she is being stalked, whether on the street or online, should completely cut off contact with the perpetrator, alert police to the problem, and document all examples of unwanted attention for possible legal action or prosecution, if necessary.

In the wake of well-publicized cases of violence, even murder, of celebrities in the 1980s, the legislatures of all fifty states developed and adopted antistalking measures. Additionally, if a stalker follows his or her victim from one state to another or harasses a person living in another state, federal antiterrorism laws may apply. If you feel you are the victim of a stalker, it's important that you familiarize yourself with any and all laws that may protect you. Local law enforcement officials may not be familiar with the full extent and intent of these laws, especially if they have never had to deal with a stalking case before. It's also important that you understand something about the stalker. Ultimately, stalking is about power and a need to control another's life. Whether the stalker be a former partner or lover or a complete stranger, he or she looks to the victims to fill a void in him- or herself. Somehow, in their thinking their own self-worth and identity are tied to their victim's. But unlike a lover or friend, stalkers have a prescribed role the victim must fill, rooted in fantasy. They may even see their own role as somehow controlling or punishing the victim for imaginary wrongs or personal failings. Normal people who suffer from infatuation or unrequited love can in time accept the pain of defeat and redirect their lives. For the stalker, however, such a defeat can be an affirmation that he or she is right and must continue the pursuit, whatever the cost. Any contact, any reaction from the victim, only encourages the fantasy. The danger is real, as some stalkers can suddenly turn violent and blame their failings on the victim's unwillingness to cooperate in the fantasy. No one knows what will flip that switch. If you even sense you are being stalked by someone, take appropriate action to protect yourself and your family, and make law enforcement officials and those around you aware of the problem.

Cyberstalking: Electronically stalking someone online. Through sophisticated use of technology a cyberstalker can track every move the victim makes online, gather personal information about the victim from databases, and use this knowledge to terrorize and disrupt the lives of the victim.

Restraining order/order of protection: A court order, requested by the victim, that stipulates that the offender is to stay away from and not interfere with or have any contact with the victim. This court order makes the stalker subject to immediate arrest or incarceration if it is violated.

Stalking is any persistent unwanted attention, and victims sometimes blame themselves for creating the situation. If a someone persists in bothering you after you've asked him or her to stop, treat him or her as an unwanted intruder into your life. State statutes vary widely on how to deal with stalkers, the rights of victims, and the types of charges that can be filed. Read and understand all applicable laws so you can develop an appropriate response. Anyone who regularly participates in online newsgroups or chat rooms should recognize that cyberstalking is one of the dangers of this activity, especially when you dismiss or ridicule other participants or post unpopular views. Be cautious about what you tell others about yourself online and what you say. You never know who you are dealing with in cyberspace.

Unfortunately, with stalking, as in some cases of rape, the initial burden of proof often falls on the victim before law enforcement officials will take action. Document all phone calls, messages, and gifts—any evidence of unwanted attention—and it will be easier to convince them that your complaint is justified. The worst thing you can do is involve yourself in any way with the stalker. Once you know you are being stalked, have absolutely no contact with the perpetrator, even to express your anger or frustration. Refuse any letters, gifts, and calls, and do all you can to distance yourself from the person. If the problem persists, alert your family and friends to the person's identity, seek an order of protection from the police, and develop contingency plans as to what you will do and who you will call should you find yourself in a dangerous situation. Make it difficult for the stalker to keep track of you by regularly changing your routine. Leave for and depart from work at different times, take alternate routes home—whatever it takes to make it more difficult for him or her to keep up with you.

Stalking: A Handbook for Victims by Emily Spence-Diehl (Learning Publication 1999): This guide discusses the rights of and options available to stalking victims to help them regain control of their lives.

Stopping a Stalker: A Cop's Guide to Making the System Work for You by Robert L. Snow (Perseus Press, 1998): The author discusses different types of threatening behavior and provides advice on how to deal with each drawn from actual case histories.

1. If a person is bothering you or showering you with unwanted attention, ask him or her to stop.

2. If the attention or intrusion continues, consider and treat him or her as a stalker.

3. Contact local law enforcement officials and ask about the applicable laws against stalking in your state. If the stalker is out of state, contact the nearest federal district court and ask about any federal laws that may apply.

12. Contact a local victim's rights or rape crisis center for assistance or advice on developing a strategy for dealing with the stalker.

11. Explain your problem and show the police your proof.

10. Contact police and seek a restraining order or order of protection against the person.

13. Change your telephone number and e-mail address.

14. Change your daily and weekly routines so the stalker doesn't know where or when to expect you.

15. Remove shrubs and add lighting around your house.

22. If you sense a real danger to you or loved ones, consider relocating and if you do, leave no forwarding address.

4. Get and read a copy of the applicable laws, and gain an understanding of your rights and the measures you can take to stop harassment.

5. Completely cut off all contact with the stalker.

6. Refuse any calls, letters, and gifts, but document each incident.

9. Ask that they alert you whenever the person is in the area or asks about you, and document the date and time.

8. Explain that under no circumstances are they to give the person any information about you or accept any messages or gifts from the stalker to you.

7. Alert family, friends, and coworkers to the problem and the perpetrator.

16. Get a watchdog.

17. Recognize the threat the stalker could pose to other family members, especially schoolchildren.

18. Alert school officials to the problem and the identity of the stalker.

21. Consider carrying mace or some other personal protective measure.

20. Get a cellular telephone and make arrangements about who you will call.

19. Develop a contingency plan if the stalker persists in following you.

how to deal with problem neighbors

100

The neighbors party late into the night, and then their dog starts barking; they've built the extension to their garage on your side of the property line; and that tree in their front yard looks as though it's going to come through your roof with the next strong wind. Unless you're planning a move, all of the above—or any disagreement with your neighbors—can make life miserable until you can resolve the problem amicably. That's not necessarily as difficult as it sounds, but you won't know until you approach them about the problem. It may be that they are oblivious to the situation or your concern; or they may greet your honest complaint as "fighting words" and cause for a physical challenge. Only when such an effort fails should you consider taking your dispute to the law.

Humans have been having problems with their neighbors since they wandered off the savanna and settled in villages. And wise men have been settling these since the first laws were written. You don't want to haul your neighbor before a judge until you've exhausted every reasonable effort to resolve your dispute. The fact is, if you like your home and your neighbors like theirs, be it on a suburban street or the twelfth floor of an apartment complex, you're going to be living alongside each other for years to come. So you might as well try to get along and set your differences aside. If the neighbors don't respond, you should be prepared to inform them what local law has to say about this particular problem. Know the law. You may have to call the police to determine how late your neighbor can practice the saxophone or if it's legal to shoot at cans within the city limits. A visit to city hall and the planning or zoning board may be required to find out how high the neighbor's fence can be or how many cars can be parked on his lawn. If you explain the law regarding any nuisance to the neighbors and they don't respond, it's time for outside help. Call the police with your complaint or inform the neighbors in writing of the problem and the applicable laws. If that still doesn't have any effect, consider the merits of taking them to court or hauling them before the zoning board. Be aware, however, that such a move certainly won't do anything to improve your relations.

jargon

Local ordinances: Local laws governing specific activities. There may be a local ordinance establishing quiet hours, the height of fences, or the number of nonworking vehicles your neighbors may keep on their lawn.

Zoning codes: A series of local codes, based on recommendations by the local planning or zoning board, that are used to classify an area of a city, and stipulate what type of buildings and related activity can be conducted within an area.

fyi

Every municipality has its own statutes and codes that govern how people can act and what they can do on their property. It's a good idea to know what any applicable local ordinance or zoning restrictions say before you approach your neighbors about a perceived problem. When all else fails, you can sue or take your neighbors to court if they are unresponsive to your complaints. Such disputes can usually be resolved in small claims court. If you can demonstrate to the judge that you've have made every reasonable effort to resolve the problem outside court, it will help your case. If there's a persistent problem, keep a log and document it and your efforts to get your neighbor to address the issue.

warning •

An angry reproach will elicit an angry response. Try talking to your neighbors amicably at first to get them to address your problem. If they make any physical threat against you or any member of your household, report it to the police immediately. If you discover that the neighbors are acting within the law, accept defeat, lobby for a change in the laws, or move. Your home is your life; if you're not happy with the situation there, it will affect all other aspects of your life.

resources •

Neighbor Vs. Neighbor: Over 400 Informative and Outrageous Cases of Neighbor Disputes by Mark Warda (Sphinx Publishing, 1999): A practical guide to solving neighbor disputes, using 450 true court cases from more than four hundred years of neighbor disputes to make its points. Explains laws that apply to neighbor disputes, such as noise, animals, offensive odors, tree branches, trespassing, and boundary disputes.

Neighbor Law: Fences, Trees, Boundaries & Noise by Cora Jordan (Nolo Press, 2001): A guide to many of the simple and complicated differences that can arise between neighbors, with help and advice in solving disputes and preventing problems from happening in the first place.

1. Define the problem and its source.

2. Check with the police, at city hall, or with the planning or zoning commission to determine what local laws and zoning regulations apply to the problem.

3. Discuss the problem with other area residents or tenants to see if they share your concerns.

6. Explain the problem and suggest how you would like it addressed.

5. Whether or not any laws apply, approach the neighbors in a friendly manner.

4. Discuss the remedies.

7. Try to reach a mutually acceptable compromise

8. If the neighbors argue, inform them of the applicable local ordinance or zoning code.

9. Explain that if they will not comply with the law, you will need to contact the police or take them to court.

12. Draft a letter or have your attorney draft a letter stating the problem, the applicable laws, and how you would like the problem resolved.

11. Explain that you have already brought this to the tenants' attention, their response, and how you want the issue addressed.

10. If the neighbors rent, or you live in an apartment, contact the landlord with your complaint.

13. If the problem persists, take appropriate action.

14. If the complaint can be handled by the police, call and register the complaint.

15. Document when they respond and note the responding officers' names.

18. If the problem persists, consider bringing the neighbors before the zoning board or small claims court.

17. If he or she is still uncooperative, contact a superior officer and register a complaint.

16. If a police officer balks at addressing the complaint, cite the applicable law.

19. Carefully weigh the potential long-term repercussions of such action.

20. Consider seeking the help of an outside mediator to help resolve the dispute.

21. If the neighbors are unwilling, proceed with filing suit, in small claims court if applicable (see Lifemap 81).

22. If the problems persist or other problems with the neighbors result from your taking action, consider relocating to retain your peace of mind.

how to get the police to act on a complaint

101

the basics

Police and law enforcement agencies are constantly inundated with calls. Of course, all callers expect immediate action, whether they are complaining about the crowd of kids playing the radio too loud on the corner or reporting a robbery in progress at a nearby store. If there's one officer available and two calls, it's the dire situation that usually gets the quick response. But not always. In fact, sometimes it's necessary to place more than one call to get a response, even in an emergency. And if all you're calling about is a problem with your neighbors' dog, or you keep calling about minor nuisances, it may take days for a response if the police are especially busy. Sometimes things fall through the cracks, too. So whenever you call about an emergency situation, insist that police are needed on the scene, right away.

When you call the police for help, your assessment of the situation is all they have to go by. How you present your complaint can also determine how soon they respond. Keep your call brief and to the point: tell them where you are, the nature of your complaint, who's involved, whether anyone is in imminent danger, and what is happening at the time you call. Always alert the police to the presence of weapons and if anyone has threatened to use them. When calling for assistance, alert them to how they can identify you, where you are, and if you have any injuries. Let them know if you feel threatened or are in any imminent danger because of someone on the scene. Explain how to identify this person and if you have an order of protection or a restraining order against the person. When you are calling about a nuisance, a persistent problem with your neighbor such as a barking dog, you'll get a quicker response if you know any applicable local laws before you call. The police may be reluctant or slow to act until you cite what law is being broken. If the police do not respond or fail to act on a complaint, you should call back. On an emergency call, if help is not on the scene within ten minutes, place another call. For nonemergency disputes or complaints, expect a response within a day. Always note the name of the responding officer and when he or she arrives. If, after you explain the situation, he or she refuses to do anything, request the name of his or her superior. Contact the superior and explain the situation; explain why he or she should respond now and what you believe needs to be done. Persist until the issue is addressed to your satisfaction. In the vast majority of incidents, the police are quick to respond appropriately. But there may be cases when your own knowledge of the law—and insistence—may be required.

Nonemergency call: Any complaint that does not pose imminent danger may be considered a nonemergency and get a slower response. Many municipalities now urge consumers not to use 911 for nonemergency calls.

Review board: Police action and response can be subject to hearings by internal or departmental review boards, as well as citizens' review boards. These should be used only after you've done everything within reason to get a response to a complaint.

Police are trained to assess situations quickly and respond based on what they observe and know. The more you can tell them about any situation and the parties involved, the easier it is for them to make the proper assessment. In a dangerous or life-threatening situation, the best help you can offer is to stay safely out of the way. Otherwise you force the police to worry about your safety as well as the call or complaint that brought them there. When you can't get the police to respond to or resolve an ongoing problem, contact your elected representative in your local or county government and explain the problem. His or her backing will add weight to your complaint.

If you believe the responding officer is not adequately acting on your complaint, don't get into an argument or launch an assault or accusation. Note his or her name, and contact his or her superior and explain the situation. Call the police emergency 911 number for help only when a real need exists. A frivolous call to 911 could prevent police help reaching someone who desperately needs it. A person who makes a pest of him- or herself and keeps calling with complaints about everyone and everything around him or her only gains a reputation as a troublemaker. The police will still respond to calls but may be slow about getting there.

1. Call 911 only when a real emergency exists; for other calls or complaints, call the nearest station house or the police department's main number.

2. With nuisance calls, familiarize yourself with applicable laws before you call to make sure the police have the authority to act on the complaint.

3. Explain to the operator the nature of your call, where you are, and how many people are involved.

12. If the call concerns a fight or argument, identify, as best you can, those involved and whether any are armed.

11. Meet the responding officer, identify yourself as the caller, and explain the situation.

10. Again get the operator's name.

13. Let the officer know if you have any restraining orders or orders of protection against the other party.

14. Follow the officer's instructions.

15. If the officer doesn't take what you believe is the appropriate action, contact his or her superior and register a compliant.

4. Alert the operator if anyone is injured or faces imminent danger.

5. If this is a fight or any form of violent confrontation, describe, as best you can, the number of perpetrators, how to identify them, and whether any weapons are present.

6. Get the name of the 911 operator before you hang up the phone.

9. Alert the operator to any deterioration in the situation since the first call.

8. Ask if an officer is en route.

7. If there is no response within ten minutes, place another call.

16. Stay out of the way, but be prepared to speak with an officer for his report.

17. When calling about a nuisance, document a pattern of behavior before making the call.

18. Show proof to the responding officer and explain the situation and your reading of any applicable laws.

20. If the police fail to take appropriate action, consider presenting your case, along with supporting documents, to the local police or civilian review board.

19. Pursue the matter until it is resolved.

about the authors

MICHAEL ANTONIAK is a freelance writer and the author of two previous books, *How to Open Your Own Store* and *How to Start a Home Business*.

STEPHEN M. POLLAN has been offering pragmatic business, legal, and career advice to individuals and businesses for more than forty years and has appeared on CNBC as a financial expert. He and MARK LEVINE have collaborated on the Lifescripts series and many other business and personal finance books.